THE FUTURE OF COMPETITION

Also by C. K. Prahalad

Competing for the Future
(with Gary Hamel)
Harvard Business School Press, 1994

The Multinational Mission
(with Yves Doz)
The Free Press, 1987

THE FUTURE OF COMPETITION

Co-Creating Unique Value

with Customers

C. K. Prahalad

Venkat Ramaswamy

HARVARD BUSINESS SCHOOL PRESS

BOSTON, MASSACHUSETTS

Library of Congress Cataloging-in-Publication Data

Prahalad, C. K.
    The future of competition : co-creating unique value with customers /
C. K. Prahalad, Venkat Ramaswamy.
      p. cm.
    ISBN 1-57851-953-5 (alk. paper)
    1. Competition. 2. Customer relations. 3. Customer services. 4. Strategic
planning. 5. Economic value added. 6. Success in business. I. Ramaswamy,
Venkat. II. Title.
HD41.P73 2004
658.4—dc22

                              2003016949

This book is dedicated
To our parents with gratitude,
To our wives with love,
and
To our children—
co-creators of the future—
with hope.

CONTENTS

PREFACE

THIS BOOK RESULTS from an unusual six-year collaboration between a nontraditional strategy researcher and an eclectic marketing scholar. Both of us were searching for meaning in the changes stirring in our economy in the late 1990s. Chance encounters brought us together. Concerns about the underlying causes of these changes dominated our initial encounters. Early on, we agreed that both the constant fear of discontinuities and the wild exuberance were equally unjustified.

In 1999 and again in 2000, one of us taught an M.B.A. course called "Emerging Issues in Strategy." Its basic premise was straightforward: The old, established corporations (let's call them "A-type" firms) would not disappear. The new, energetic dot-coms ("B-type" firms) would not necessarily survive. A new class of firms ("C-type") would emerge, signifying a morphing and evolving of both the A-type incumbents and the B-type start-ups. The changes underway appeared more subtle and profound. Dot-coms weren't simply toppling long-standing firms or vice versa. Both of us implicitly agreed that the phenomenon deserved more active and thoughtful investigation. Thus began our journey together, a period of intense collaboration and research.

We came to some early conclusions. The phenomenon was indeed not cosmetic. It cut across rich and poor, across developed and developing countries, and across private and public sectors. It challenged the distinction between enterprises and households. The phenomenon seemed universal, forcing change in governments and industries alike. In nearly

ix

all cases, there was a portending shift in the balance of influence between the individual and the institution—be it the legislature, the hospital, the university, or the corporation. More important, the individual could actively participate in the process by which all these institutions generated value, almost as if one were combining the efficiencies of the modern era with what the English so nostalgically call the "bespoke" world. The consumer and the firm are intimately involved in *jointly creating value that is unique to the individual consumer* and sustainable to the firm.

In this book, we take a cohesive approach to understanding the nature of this emerging reality. Our task here is to "amplify weak signals" from a diversity of institutions, industries, and countries and to present readers with a *new frame of reference* for value creation. The question is: How can we go from A-type and B-type firms to the C-type firm without exacting an unreasonable human cost? If you want a set of checklists and commandments based on current business fads, then don't read this book. But if you want to understand how the industrial system as we have known it is morphing and evolving, and want a consistent point of view on how it will change the way we compete in the future, then this book is for you.

While we do not suggest a revolution, we do see wide departures from traditional ways of sensing, thinking, and doing. For example, in the conventional realm of A-type and B-type firms, almost all of the work has centered on the firm. It is traditional to categorize enterprises as business-to-business (B2B) or business-to-consumer (B2C), decidedly putting "business" first and taking a firm-centric view of the economy. This book challenges those conventions. What if the individual consumer (whether in an enterprise or a household) were at the center, and not the firm? What if we spoke of "consumer-to-business-to-consumer" (C2B2C) patterns of economic activity?

Consequently, we challenge the traditional notion of value and its creation, namely that firms create and exchange value with consumers. We believe that, increasingly, the joint efforts of the consumer and the firm—the firm's extended network and consumer communities together—are *co-creating* value through *personalized experiences* that are unique to each individual consumer. This proposition challenges the fundamental assumptions about our industrial system—assumptions about value itself, the value creation process, and the nature of the relationship between the firm and the consumer. In this new paradigm, the firm and the consumer co-create value at *points of interaction*. Firms cannot think and act unilaterally.

This book reveals unprecedented opportunities for value creation and innovation. But to recognize these prospects, we must regard the world through new lenses and with a deep understanding of our existing framework of value creation. Which ideas from the past must we discard? What new perspectives are needed to comprehend the evolving industrial system? Throughout this book, we present new lenses and contrast them with the old set—the point of departure.

This book's purpose is clear: *to guide business leaders in their search for new strategic capital*, helping them to break out of their old entrenched ways and discover new ones. To move into the new "zones of opportunity," all of us must recognize the limitations of what we know, our "zones of comfort."

Throughout this book, we use a lot of examples as *thinking props* to convey our perspective and key ideas, not to illustrate best practices. Instead, we strive to discover *next* practices, and so no single example could possibly exemplify the entire framework. We neither prescribe "one best way" nor glorify any one company as the model of the future. We recognize a wide array of options that institutions and individuals can explore and "co-shape," to cope with and capture the opportunities available to everyone reading this book.

This book is more than an invitation to think differently; it is a clarion call to action—to help co-create a new world of possibilities. While we focus primarily on the implications for managers, we believe that, ultimately, all of us will have to behave differently—not just as business leaders, but as consumers, employees, investors, and global citizens—thereby rebalancing the relative influence of the individual and the large institution. We expect a long but exciting journey through the unfamiliar that will force us out of our comfort zones.

We expect you to raise your own specific questions as you peruse each chapter. We can imagine a book like ours, someday soon, with enough embedded intelligence to adapt and evolve its contents along with you—a "living book" if you will—so that you can interact with it and co-construct a personalized experience, should you so desire. For now, you can co-create and extract greater value from this book by jotting your questions in margins and at ends of chapters, to review them periodically as you move along.

N<small>O BOOK OF THIS KIND</small> can be written without help and significant dialogue with a large number of colleagues and managers. We owe a special debt to several who read early versions of the manuscript and shared with us their suggestions for improvement. Our colleagues Gordon Hewitt, M. S. Krishnan, Gautum Ahuja, Richard Bagozzi, Vikram Nanda, and Anuradha Nagarajan provided detailed feedback and support throughout the process.

Several thoughtful managers gave us their perspective and unstinted support: Larry Keeley (Doblin Group), Jan Oosterveld (Philips), C. V. Nataraj (Unilever), Roy Dunbar (Eli Lilly), Vince Barabba (General Motors), Herbert Schmitz (formerly of P&G Europe), Ron Bendersky (UMBS Executive Education), Debra Dunn (Hewlett Packard), Neerja Raman (HP Imaging Labs), Scott Fingerhut and Stefano Malnati (formerly of PRAJA), S. Ramachander (ACME), V. Sriram (Indian Railways), and Jorge Lopez, Tim Enwall, Lauren Shu, and Steve Bell (all at GartnerG2).

We have also benefited from interactions with Diane Coutu and David Champion *(Harvard Business Review)*, Bob Evans and Stephanie Stahl *(Information Week)*, Brian Gilhooly *(Optimize)*, and Ann Graham *(Strategy and Business)*.

We have particularly benefited from the contributions of Kerimcan Ozcan, a doctoral student, who has interacted with us very closely, engaging in scholarly debate. Thanks also to Venkatesh Rajah and Sukumar Ramanathan for providing feedback in the early stages of our research.

More than four hundred students in our M.B.A. classes read early versions of the manuscript and provided detailed comments. We extend our gratitude to all of them. We especially thank Kunal Mehra for his persistence and untiring willingness to provide feedback. We have benefited from all the generous and thoughtful suggestions.

Needless to say, we build on the work of several other scholars and writers. Peter Drucker has always inspired us with his ability to see developments in their historical context. We have benefited from the work of Wroe Alderson, John Seely Brown, Frances Cairncross, Manuel Castells, Clayton Christensen, Jim Collins, Thomas Davenport, Stan Davis and Chris Meyer, Michael Dertouzos, Yves Doz, Kathleen Eisenhardt, Philip Evans and Thomas Wurster, Richard Foster, Sumantra Goshal, Andrew Grove, Stephan Haeckel, John Hagel III, Gary Hamel, Charles Handy, F. A. von Hayek, Tom Kelley, Kevin Kelly, Chan Kim and Renée Mauborgne, Philip Kotler, Dorothy Leonard-Barton, Regis

McKenna, Henry Mintzberg, John Naisbitt, Nicholas Negroponte, Ikujiro Nonaka and Hirotaka Takeuchi, Richard Normann and Rafael Ramirez, Don Peppers and Martha Rogers, Tom Peters, B. Joseph Pine II and James Gilmore, Michael E. Porter, Howard Rheingold, Mohanbir Sawhney, Bernd Schmitt, Michael Schrage, Joseph Schumpeter, Peter Senge, Patricia Seybold, Carl Shapiro and Hal Varian, Michael J. Silverstein and George Stalk Jr., Adrian Slywotzky, Thomas Stewart, Don Tapscott, Stefan Thomke, Noel Tichy, Alvin Toffler, David Ulrich, Sandra Vandermerwe, Eric von Hippel, Gerald Zaltman, Shoshana Zuboff and James Maxmin, and many more. While we have benefited from the work of others and owe them an intellectual debt, this book represents our synthesis and our point of view.

A good editor is a co-creator. Kirsten Sandberg, our editor, continuously and untiringly cajoled and coaxed us to refine the argument. Karl Weber helped us in clearing the underbrush, making the argument simpler without simplifying it. We owe them a deep debt for their persistence and commitment in bringing clarity to a complex argument.

We would also like to thank Susan Catterall, Sharon Rice, Jennifer Waring, and the entire production and marketing team at Harvard Business School Press.

Finally, we could not have done this work without the unwavering support of our wives—Gayatri and Bindu. Their belief in our search and its importance was unwavering. By taking on a disproportionate part of the duties of parenting, they gave us the privilege of time and the peace of mind required for research and writing. Our children—Deepa, Murali, and Lalitha—were a constant source of inspiration and encouragement.

While we are grateful to many who helped us with this book, we alone are responsible for all its shortcomings.

C. K. Prahalad
Venkat Ramaswamy

Chapter One

CO-CREATION OF VALUE

A PROFOUND, BUT SILENT, transformation of our society is afoot. Our industrial system is generating more goods and services than at any point in history, delivered through an ever-growing number of channels. Superstores, boutiques, online retailers, and discount stores proliferate, offering thousands of distinct products and services. This product variety is overwhelming to consumers. Am I buying the right digital camera? Am I getting the best treatment for my chronic ulcer? Am I signing up for the right service? Simultaneously, thanks to the propagation of cell phones, Web sites, and media channels, consumers have increased access to more information, at greater speed and lower cost, than ever before. But who has the leisure and the proficiency needed to sort through and evaluate all these products and services? The burgeoning complexity of offerings, as well as the associated risks and rewards, confounds and frustrates most time-starved consumers. *Product variety has not necessarily resulted in better consumer experiences.*

For senior management, the situation is no better. Advances in digitization, biotechnology, and smart materials are increasing opportunities to create fundamentally new products and services and transform businesses. Major discontinuities in the competitive landscape—ubiquitous connectivity, globalization, industry deregulation, and technology convergence—are blurring industry boundaries and product definitions. These discontinuities are releasing worldwide flows of information, capital, products, and ideas, allowing nontraditional competitors to upend the status quo. At the same time, competition is intensifying and profit margins are shrinking. Managers can no longer focus solely on costs, product and process quality, speed, and efficiency. For profitable growth, managers must *also* strive for new sources of innovation and creativity.

Thus, the paradox of the twenty-first-century economy: Consumers have more choices that yield less satisfaction. Top management has more strategic options that yield less value. Are we on the cusp of a new industrial system with characteristics different from those we now take for granted? This question lies at the heart of this book.

The emerging reality is forcing us to reexamine the traditional system of company-centric value creation that has served us so well over the past hundred years. We now need a new frame of reference for value creation. The answer, we believe, lies in a different premise centered on *co-creation* of value. It begins with the changing role of the consumer in the industrial system.

The Changing Role of the Consumer

The most basic change has been a shift in the role of the consumer— from isolated to connected, from unaware to informed, from passive to active. The impact of the connected, informed, and active consumer is manifest in many ways. Let us examine some of them.[1]

Information Access

With access to unprecedented amounts of information, knowledge-able consumers can make more informed decisions. For companies accustomed to restricting the flow of information to consumers, this shift is radical. Millions of networked consumers are now collectively challenging the traditions of industries as varied as entertainment, financial services, and health care.

For instance, active health care consumers (no longer the passive recipients of treatment, a.k.a., *patients*) are using the Internet to learn about diseases and treatments; the track records of doctors, hospitals, and clinics; and the latest clinical drug trials and experimental procedures—and to share their personal experiences with others. Consumers can now question their physicians more aggressively and participate more fully in their own treatment modalities.

Global View

Consumers can also access information on firms, products, technologies, performance, prices, and consumer actions and reactions from around the world. Twenty years ago, the two car dealerships (General Motors and Ford) in small towns in North America would probably have influenced the driving aspirations of a local teenager. Today, a teen anywhere can dream about owning one of more than seven hundred car models listed on the Internet, creating a serious gap between what is immediately available in the neighborhood and what is most desirable.

Geographical limits on information still exist, but they are eroding fast, changing the rules of business competition. For example, broader consumer scrutiny of product range, price, and performance across geographic borders is limiting multinational firms' freedom to vary the price or quality of products from one location to another.

Networking

Human beings have a natural desire to coalesce around common interests, needs, and experiences. The explosion of the Internet and advances in messaging and telephony—the number of mobile phone users is already over one billion—is fueling this desire, creating an unparalleled ease and openness of communication among consumers. Consequently, "thematic consumer communities," in which individuals share ideas and feelings without regard for geographic or social barriers, are revolutionizing emerging markets and transforming established ones.

The power of consumer communities comes from their independence from the firm. In the pharmaceutical industry, for instance, word of mouth about actual consumer experiences with a drug, and not its claimed benefits, is increasingly affecting patient demands. Thus, consumer networking inverts the traditional top-down pattern of marketing communications.

Experimentation

Consumers can also use the Internet to experiment with and develop products, especially digital ones. Consider MP3, the compression standard for encoding digital audio developed by a student Karlheinz

Brandenburg and released to the public by the Fraunhofer Institute in Germany. Once technology-savvy consumers began experimenting with MP3, a veritable audio-file-sharing movement surged to challenge the music industry. The collective genius of software users the world over has similarly enabled the co-development of such popular products as the Apache Web server software and the Linux operating system.

Of course, the Internet facilitates consumer sharing in nondigital spheres as well: Aspiring chefs swap recipes, gardening enthusiasts share tips on growing organic vegetables, and homeowners share insights into home improvements. More crucial, consumer networks allow proxy experimentation—that is, learning from the experiences of others. The diversity of informed consumers around the world creates a wide base of skills, sophistication, and interests that any individual can tap into.

Activism

As people learn, they can better discriminate when making choices; and, as they network, they embolden each other to act and speak out. Consumers increasingly provide unsolicited feedback to companies and to each other. Already, hundreds of Web sites are perpetuating consumer activism, many targeting specific companies and brands. America Online's AOL Watch, for example, posts complaints from former and current AOL customers. Blogs (Web logs) that present an individual's worldview through texts, images, and Web links, facilitate public expression and debate.

The Web has also become a powerful tool by which groups focused on issues such as child labor and environmental protection seek corporate and governmental attention and promote reforms. Consumer advocacy through online groups may have even greater impact than company marketing. When Novartis AG launched clinical trials of a promising leukemia drug, Gleevec, word spread so fast on the Internet that the company was inundated by demand from patients wanting to participate. Activism by leukemia patients who were on the early clinical trials for this drug led to a highly effective lobbying effort via Internet support groups to speed up its production, and even get the Food & Drug Administration (FDA) to expedite its approval.[2]

What is the net result of the changing role of consumers? Companies can no longer act autonomously, designing products, developing production processes, crafting marketing messages, and controlling sales channels with little or no interference from consumers. Consumers now seek to exercise their influence in every part of the business system. Armed with new tools and dissatisfied with available choices, consumers want to interact with firms and thereby co-create value. The use of *interaction* as a basis for co-creation is at the crux of our emerging reality.

Consumer-Company Interactions: The Emerging Reality of Value Creation

Consider the evolution of the health care industry. Innovations in pharmaceuticals, biotechnology, nutrition, cosmetics, and alternative therapies are creating various treatment modalities and transforming our concepts of health. As both consumers and technologies advance, traditional medicine ("curing sickness"), preventive medicine, and improvements in the quality of life are rapidly merging into a "wellness space." Let us examine the changing dynamics of interaction between a consumer and the firms that participate in the wellness space.

Twenty years ago, when I was feeling ill and visited my doctor, I might have undergone a battery of tests that would have informed my doctor's diagnosis, which he would explain to me only if he had to. He would then choose a treatment modality, prescribe some medications, and schedule a follow-up examination. Health care back then was generally doctor-centric, just as commerce was company-centric. Doctors thought that they knew how to treat me, and since I wasn't a physician myself, I probably agreed. Similarly, most businesses figured that they knew how to create customer value—and most customers agreed.

Now, the health care process is far more complex. As soon as I feel ill, I can tap into the expertise and experience of other patients and health care professionals. I can access an abundance of information, some of it reliable, some not. I can learn what I want about breast cancer or high cholesterol or liposuction. I can investigate alternative treatments for any condition and develop an opinion about what might and might not work for me.

Ultimately, I can cut my own path through the wellness space, thereby constructing a personal wellness portfolio. If I'm grappling with high cholesterol, then I can include pharmaceuticals for blood pressure and cholesterol approved by the FDA, health supplements not approved by the FDA, a fitness regimen developed with an instructor, and genetic screening for hereditary heart disease.

Notice that my wellness portfolio does not fit neatly into any traditional industry classification. Yes, I visit my doctor. I get tests and medications and submit the bills to my medical insurance, provided through my employer. But other services in my wellness portfolio fall outside the conventional doctor-based health care, pharmaceutical, or insurance industries. *My* wellness space springs from *my* view of wellness, my biases, values, expertise, preferences, expectations, experiences, and financial wherewithal. My spouse, meanwhile, can construct her own wellness portfolio.

Rather than rely solely on my doctors' expertise, I can seek experts among my peers—other health care consumers—organized into thematic communities, such as a high-cholesterol group. This networked knowledge encompasses not just the medical aspects pertinent to my condition but its sociology, psychology, and likely impact on me, my family, and the community at large.

Thus, my next visit to the doctor can differ dramatically from the conventional checkup. I can ask, Why did you prescribe this treatment? Why not the alternative that I found through my exploration with other consumers and the Web? My doctor probably won't enjoy my challenging his expertise and authority. After all, I'm asking him to explain and defend his approach, which takes time and energy. What's more, I'm testing the depth, breadth, and currency of his knowledge. What if I'm experimenting with alternatives—herbs, dietary supplements, and so on—that he may not yet understand? Will he know of any complex interactions between these treatment modalities? Should he?

Of course, health care consumers have always shaped their own treatment to a certain extent. Remember Grandma's prescribing a remedy such as chicken soup for a cold? But with today's access to information, consumer war stories, and advice from an experienced peer group, consumers are far more likely to network and experiment than ever before. As a health care consumer, I can more actively determine the "value bundle" that is appropriate for *me*, cutting across customary industry boundaries.

Now position yourself as a manager in a pharmaceutical firm. The commingling of traditional industries into a complex, evolving wellness space challenges deeply entrenched and implicit assumptions in managerial tradition, which have evolved over decades. For starters, what constitutes or defines a product or service? Is an antiwrinkle cream with

Retinol a cosmetic, a fashion, or a pharmaceutical product? With unclear industry boundaries, how do we identify the nature of our competitive advantage?

More important, what value does the pharmaceutical firm provide in the wellness space of an active, involved consumer? How does the consumer's increasing desire to interact with both the providers and their provisions affect the various parties involved in that consumer's wellness space? Who bears the risk—the doctor, the hospital, or the patient? Patients will likely hold doctors, as experts, accountable.

Let's move beyond doctors and patients. What if consumers inappropriately use or modify your products and then hold you responsible for any resulting damage? Increasingly, consumers seem to want power without accountability. They want to choose for themselves but not be liable for the consequences of their choice. Are you as a manager responsible for the product's performance even though you cannot control the consumer's usage? How do you protect yourself? Is this risk a new cost of doing business? No matter how the future unfolds in terms of the roles, rights, and responsibilities of companies and consumers, companies *will* have to engage consumers in co-creation of value.

Thus, when we scrutinize consumer-company interactions and amplify the weak signals reverberating in the wellness space, we glimpse the emerging reality of the active involvement of consumers, whether as thematic communities or as informed individuals. This fundamentally challenges two deeply embedded, traditional business assumptions: (1) that any given company or industry can create value unilaterally; and (2) that value resides exclusively in the company's or industry's products and services. What new concepts do we need to understand the implications of the emerging pattern of interactions between consumers and the firm?

Co-Creation of Value

Let us stay with the wellness space and look at cardiac pacemakers. More than five million adults in the United States suffer from various cardiac maladies. Many of them could get a pacemaker that monitors and manages their heart rhythm and performance, a valuable benefit. However, a patient's comfort level would increase substantially if someone or something monitored his heart remotely, and alerted him and his doctor simultaneously of any deviations from a predetermined

bandwidth of performance, relevant to his condition. Doctor and patient together could decide on the remedial response.

The scenario gets more complicated when the patient travels far
from home. A mere alert will not suffice. The patient needs directions
to the best nearby hospital, and the attending physician needs access to
the patient's medical history. How do the two doctors—his primary
care provider back home and the physician on call at the out-of-town
hospital—coordinate their diagnosis and treatment? Should he call his
spouse? How can he recognize and assess the risks and develop an approach to compliance and cooperation with these medical professionals? Are the doctors, the facilities and services, and the pacemaker all
part of a network centered on the patient and his well-being?

Companies are already installing elements of these network capabilities. Consider Medtronic, Inc., a world leader in cardiac rhythm
management that seeks to offer lifelong solutions for patients with
chronic heart disease. It has developed a system of "virtual office visits"
that enables physicians to check patients' implanted cardiac devices via
the Internet. With the Medtronic CareLink Monitor, the patient can
collect data by holding a small antenna over his implanted device. The
data are captured by the antenna, downloaded by the monitor, and
transmitted by a standard telephone line to the Medtronic CareLink
Network. On a dedicated secure Web site, physicians can review patient data and patients can check on their own conditions—but no one
else's—and grant access to family members or other caregivers.[3]

Medtronic's CareLink system goes beyond the cardiac device itself
and unleashes opportunities for an expanding range of value creation
activities. For example, each person's heart responds to stimulation
slightly differently, and the response can change over time. In the future,
doctors will be able to respond to such changes by adjusting the patient's
pacemaker remotely. Furthermore, Medtronic's technology platform can
support a wide range of devices and remote monitoring/diagnostic systems, potentially used for monitoring blood sugar readings, brain activity, blood pressure, and other important physiological measures.

We believe that the pacemaker story, as summarized in figure 1-1, is
a prototype of the emerging process of value creation.

Now, as a manager, consider the following questions:

1. How does the patient *actively* participate in the process of
co-creating value?

FIGURE 1 - 1

Cardiac Pacemakers and the Patient Co-Creation Experience

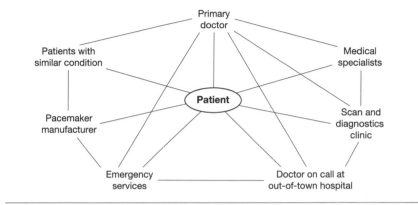

2. How does the quality of the patient's *interactions* with the doctor, the family, and the staff of the out-of-town hospital affect the quality of the patient's overall experience?

3. What is the basis of value creation here? What role does the total *network* of related products, services, and caregivers play in creating value? How can any one of them create *unique value* with the patient at any given point in time? What if the patient values the whole experience co-created with the network, and not simply with the pacemaker?

4. How does the network's ability to accommodate different situations affect the patient experience—different time and location of the *event* of an irregular heartbeat? Can the same individual have a different experience with the network under different circumstances, depending on the context of the event and his personal preferences at that moment in time?

5. Are experiences therefore *contextual?* Given the same network, can an individual have different experiences, depending not only on the situational *context* (time and space) of the event, but also on the social and cultural context of the event? How much do intangible aspects of a patient's context influence the experience?

6. Do patients as individuals react differently to similar problems? Given the same network, similar medical problems, and even similar circumstances, can different individuals have different experiences? How does patient *heterogeneity* influence the nature and quality of experience?

7. Can companies create an environment that generates *experience variety* without burdening the consumer with a variety of products and services?

The pacemaker story illustrates the new value creation space: a competitive space centered on *personalized co-creation experiences* developed through purposeful interactions between the consumer and a network of companies and consumer communities.

Value does not stem from the physical product, the pacemaker, or from the communication and IT network that supports the system, and not even from the social and skill network that includes doctors, hospitals, the family, and the broader consumer community. *Value lies in the co-creation experience of a specific patient, at a specific point in time, in a specific location, in the context of a specific event.*

The co-creation experience originates in the patient's interaction with the network. It cannot occur without a network of firms collaborating to create the environment that allows the patient to undergo that unique co-creation experience. The network, not owned by any single firm, multiplies the value of the pacemaker to the patient, his family, and his doctors. The patient, by co-creating with the network, is an active stakeholder in defining the interaction and the context of the event. The total co-creation experience with the network results in value that is more personal and unique for each individual.

In the conventional value creation process, companies and consumers had distinct roles of production and consumption. Products and services contained value, and markets exchanged this value, from the producer to the consumer. Value creation occurred outside the markets. But as we move toward co-creation, as with the pacemaker, this distinction disappears. Increasingly, consumers engage in the processes of both defining and creating value. The co-creation experience of the consumer becomes the very basis of value.

At a basic level, the pacemaker example encapsulates the changed relationship between the firm and its consumers. As we saw in the patient-doctor interaction, we find that the consumer (pacemaker patient) and all the firms in the network interact intensely, involving *access* to information on all sides, a level of *transparency*, and, more important, human *dialogue* and an ongoing *assessment of risk*.

However, the pacemaker firm must deal with a large number of consumers, inevitably a heterogeneous lot, with different approaches to the interaction. Consumers can also interact with multiple thematic communities. The firm also interacts with multiple communities in the network, including those of health care professionals and the service providers that operate and maintain the IT and Internet infrastructure. The pacemaker firm may have little influence over these groups. Finally, for the same consumer, the co-creation experience at two different times will not be the same. The event's context in space and time, as well as the eagerness and level of involvement of the individual, influences the experience.

We can conceptualize these increasingly complex patterns of interaction between the consumer and the firm, as shown in figure 1-2. In the emerging reality, these patterns of interactions between the consumer

FIGURE 1 - 2

The Spectrum of Co-Creation Experiences

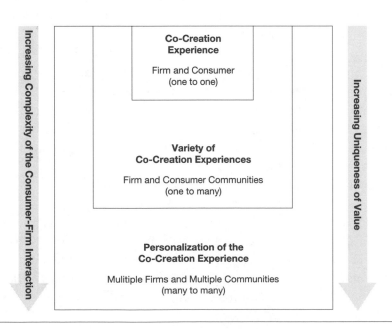

and the firm will shape the value creation process, challenging existing ways of doing business and creating value. Simultaneously, they create tremendous new opportunities.

But to see these opportunities, we must suspend the traditional distinction between B2"B" and B2"C" customers. In the world of co-creation, we have to imagine every individual who interacts with the company as a "consumer," whether that individual is a fork-lift opera-tor, a pilot, a design engineer, a beautician, a clinical researcher, an instructor, a contractor, a paralegal, or a civic worker. This perspective forces us to discard the artificial distinctions among enterprises and households. Furthermore, historically we have started with "B"—our business—and not the individual consumer. This company-centric view of value creation is deep-rooted, as it has been the very foundation of competition in the industrial era.

The future of competition, however, lies in an altogether new ap-proach to value creation, based on *an individual-centered co-creation of value between consumers and companies.* To see this future, we must escape the past. And to escape the past, we must understand it—that is, we must recognize the belief structures that underlie our actions as managers.

Escaping the Past:
The Traditional System of Value Creation

The traditional belief structure that has served business leaders so well for the past hundred years is shown in figure 1-3.

The relationships between the rows and the columns in the chart depict the internal consistency of the traditional logic of value creation. Let us start with the premises in the top row of the figure.

Traditional business thinking starts with the premise that the firm creates value. A firm autonomously determines the value that it will provide through its choice of products and services. Consumers repre-sent demand for the firm's offerings.

The implications for business follow from these premises. The firm needs an interface with consumers—an exchange process—to move its goods and services. This firm-customer interface has long been the locus of the producer's extracting economic value from the consumer. Firms have developed multiple approaches to extracting this value—by increasing the variety of offerings, by efficiently delivering and servic-ing those offerings, by customizing them for individual consumers, or

FIGURE 1 - 3

The Traditional Frame of Reference for Value Creation

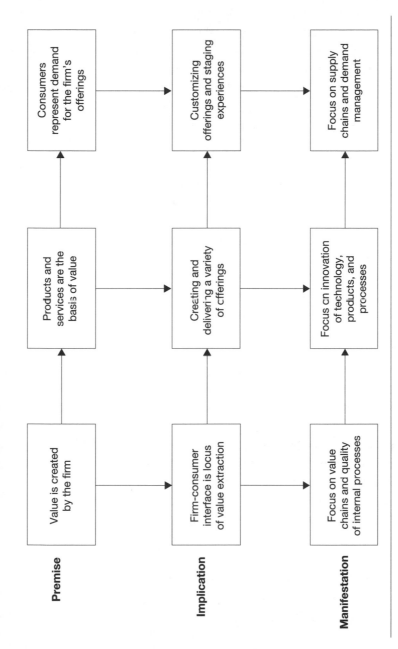

by wrapping contexts around them and staging the value creation process, as themed restaurants do.

These premises and implications manifest themselves in the perspectives and practices of firms in the industrial system. Managers focus on the "value chain" that captures the flow of products and services through operations that the firm controls or influences. This value chain system essentially represents the "linear cost build" of products and services. Decisions on what to make, what to buy from suppliers, where to assemble and service products, and a host of other supply and logistics decisions all emanate from this perspective. Employees focus on the quality of the firm's products and processes, potentially enhanced through internal disciplines such as Six Sigma and Total Quality Management. Innovation involves technology, products, and processes.

Thus, we have a coherent system for value creation. The rows and columns are internally consistent. If the firm creates value, then the value creation process is separate from the market, where various parties simply exchange this value. The importance of efficiently matching supply from the firm's value chain with demand from consumers becomes obvious. In fact, matching supply and demand has long been the bedrock of the value creation process.

But the cardiac pacemaker case signals a different starting point. Consider the shifts in thinking identified thus far. Consumers are overwhelmed and dissatisfied by the product variety available today. Armed with new connective tools, consumers want to interact and co-create value, not just with one firm but with whole communities of professionals, service providers, and other consumers. The co-creation experience depends highly on individuals. Each person's uniqueness affects the co-creation process as well as the co-creation experience. A firm cannot create anything of value without the engagement of individuals. Co-creation supplants the exchange process.

The New Frame of Reference for Value Creation

What might a new, internally consistent system based on co-creation of value look like? We present such a system in figure 1-4.

The new starting premise is that the consumer and the firm co-create value, and so the co-creation experience becomes the very basis of value. The value creation process centers on individuals and their co-creation experiences.

FIGURE 1 - 4

The New Frame of Reference for Value Creation

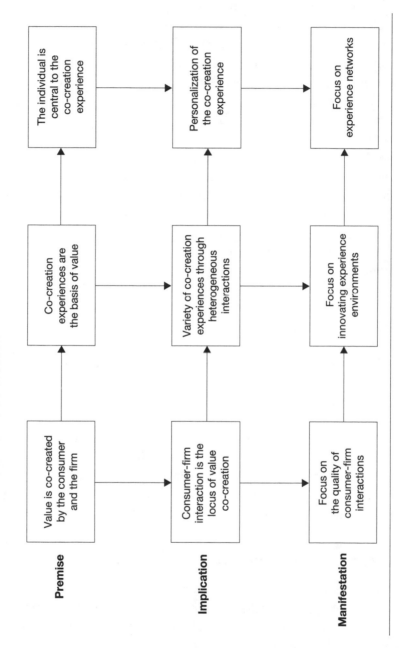

	Premise	**Implication**	**Manifestation**
	Value is co-created by the consumer and the firm	Consumer-firm interaction is the locus of value co-creation	Focus on the quality of consumer-firm interactions
	Co-creation experiences are the basis of value	Variety of co-creation experiences through heterogeneous interactions	Focus on innovating experience environments
	The individual is central to the co-creation experience	Personalization of the co-creation experience	Focus on experience networks

New premises inevitably lead to new implications for business. The interaction between consumers and firms becomes the new locus of co-creation of value. Since millions of consumers will undoubtedly seek different interactions, the value creation process must accommodate a variety of co-creation experiences. Context and consumer involvement contribute to the meaning of a given experience to the individual and to the uniqueness of the value co-created.

These premises and implications suggest new capabilities for firms. Managers must attend to the quality of co-creation experiences, not just to the quality of the firm's products and processes. Quality depends on the infrastructure for interaction between companies and consumers, oriented around the capacity to create a variety of experiences. The firm must efficiently innovate "experience environments" that enable a diversity of co-creation experiences. It must build a flexible "experience network" that allows individuals to co-construct and personalize their experiences. Eventually, the roles of the company and the consumer converge toward a unique co-creation experience, or an "experience of one."

Notice what co-creation is *not*. It is neither the transfer nor outsourcing of activities to customers nor a marginal customization of products and services. Nor is it a scripting or staging of customer events around the firm's various offerings. That kind of company-customer interaction no longer satisfies most consumers today.[4]

The change that we are describing is far more fundamental. It involves the co-creation of value through personalized interactions that are meaningful and sensitive to a specific consumer. The co-creation experience (not the offering) is the basis of unique value for each individual. The market begins to resemble a *forum* organized around individuals and their co-creation experiences rather than around passive pockets of demand for the firm's offerings.

Discovering Next Practices

Managers are under intense pressure to create value. But value creation by improving operational efficiency—through such initiatives as outsourcing, business process reengineering, and work force reduction—has natural limits in terms of morale and potential. Firms must couple such efficiencies with innovation and new business development. Internally generated profitable growth is at a premium. Even the best firms have struggled and are still struggling to create new markets or sustain a high rate of commercially successful innovations.

Obviously, managers need a radically different approach for reigniting the growth and innovation capabilities of their firms. We see a new frontier in value creation emerging, replete with fresh opportunities. But successful prospecting will require framing and practicing value creation in a fundamentally different way from that of the past.

Recognizing that the traditional system is becoming obsolete, many firms are already testing new business assumptions. As we reveal later in this book, these experiments can both guide and enlighten managers, when viewed through the new frame of co-creation. But innovation by extrapolation from the past, using those dusty one-way lenses, will likely fail to create the fundamental change required to compete in a world of co-creation.

In the emergent economy, competition will center on personalized co-creation experiences, resulting in value that is truly unique to each individual. This book provides a road map to that future, a map for a journey that we believe all business leaders must eventually and boldly make.

Chapter Two

BUILDING BLOCKS OF
CO-CREATION

I N THE PREVIOUS CHAPTER, we identified the dynamics of the active role of consumers and the changing relationship between the consumer and the firm. At the heart of this change is the emerging pattern of interactions between them. These interactions are the *locus* for the co-creation of value.

Consumer-Company Interaction in Co-Creating Value: The Sumerset Example

To illustrate the nature of deep interactions between a consumer and a firm in co-creating value, let's consider custom home building. Consumers expect to join in every step of the design and building process—indeed, they demand it. They want a home uniquely tailored to their needs and wishes, and they expect the builder to adapt, change, redesign, and re-imagine the project as many times as necessary to achieve this personalization. In customized construction, intense involvement with consumers is not optional; it is compulsory. Dominated by local firms, this business demands considerable face time between builders and consumers; and the finished product—the custom home—costs far more than a ready-made house.

One company has found a way to capture the spirit of custom home building remotely. Sumerset, a Kentucky-based company, is the world's largest builder of house*boats*, with over $30 million in annual sales.[1]

What if I wanted Sumerset to work with me in designing and building a unique houseboat that would serve not only as a recreational vehicle but also as my home? I would contact Sumerset's development group and discuss my ideas for the boat—size, furnishings, amenities, special features, and, of course, my budget. Over several conversations, their engineers and I would co-develop specifications for a boat that fits my needs.

Once we agreed on the specifications, the manufacturing process would begin. I could access the manufacturing plant through the Web, watch my boat being built, and track its progress. Ultimately, as a Sumerset customer, I could join a community of houseboaters. Through dialogue with this community, I could glean new ideas about how to design, accessorize, and enjoy my boat further.

Because the product development process is transparent to customers, they can intervene more often and more intensely than usual. This intensity requires Sumerset's engineers to be especially responsive, creative, and articulate. For example, suppose I wanted extra-large windows on my houseboat. Sumerset's engineers would discuss the pros and cons with me, including the associated risks. Then we could jointly decide on the window, based on the principle of informed choice.

Occasionally, as a customer, I might demand a feature that is dangerous or simply impractical. Given the high risks to the boat's structural soundness, Sumerset could refuse to incorporate it, but in the spirit of co-creation, would fully explain why.

The continuous dialogue between Sumerset and other customers like me helps the firm to identify and correct problems proactively rather than reactively. For example, motor exhausts, situated at the rear of most boats, are extremely toxic. Although Sumerset had switched to a side exhaust in 1996, houseboaters often tie their boats alongside other boats, and children usually play on the rear deck. When Sumerset learned that a couple tragically lost two sons to carbon monoxide poisoning in 2000, it redesigned the exhaust system. A new "dry stack" system introduced in 2002 separates the wet exhaust from the onboard generator and pumps harmless water from the side of the boat. The carbon monoxide now escapes via a top-mounted stack nine feet above the deck. Sumerset has volunteered to retrofit any boat, even those manufactured by others, with the dry stack system and has vigorously lobbied for adoption of the system as a new industry standard.[2] The involvement of Sumerset's customers in co-creation of value has enabled the firm to reduce risk very publicly and positively, no doubt saving more lives. Of course, the company also benefits financially from creating a unique new technology.

Let us now analyze the underlying dynamics between Sumerset and its customers. As in traditional manufacturing, the process involves a physical product—a houseboat. But the process of acquiring a boat differs from that of buying a car or television from a traditional manufacturer. Before customers even sign a contract, they interact intensely with Sumerset. The nature of the dialogue depends on the specific customer—individual needs, expertise, and desire for involvement—and usually evolves over time. To foster this dialogue, the company not only provides customers with access to the firm's employees and knowledge, but also clearly explains the risks and trade-offs of every customer choice throughout the process. Transparency on both sides characterizes the relationship: The customer must know what is happening at all times and why, while the firm must know the customer's desires, concerns, and requirements.

Not everyone enjoys such an interactive co-creation process. Some customers—including houseboat purchasers—elect not to dialogue at length about the product. Nor are all co-creation experiences positive. If the customer believes that her dialogue with the company has been unilateral or that the firm behaved unfairly or opaquely, or else failed to reveal and discuss the risks candidly, then the customer's co-creation experience may be very negative.

Nonetheless, customers who buy boats exclusively from Sumerset enjoy a number of distinct benefits:

- The co-creation process gives the customer a greater level of knowledge and expertise about houseboats, and with it a greater degree of self-esteem.

- Dialoguing with Sumerset's employees and tracking the progress of the boat along the factory floor creates a sense of emotional bonding with the product and the company.

- Sumerset's transparency and willingness to dialogue enhances the customer's readiness to trust the company and believe in the quality of its product.

- Access to the community of Sumerset customers increases the consumer's enjoyment of the houseboat.

Thus, the quality of the experience involved in co-creation differs markedly from that of a traditional product purchase. The basis of value for the customer shifts from a physical product (with or without ancillary services) to the total *co-creation experience*, which includes co-designing as well as all the other interactions among the consumer, the company, and the larger community of houseboaters. Thus, the co-creation experience depends on the nature and level of access to the company's employees and extended community, as well as the level of transparency of all parties.

Consider the same co-creation experience from Sumerset's perspective. The firm and its suppliers can learn more about consumers and get new ideas for design, engineering, and manufacturing. Sumerset's employees—from design engineers to carpenters—can more deeply understand consumer aspirations, desires, motivations, behaviors, and agreeable trade-offs regarding features and functions. Through continuous dialogue, employees can relate their efforts to individual consumers. The company can reduce uncertainty in capital commitments and even spot and eliminate sources of environmental risk.

But the co-creation process, demanding as it is, raises important questions for managers:

- In-depth dialogue with customers is very time-intensive. What if my firm has a million consumers—or ten million? My staff can barely keep up with current interactions with customers, suppliers, and each other. How can my firm interact so intensely with each consumer *and* maintain operational efficiency?

- Co-creation allows for an unusual degree of customer input into product design. How do I maintain consistently high standards of product quality *and* cede some control over design?

- Transparency allows customers to interact with my firm in potentially intrusive ways. How much access up and down the supply chain do I allow customers?

- Individual consumers are at the very heart of the co-creation experience. How do I deal with the heterogeneous demands of my customer base?

- Discussing options openly gives customers a degree of control over the risks that they assume—but not necessarily the liabilities.

Where do I draw the line on acceptable risks—and where do my legal responsibilities begin and end?

- Co-creation moves the firm toward an individual-centered view of demand. How does demand forecasting work under such unpredictable circumstances?

These difficult questions breach the very meaning of value and the process by which a firm co-creates value. In the chapters that follow, we will explore how that meaning and that process are evolving, and we will consider possible answers for the important questions that managers must confront.

The Building Blocks of Co-Creation

The Sumerset story exemplifies the emerging reality of the consumer-company interaction as the locus of value creation. It also illustrates the need to concentrate on the total co-creation experience, as well as the process of co-creation through its key building blocks: dialogue, access, risk assessment, and transparency, which we will refer to by the acronym DART. Let's discuss each of these key elements in more detail.

Dialogue

Dialogue means interactivity, deep engagement, and a propensity to act—on both sides. Dialogue is more than listening to customers: It entails empathic understanding built around experiencing what consumers experience, and recognizing the emotional, social, and cultural context of experiences. It implies shared learning and communication between two *equal* problem solvers. Dialogue creates and maintains a loyal community.

The dialogue involved in co-creation has several specific features:

- It focuses on issues that interest both the consumer and the firm.

- It requires a forum in which dialogue can occur.

- It also requires rules of engagement (explicit or implicit) that make for an orderly, productive interaction.

To illustrate why an effective co-creation dialogue requires these elements, consider the venerable golf industry. Three interested parties—

the Royal and Ancient Golf Club of St. Andrews (R&A), the United States Golf Association (USGA), and the manufacturers of golf clubs—have been battling over the effect of club heads on the length of golf drives. USGA rules control golfing in North America; R&A rules govern everywhere else.[3]

Since 1976, the USGA has tested drivers for "spring-like effect," which its rules prohibit ("the face or club head shall not have the effect at impact of a spring").[4] Nonetheless, club manufacturers have developed drivers whose flexibility produced the banned "spring-like effect," and some amateur golfers outside the United States eagerly bought and used the clubs to add length to their drives. In early fall of 2000, the R&A announced that it would neither test nor limit the flexibility of driver club heads.

Meanwhile, Callaway announced that it would become the first major manufacturer to market a "nonconforming" driver (the ERC II Forged Titanium Driver) in the United States. According to founder and chairman Ely Callaway, "We intend to give an unprecedented choice to U.S. golfers. It should not be considered a sin to play a nonconforming driver for fun."[5]

While the golfing associations and manufacturers debate the issue, no one knows where the interests of ordinary golfers lie. Weekend golfers have no real forum to express their views. The industry is, in effect, a closed circle in which the established organizations talk to one another but the consumer is excluded.

We see a similar pattern of exclusion in the music industry, roiled by debates over file sharing, copyright infringement, and the conflicting rights of artists, record companies, and consumers. The Recording Industry Association of America (RIAA) has a voice in these debates; so do the songwriters (through ASCAP, the American Society of Composers, Authors and Publishers), the media conglomerates, and the Internet companies. But consumers of music have no real opportunity to enter the dialogue beyond their support of (arguably illegal) peer-to-peer software and file-sharing networks like Kazaa and other successors to the now-defunct Napster.

Contrast those situations with the software community's "open source" movement. Free dialogue has significantly influenced evolving standards and developed a self-governing process to establish quality guidelines. Traditional industry players have perceived the dialogue's many benefits. In 2001, IBM committed about 20 percent of its R&D budget ($1 billion) to Linux and Apache Web servers.[6]

Similar initiatives are popping up in unlikely places. For example, Eli Lilly and Company launched the research venture InnoCentive LLC in June 2001. Via its Web site, this venture brings together companies and researchers from around the world to solve specific scientific problems.[7] Researchers who offer the solution judged best by the company posting the problem receive significant cash incentives. InnoCentive represents a bold open source approach to innovation for previously closed industries, opening up complex problems to the scientific community at large.

Dialogue also involves building thematic communities. Consider America Online (AOL), which long ago recognized the importance of cultivating a forum for dialogue among its customers. While telecommunications companies were vying to become Internet service providers, AOL was allowing its subscribers to engage with other consumers online through live chats, message boards, and newsgroups, and later through buddy lists and instant messaging enabled by AOL Instant Messenger protocol and ICQ ("I seek you") software. AOL recognized that individuals like to connect with each other and belong to a social network. With a buddy list, individuals can invite others selectively, giving the group a sense of privacy. This desire to be unique and uniquely connected to a social network is widespread.

Access

The traditional focus of the firm and its value chain was to create and transfer ownership of products to consumers. Increasingly, the goal of consumers is access to desirable experiences—not necessarily ownership of the product. One need not own something to access an experience. We must uncouple the notion of access from ownership.

Access begins with information and tools. Consider Taiwan Semiconductor Manufacturing Company (TSMC), one of the world's largest and more creative semiconductor firms. TSMC has given its customers access to data on its manufacturing processes, design and fabrication libraries, and quality processes.[8] Thus, as the semiconductor business becomes more software-oriented, even small software firms can access the knowledge base of large manufacturing facilities like TSMC, reducing the investment needed to participate effectively in the semiconductor business.

Access can also involve on-demand resources such as computing. Gateway's experimental Processing on Demand is slated to offer access to massive computational services rivaling those of supercomputers by harnessing the processing power of 8,000 PCs in 272 Gateway stores. Price: about fifteen cents per processor hour.[9] IBM's $10 billion on-demand computing initiative envisions a world in which companies can access computing power just like electricity, and get various information technology services as needed.[10]

Consumers may also want access to a lifestyle. Automobile leasing, for example, allows consumers to have the lifestyle of a car owner without the responsibilities of ownership. New forms of access to mobility are emerging. Why can't I sign a contract with General Motors or Ford that lets me drive four different types of cars, depending on what I am doing on any particular day? On Friday night, I'll drive a luxury car to a fancy restaurant; on Saturday morning, I'll take my daughter's soccer team to practice in an SUV; on Tuesday, I'll use a pickup to haul firewood; on Thursday, I'll drive an easy-to-park compact car to the mall. I'll pay a lump sum of, say, $5,000 per year for the privilege. I receive access to multiple lifestyles, through access to a pool of varied vehicles without the hassles of investment, ownership, and maintenance.

Over the past decade, numerous companies serving European and U.S. cities have begun to offer analogous services to people who prefer access over ownership. For example, in Switzerland, people who join Mobility CarSharing receive a personal access device that unlocks a dedicated pool of cars, rented on a pay-as-you-drive basis, making the service ideal for running short errands, visiting friends in the suburbs, and the like.[11] This new, urban lifestyle experience not only saves time and money but reduces pollution and parking problems. The travel and leisure industry employs similar access models in holiday time-share homes and partial lease arrangements for executive aircraft.

Access can create new opportunities in emerging markets.[12] The debate about the "digital divide" between the wealthy (who own computers) and the poor (who do not) assumes that ownership is a prerequisite for access. But in every big emerging market, cyber cafes and Internet kiosks are making online access available on a pay-per-use basis. In India, for example, one can use the Internet for about thirty cents an hour. That beats purchasing a PC for $1,000, the annual income of many Indian families. A single Internet connection in an Indian village provides a community of fishermen with access to weather forecasts, satellite images of fish shoals, and the latest market prices for their catch. The world's poorest are not the only beneficiaries. Using Web sites such as Healthnet.org, doctors in poor countries can easily and cheaply keep up to speed with the latest medical developments. In Bangladesh, the local Medinet system provides physicians with access to hundreds of expensive medical journals for less than $1.50 a month.

Access can also transform the capacity for self-expression. Thanks to rapid advances in technology, consumers now also have access to the value chains of entire industries that were traditionally company-controlled. For example, using new print on demand (POD) technology, anyone can publish a book for less than $400. The consumer accesses a POD publisher to design a cover and transmits the text to a book distributor, who digitally stores it. When readers order copies of the book, the distributor prints them individually at speeds exceeding a thousand pages per minute—most books take less than thirty seconds. The POD system radically alters the economics of book publishing, with no minimum print quantities, no inventories to warehouse, and no costly returns of unsold copies, which sometimes require shredding 30 to 40 percent of a printing.[13] The consumer can become author, publisher, and manager of the value creation process, and the reading public has access to many more books by budding authors. Finding the best new titles among the stacks is another matter.

Risk Assessment

Risk here refers to the probability of harm to the consumer. Managers have traditionally assumed that firms can better assess and manage risk than consumers can. Therefore, when communicating with consumers, marketers have focused almost entirely on articulating benefits, largely ignoring risks.

Today, however, there is a growing debate about risk and the trade-off between risks and benefits—a debate that the move to co-creation will intensify. Can firms unilaterally manage risks in an environment of co-creation? On the other hand, if consumers are active co-creators, should they shoulder responsibility for risks as well?

Consider hormone replacement therapy, a sixty-year-old business with revenues of $2.75 billion in 2000. Millions of women have found relief from menopausal symptoms such as sleeplessness and hot flashes by taking hormones. But new studies are revealing previously unknown risks to these treatments. One study from the Women's Health Initiative found that the risk of heart attack, breast cancer, stroke, and blood clots increased among women using hormone replacement therapy. Partly from these revelations, sales of Prempro, a dominant therapy in the menopause market used by six million American women in 2002, declined by 25 to 30 percent.[14]

Risk disclosure is emerging as a major bone of contention between consumers and businesses. Consider the debate over genetically modified (GM) food. Humans have been modifying plants and animals using breeding techniques for millennia. However, during the past twenty years, scientists have developed ways of identifying genes that produce specific characteristics and incorporating those genes directly into living organisms. The new made-to-order plants—from soybeans with specified protein content to pest-resistant strains of cotton—may prove significant to the world's poor. Feeding six billion people around the world is certainly a noble goal. But firms at the forefront of the GM business such as Monsanto failed to anticipate the concerns that many scientists and lay people would raise. Within a few years, Monsanto found itself cast as the villain in a battle over the supposed environmental and medical threats posed by Frankenfood ("Frankenstein food").[15]

Monsanto failed to recognize that today's consumers increasingly want to know about and debate the risks. A generation ago if Monsanto had stated, "We've assessed the risks, and the FDA has studied our products and approved them for sale," most consumers would have been satisfied. No longer. Today, people want to know the limits of our knowledge about GM food and the potential risks of rushing headlong into its production.

How deep is the skepticism about GM food? A poll found that readers of *Scientific American* magazine were equally divided on the merits and risks.[16] If this group—a relatively well informed and scientifically literate group—has qualms about GM food, then the general public will likely be even more anxious. In retrospect, Monsanto should have involved other agricultural and food organizations, government agencies, regulatory bodies, nongovernmental organizations (NGOs), and lay groups in debating the risk/reward trade-offs, potentially avoiding the development of a polarized, suspicious public.

Contrast that situation with the story of DeCode, a commercial venture that proposed conducting a detailed genetic study of the entire population of Iceland. This idea involved sensitive issues of privacy and individual freedom—potentially as controversial as GM food. In this case, however, DeCode conducted a public debate about the benefits and risks. Three major Icelandic newspapers published more than seven hundred articles. More than one hundred television and radio programs were also aired on the issue. The population had a chance to learn, debate, and build a consensus. As a result, the Icelandic parliament approved the project, passing a law to enable the collection of DNA data and make it available to researchers and pharmaceutical firms with adequate privacy guarantees.[17]

Risk assessment and informed choice got a boost from the U.S. Food and Drug Administration's decision to reintroduce Lotronex, a drug used in treating irritable bowel syndrome. After Lotronex was first introduced by GlaxoSmithKline in 2000, more than 275,000 patients used it. When significant side effects led to several deaths, Glaxo withdrew the drug from the market, less than ten months after its introduction.[18]

The story could have ended here. Not in the age of the active consumer. Thousands of irritable bowel sufferers protested, demanding that the FDA reapprove the drug's usage under stricter controls. In 2002, the FDA agreed: The approved dosage is now half its former level. Doctors may prescribe Lotronex after meeting several criteria. Doctors must enroll in a training program organized by GlaxoSmithKline and "self-attest" their understanding of the symptoms and risks involved. They must also agree to explain those risks clearly to their patients, who in turn must sign an agreement acknowledging their own understanding of the risks.

The Lotronex controversy was resolved through an active dialogue about risk among Glaxo, consumers, doctors, the FDA, pharmacists, and health care advocacy groups. But who bears the ultimate responsibility for the risk that Lotronex consumers assume? The answer is far from clear. Consumers are saying, "Give us the information, the tools, and the freedom to choose," but not necessarily, "We'll take responsibility for our choices."

The debate about informed consent and the responsibilities of companies and consumers will likely continue for years. However, we can safely assume that consumers will increasingly participate in co-creation of value. They will not cede their right to choose. However, they will insist that businesses inform them fully about risks, providing not just data but appropriate methodologies for assessing the personal and societal risk associated with products and services.

For their part, business leaders must ensure that the focus on risk assessment and harm reduction does not lead to a defensive mentality within the firm. On the contrary, risk management offers new opportunities for firms to differentiate themselves. An active dialogue on the risks and benefits involved in using products and services can create a new level of trust between the consumer and the company. For example, recent studies are divided on the benefits (as well as the risks) of breast cancer screening through mammograms. A study of more than ninety thousand Canadian women suggested that women in their forties reap no real benefits from mammography but suffer greatly from unnecessary treatment. Such issues put a premium on discussing the evidence concerning risks and benefits to consumers, even when the evidence is complex or contradictory, thus helping individuals make informed risk-benefit trade-offs.

Transparency

Companies have traditionally benefited from information asymmetry between the consumer and the firm. That asymmetry is rapidly disappearing. Firms can no longer assume opaqueness of prices, costs, and profit margins. And as information about products, technologies, and business systems becomes more accessible, creating new levels of transparency becomes increasingly desirable.

Consider the ongoing revolution in securities trading. Instinet, a global agency broker, uses advanced technology to enable managers of retail mutual funds, 401(k)s, IRAs, and other investment plans to negotiate the best execution price for a trade directly with each other, twenty-four hours a day, in more than forty markets worldwide.[19] The new level of transparency from the beginning of the trading cycle through post-trade cost assessment and settlement lets Instinet's customers measure the real-time costs of their trading. Such transparency of trading is now attracting individual investors, empowering many of them to trade alongside institutions.

Or consider Celera Genomics and the Human Genome Project, the historic transcription of "the book of life." Although the basic structure of the human genome has now been decoded, the process of finding distinct genes, understanding what they do, and tracing their links to various health conditions has just begun. An unprecedented level of transparency is impressively facilitating this work. Scientists can now use electronic research agents to conduct sophisticated analyses of the proteins formed by genes, even as they track similar ongoing work around the globe, thereby identifying potential targets for drug development. Thus, increased transparency in the scientific research process is enabling new patterns of discovery and development.[20]

Let us return to Taiwan Semiconductor Manufacturing Company (TSMC). By building transparency into its state-of-the-art Virtual Fab, TSMC is giving its "fabless" customers greater control of the design cycle and manufacturing process. The online system gives customers complete visibility of the manufacturing process for their products while supplying them with a full array of up-to-date information supporting their design needs. Customers can access TSMC engineering and supply chain information, its advanced technologies and processes, technology road maps, product planning support, yield analysis, monitoring of process reliability data, and more.

Combining the building blocks of transparency, risk assessment, access, and dialogue enables companies to better engage customers as collaborators. Transparency facilitates collaborative dialogue with consumers. Constant experimentation, coupled with access and risk assessment on both sides, can lead to new business models and functionalities designed to enable compelling co-creation experiences. Even conventional companies such as Sony now engage in collaborative dialogues with consumers, who helped co-develop Sony's PlayStation 2. From Intel to Microsoft to Nokia, consumers are helping to shape new technology, ranging from Web-enabled devices and networking software to cellular phones. They contribute to the debate, both technically and in terms of their expectations and views of value. In so doing, they are co-shaping the future.

The Building Blocks in Combination

Let's recapitulate. The four building blocks of co-creation are dialogue, access, risk assessment, and transparency—DART. *Dialogue* encourages not just knowledge sharing but, even more important, qualitatively new levels of understanding between companies and consumers. It also allows consumers to interject their views of value into the value creation process. *Access* challenges the notion that consumers can experience value only through ownership. By focusing on access to experiences at multiple points of interaction, as opposed to simply ownership of products, companies can broaden their business opportunities. *Risk assessment* assumes that if consumers become co-creators of value with companies, then they will demand more information about potential risks of goods and services; but they may also bear more responsibility for dealing with those risks. *Transparency* of information is necessary to create trust between institutions and individuals.

When companies combine the four building blocks in different ways, they can create the following new and important capabilities.

Access and Transparency

Coupling access with transparency enhances the consumer's ability to make informed choices. For instance, consumers in the United States now have instant access to yield rates of investment options offered by most financial services firms. They also have a reasonable level of transparency regarding the track record of various investment options and the quality of services offered, particularly the experiences of other customers with each firm. Consumers can therefore make better choices among investment options and firms.

Dialogue and Risk Assessment

Combining dialogue with risk assessment enhances the ability to debate and co-develop public and private policy choices. For instance, the existence of a broad-based dialogue, more scrutiny of companies, and widely disseminated information concerning the risks associated with cigarette smoking is increasingly leading society to develop new policies as well as facilitating more informed private choices. Ongoing debates concern such questions as: Should we let tobacco firms market their products in ways that attract children and young teenagers? Should cigarettes be sold in vending machines or on the Internet? Should we regulate and control tobacco as strictly as alcohol or prescription drugs? Acting as citizens, individuals are significantly affecting public policy even as they are making informed private decisions as consumers.

Access and Dialogue

Coupling access with dialogue enhances the ability to develop and maintain thematic communities. For instance, fans of NASCAR auto racing can use the Internet to learn about upcoming events, the favorites for each race, and the statistics of their favorite racers. They can join any of the number of online communities interested in dissecting the races, swapping stories about NASCAR events, and buying and selling memorabilia. Similar communities of interest form around themes ranging from fly fishing to the study of the musical instruments of twelfth-century China.

Transparency and Risk Assessment

Combining transparency with risk assessment enhances the ability to co-develop trust. For instance, the debate in the Firestone–Ford tire liability case centered on the amount of information Ford and/or Firestone had about risks associated with the combination of vehicles, tire pressure, and driving conditions. Should Firestone have revealed all the information about well-documented risks only, or also about the suspected but undocumented risks worth legitimate debate? Very few industries and firms volunteer to disclose risks and debate them with consumer groups. Should financial services firms have a "consumer bill of rights"? Should investors be informed about risks in clear English (or other local language), instead of legal jargon? Consumers must trust the firms with which they engage in co-creation.[21] The motto for smart companies is rapidly becoming "When in doubt, disclose."

The New Dynamics of Co-Creation

As we have seen, the elements of DART—dialogue, access, risk assessment, and transparency—are the basic building blocks of value co-creation, and managers can combine them in different ways. Although many firms and industries are experimenting with these elements, and the evidence of the changing nature of value creation accumulates, many companies are unable to embrace the new framework of co-creation. Why?

A large part of the answer is that co-creation fundamentally challenges the traditional roles of the firm and the consumer. The tension manifests itself at *points of interaction* between the consumer and the company—where the co-creation experience occurs, where individuals exercise choice, and where value is co-created. Points of interaction provide opportunities for collaboration and negotiation, explicit or implicit, between the consumer and the company—as well as opportunities for those processes to break down.

In the next chapter, we will examine the emerging dynamics at points of consumer-company interactions as well as the tensions inherent in them.

Chapter Three

THE CO-CREATION EXPERIENCE

A S WE HAVE SEEN, many companies have begun to experiment with co-creation of value. Still, most managers are reluctant to let go of familiar practices and tools—their zone of comfort. The result is an emerging tension between the traditional "company think" and the emerging "consumer think" around the issue of whether the firm can unilaterally control the choice of experiences in the co-creation process. We believe the answer is *no*.

The Co-Creation Experience as the Basis for Value: The Napster Example

In May 1999, Shawn Fanning created Napster, which allowed individuals to share digitized music files on the Internet. In effect, it fostered compelling new experiences for consumers, focusing on access, choice, and an individual-centric view of value, rather than the conventional company-controlled exchange built around predetermined packaging and distribution.

Napster attracted more than 40 million consumers before legal action by the established music industry shut it down.[1] We can debate the legality and even the morality of Napster's approach to music distribution—but not its popularity. Several successor firms have emerged and are thriving on the Internet. Obviously, millions of music fans are eager to proclaim, "I, the consumer, will choose and use the music I like in my own way."

For the entertainment establishment, Napster and its successors represent piracy, theft, and an enormous financial threat. But interpreted differently, the Napster story represents the best hope for the music industry's future. Napster demonstrated that consumers really like the music industry's products and want to consume more—but in their own way. They want open access to the world's music libraries so that they can select and experience music according to their current preferences, contexts, and communities.

Would any of Napster's users have willingly paid for downloaded songs? Probably, but the music industry offered no mechanism for doing so. Nor did music retailers permit consumers to sample songs, buy their favorites, burn them into CDs, and pay for their selections. Instead, music firms stuck to their traditional "We package it, you buy it" mode, which they sought to defend at all costs. They believed that the new technology would reduce music sales and perhaps kill the industry. The movie industry, which similarly feared VCRs a decade earlier, now fears digital video recorders and file sharing technology.[2]

Napster exposed the tensions between the traditional "company and product-centric" business system and the emerging "consumer and experience-centric" system:

- by removing the music industry's multiple levels of distribution, exposing the fault lines between the company and the consumer.

- by challenging the kinds of options available to consumers, showing that many music lovers want to wrest the choice of music—available only as pre-packaged products—away from company executives and brand managers.

- by questioning the appropriate price-experience relationship, forcing consumers and companies to measure the value added to the consumer experience from all the intermediate steps between recording and consumption, such as packaging, distribution, marketing, advertising, and promotion.

- by revealing the heterogeneity of music consumers, forcing the industry to imagine consumer-centric experiences for the first time.

The Napster story suggests that the tension between consumer and company in the music industry centers on the quality and the nature of the interaction between the two. Consumers will no longer pay for prepackaged selections of music. They want to exercise their choice and experience the music before they pay for it.

Napster may be dead, but Kazaa (with over 200 million downloads) and other peer-to-peer software and file-sharing companies are continuing to transform the music industry. Established firms not typically associated with the music industry are entering the fray. A case in point is Steve Jobs's new Applemusic initiative. In about two months since the launch of iTunes, over 5 million songs were downloaded at ninety-nine cents each.[3] In principle, in the emerging "fun space"—wrought by the convergence of electronics, computers, communications, and entertainment, initiatives such as Applemusic can evolve into a potential network of musicians, music libraries, devices, and music enthusiasts, through which consumers can exercise their view of choice and co-construct their own unique experiences. Many new possibilities for co-creation experiences in this fun space are springing up, such as the Digital Club Network (DCN), which has wired some of the better-known rock clubs in the United States, and Webcasts their concerts. DCN now controls the rights to more than four thousand concerts by hundreds of bands, most of them little-known, aspiring acts happy to sign over their rights in exchange for exposure and royalty potential down the road. DCN raises some interesting possibilities. What if a band that a record company signed suddenly succeeds? Why can't I get instantaneous access to the band's performances and co-construct my own experiences, which I am willing to pay for?[4]

Company Think Versus Consumer Think

Like all humans, business managers are socialized into a *dominant logic*—shaped by the attitudes, behaviors, and assumptions that they learn in their business environments.[5] Unfortunately, most managers seem to forget that they are also consumers. Their thinking is conditioned by managerial routines, systems, processes, budgets, and incentives created under the traditional framework of value creation. They focus on technology road maps, plant scheduling, product quality, cost reduction, cycle time, and efficiency. Unsurprisingly, opportunities for interaction with consumers are approached in a similar fashion.

For example, the company call center represents a unique opportunity for interacting with the consumer. A well-run call center can transform a consumer's experience from negative to positive, not only by solving problems and answering questions but by offering entirely new ways to enjoy the product or service. Yet most firms squander the opportunity by establishing automated call centers, manned by inexperienced, narrowly focused operators whose productivity is measured in terms of calls handled per hour—not the quality of the consumer experience. The managers who develop these systems mean well. They are simply applying the customary management techniques. But most consumer experiences with call centers are unpleasant, irritating—and potentially disastrous.

Simply understanding the framework of co-creation will not suffice. *We must explicitly recognize how deeply etched ways of thinking limit our ability to shift into co-creation mode.* We must understand the differences between "company think" and "consumer think" that will drive success in the twenty-first century (see figure 3-1).[6]

The disconnect between consumer think and company think is not new. However, as we move toward co-creation, this disconnect becomes more pronounced at points of consumer-company interaction, where choice is exercised and the consumer interacts with the firm to co-create an experience.

Consider the digital camera. It represents an amazing technological breakthrough with many powerful advantages for the consumer. The digital camera works without film, eliminating trips to the store for more film or development, and users can view pictures immediately. They can delete unwanted pictures, crop and edit the good ones, print copies at home, and share images with friends on the Internet.

Despite these wonderful features, the real value for consumers lies in the ease, intuitiveness, and seamlessness of this experience, not in the product itself. Think of a mom who takes her new digital camera to the beach. If she wastes half an hour learning how to navigate the camera's complex menu of directions, if she struggles that evening to download pictures of her kids to the PC, or if she discovers that she accidentally erased some of the pictures, then the camera company will have co-created a negative experience. Mom will not likely trust her new digital camera to record her two-year-old's birthday party the following weekend.

This mom cares only about the quality of the experience. She wants easy access to memorable experiences, not to a product or even a set of features. She wants simple, satisfying answers to questions like: How easily can I access my digital pictures, or index, sort, and retrieve them? How can I show them on my TV set? Can I easily repurpose them for

FIGURE 3 - 1

Company Think Versus Consumer Think

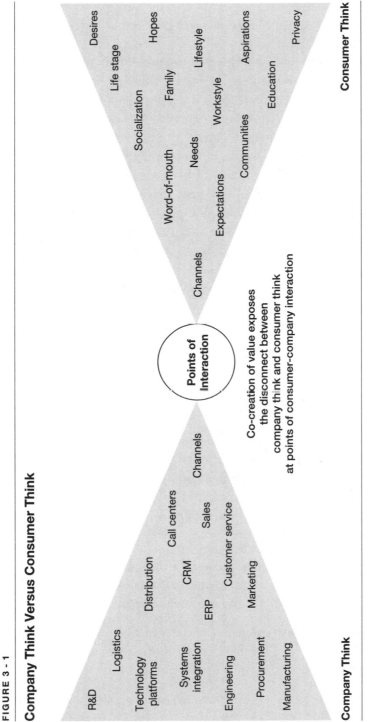

Company Think

Consumer Think

R&D

Logistics

Technology platforms

Distribution

Systems integration

CRM

Call centers

ERP

Sales

Engineering

Customer service

Procurement

Marketing

Manufacturing

Channels

Points of Interaction

Channels

Word-of-mouth

Socialization

Life stage

Desires

Needs

Family

Hopes

Expectations

Workstyle

Lifestyle

Communities

Aspirations

Education

Privacy

Co-creation of value exposes
the disconnect between
company think and consumer think
at points of consumer-company interaction

other media, like greeting cards, T-shirts, or Web sites? In short, the consumer is asking, How can my digital camera launch a series of delightful experiences?

Yet most managers implicitly assume that their physical product—the digital camera—is the vessel of value. They rarely consider the aspirations, frustrations, and wishes of the heterogeneous group of consumers who experience their product or service. Instead, they focus on the efficiency of production and logistical systems or on advanced technology for its own sake. Misled by company think, they clutter the marketplace with products that are *feature rich* but *experience poor*. For the consumer, "technology convergence" can create "experience divergence."

The continued dominance of company think explains why technological change is creating more variety in devices, features, and formats than ever before—and more confusion, doubt, and anxiety. Depending upon the consumer's level of competence and sophistication, and her tolerance for irritants, her reaction will range from mild annoyance to deep cynicism and anger.

The tensions at the points of interaction result from the disconnect between company think and consumer think. So how can we connect the two?

Dimensions of Choice in Consumer-Company Interaction

As we have seen, dialogue, access, risk assessment, and transparency—DART—form the foundation for co-creation of value. But these factors alone may not produce compelling experiences in co-creation. We also must attend to the *dimensions of choice* in consumer-company interaction that condition the co-creation experience. We have identified four such dimensions:

- Consumers want the freedom of choice to interact with the firm through a range of experience gateways. Therefore, the firm must focus on the co-creation experience across *multiple channels*.

- Consumers want to define choices in a manner that reflects their view of value. Therefore, the firm must provide experience-centric *options* that reflect consumer desires.

- Consumers want to interact and transact in their preferred language and style. They want quick, easy, convenient, and safe access to experiences. Therefore, in consummating individual choices, the firm must also focus on the co-creation experience through *transactions*.

• Consumers want to associate choice with the experiences they are willing to pay for. They want the price of these experiences to be fair. Therefore, the firm must focus on the totality of the *price-experience relationship* in co-creation.

Let's look at some of the emerging issues along these dimensions as well as the typical problems that firms with a company-think mentality will encounter.

Co-Creation Across Multiple Channels

Although most businesspeople recognize that technological change is revolutionizing channel structures across industries, they may not realize that the choice of channels by both consumers and firms fundamentally shapes the co-creation experience.

As Amazon.com illustrates, the Web potentially offers an incredibly rich channel for direct dialogue between consumers and companies, even as it offers unprecedented cost and process efficiencies. But co-creation can involve both virtual and physical environments, with traditional channels morphing to complement the new electronic channels. As multiple channels provide multiple gateways to experiences, the quality of the co-creation experience across different channels must be consistent.

Consider the experience of buying or selling shares of stock. For individual investors, the cost of a trade has decreased considerably, even as its convenience has greatly increased. A generation ago, individuals traded through full-service brokers, available at relatively high cost during restricted office hours. Now they can trade through Charles Schwab or a number of other discount brokers, paying only for desired or necessary services. They can use Schwab's telephone channel, Tele-Broker, or trade online, where they can also track the performance of their stock portfolios through Schwab's investment tools. For easy, safe, and reliable online stock transactions with an absolute minimum of other services, individuals can use companies like E*TRADE. The choice of company and channel is the individual's.

Thus, in the world of stock trading, multiple channels are a reality. The range of channels is crucial to the consumer experience. But for the uninitiated and unsophisticated consumer, even an ordinary company Web site can be intimidating. Empathetic human beings are needed for those who can't help themselves, which means that traditional branch offices, and call centers must be staffed with highly trained, knowledgeable service representatives.

Let us stay with the broad, evolving "wealth creation and protection" space. Consider Intuit, the $8 billion company best known for its personal finance software packages. Intuit's early success, Quicken, enabled consumers to track their personal finances and spending patterns using a simple, intuitive interface based on the familiar household checkbook. Later, Intuit's QuickBooks did the same for entrepreneurs and small business consumers. Intuit has continued to embed new functions in its software, such as payroll management and the ability to import bank and credit card statements, seamlessly integrating them into the consumer's experience with Intuit.

Now, Quicken and QuickBooks come with embedded browsers that weave the experience through dozens of financial resources on the Web. More than fifteen hundred financial institutions connect to Intuit's array of products and services. Consumers can access Web services that include bill payment, mortgage applications, a financial services portal, and even physical locations that process loans. Through Intuit's QuickBooks Internet gateway, a small business can easily access online payroll services, online purchasing systems, and Web design tools. The Intuit network also includes CheckFree for check processing, insurance companies such as InsWeb (partially owned by Intuit), and Fidelity Investments, the mutual fund giant, which can export a customer's data into Quicken.[7]

Now Intuit has brought the same granular understanding of consumer experiences to its TurboTax software. Filing taxes electronically requires a degree of consumer sophistication, financial know-how, and ability to navigate the complex protocols that govern tax calculations. In response, Intuit has evolved its tax preparation software with video tutorials, access to professional expertise, integration with Quicken, and a system that facilitates direct tax payments and refunds through a personal bank account. Intuit has even powered the Tax Center on Fidelity.com.

To co-create value, consumers like Intuit's will increasingly use multiple channels of their choice, a function of the consumer's competence, backgrounds, interests, and needs. Thus, companies will have to manage multiple channels and ensure a consistent quality of experience for individual consumers across these channels.

Co-Creation Through Options

At one time, consumer choice related to availability and affordability. Ford mastered the approach to choice through standardization at the turn of the last century. Its Model T was remarkably affordable and democratized car ownership for millions of working-class Americans who, as the cliché goes, could get their Model T in any color—as long as it was black.

The pendulum has now swung from standardization to mass customization of products and services. Thanks to quantum leaps in supply chain efficiency, drastic reductions in cycle time in product/service innovation, and the development of elaborately structured distribution and media channels, consumers have an enormous variety of merchandise and service options in almost every business.

More recently, information technology has opened a whole new opportunity for manufacturers to offer customized products faster, cheaper, and more cost effectively using "build-to-order" techniques facilitated by the Internet. Dell Computer mastered the build-to-order PC, using methods now emulated by Dell's rivals. BMW offers a custom car deliverable in twelve days; the Z3 roadster, for example, comes in 26 wheel designs and 123 consoles.[8]

The variety of options enabled by mass customization may impress consumers, but does it translate into a satisfying co-creation experience? Let us look at the made-to-order PCs. If I am techno-savvy, then I can visit a company's Web site and customize a computer using product configurators and choiceboards rather than choose from the available supply of PCs. But the company's view of choice still limits customization, because the company is designing and giving me only those options that fit the company's value chain rather than my own preferences.

How often do manufacturers ask how I intend to use the product before they build and sell it to me? How closely and intuitively do they connect the technical specifications to my anticipated uses and tasks? Suppose I order a printer with my new PC. If I am a graphic artist, then I will have one set of requirements. If I publish a newsletter for a local civic organization, then I will have another; if I make greeting cards from snapshots of my kids as a hobby, then I will have yet another. Why can't I test-print examples of my requirements at a retail store, rather than base my decision on a manufacturer's generic sample page, carefully designed to look attractive? Why can't I receive my chosen printer ready to use, with its components and software already configured the way I want to experience it?

As a consumer, I want companies to accommodate *my* context, my needs, preferences, sophistication, and desires. I want to inject my view of value into the menu of options, rather than accept the company's menu.

Some companies seem to understand this desire. Consider video rental, an $8 billion business in the United States in 2002. When I visit the local rental store, I may not find my first, second, or even third choices. Once I do pick one or two videos, I must watch them within the company-allotted time frame. If I find two hot releases, then I must return them together. If I want to watch both, then I must reorganize my life around the rentals or pay a late fee.

By contrast, Netflix has developed a video rental system designed around consumer think. As a Netflix customer, I pay a flat monthly fee (under $20) to choose from the firm's inventory of more than 15,000 DVD titles. At the Netflix Web site, I can explore all the available titles by genre, director, actor, top picks of critics, and so on, and create a list of what piques my interest. The first three DVDs listed arrive in my home mailbox, usually within a few days. I can keep the movies as long as I want, even take them wherever I want. When I'm done with a movie, I simply seal it in the prepaid envelope provided by Netflix and pop it in the nearest mailbox. When Netflix receives the envelope, it sends me the next one on my list. Depending on how quickly I watch the movies I receive, I can watch three—or fifteen—movies a month for the same monthly fee. As a consumer, I want options that enable me to co-construct my own experiences effectively, the way I want to. Netflix represents a pioneering step in that direction.

Netflix now has over a million customers and ships some 300,000 DVDs daily. The firm's revenues in 2002 were about $150 million.[9] Netflix not only provides a series of options unavailable in the traditional video rental business but also reflects a very different view of transactions focused on co-creating experiences.

Co-Creation Through Transactions

Transactions between the firm and the consumer are the traditional basis for the extraction of value. Transaction encompasses logistics, information, channels, and the associated costs and effort on both sides.

Companies have quickly adopted emerging technologies that reduce their transaction costs by forcing consumers to perform functions formerly handled by the firm—customer self-service. Gas stations' transition from full-service to self-service was an easy win for both gasoline retailers and consumers. Most drivers happily traded reduced service for greater convenience and, sometimes, lower prices.

But most customer self-service scenarios do not proceed this smoothly. Managers are usually so preoccupied with the cost advantages of self-service that they misjudge its consequences for the customer experience—or fail to consider the consequences at all. Anyone who has been frustrated by automated multiple-choice phone menus or who has been left on hold listening to bad music knows the limitations of call centers. And the introduction of virtual service representatives employing natural-language, voice-recognition technology may force me as a consumer to learn and use the language of the company—an imposition of "company speak" that reflects the bad habits of company think.

The move from branch banking to Internet banking neatly illustrates the divide between company think and consumer think. In branch banking, the teller interacts with the bank's internal software and provides customers with the requested information. In technical terms, the transition to Internet banking may appear as simple as turning the screen 180 degrees and presenting the application to consumers over the Web. But anyone who has shopped for a financial product without first reading a Motley Fools primer has probably been befuddled by the arcane financial jargon that some banks employ. Without a human intermediary to translate the bank's language of products, services, and procedures, online consumers can find themselves lost and angry.

Elsewhere on the Web—the ultimate self-service technology—we constantly encounter such corporate indifference to the consumer experience. Witness the high percentage of online shopping carts abandoned by shoppers who find the interface confusing or feel insecure about using a credit card online.

Important new issues are emerging for consumers as they test new ways of conducting transactions. In health care, for example, as hospitals, pharmacies, and laboratories experiment with online health records, diagnoses, and prescriptions, they are facing resistance from patients who resent hard-to-navigate interfaces and worry about privacy and security. Consumer groups, worried about the side effects of drugs like Paxil, pressured pharmaceutical firms and the FDA to provide more detailed, accurate online labeling before pharmacies shifted prescription

transactions to the Web. Health care consumers don't define the transaction narrowly, in terms of a doctor's visit or the filling of a prescription; instead, they think in terms of the continuity of their well-being,
as we saw in chapter 1. Providers must learn to experience the world as
many individual consumers do.

Thus, a key variable in the quality of the transaction experience is
consumer *heterogeneity*. For example, consumers differ widely in their
attitudes about the impact of information technology on their privacy.
While a debate rages over privacy on the Internet, consumers by the
millions are voting one interaction at a time on the type of private information that they will trade, for the convenience of one-click purchasing or instant recognition on a password-protected Web site. The
complex heterogeneity of the customer experience is lost on managers
who focus only on the cost savings of Web-based transactions.

Again, we see the deep-rooted disconnect between the company's
view of value and the consumer's view of value. For the company, transactional efficiency leads to cost reduction, which leads to value creation; for the consumer, transactional ease and openness leads to trust,
which leads to a satisfying experience. For instance, self-service, as a
mechanism for transactions, works best when applied by companies
that manage the customer experience *and* their costs with equal care.
Southwest Airlines Company strives to deliver prompt, accurate, and
friendly service regardless of whether the customer interaction with the
company occurs through an automated channel or an employee. Similarly, Lands' End Inc. has invested in self-service technology and supe-
rior agent training so that the consumer experience on its Web site
matches that of its catalog operations. Consumers may appreciate cost
reduction when firms pass along the savings, but cost cutting cannot be
isolated from its consequences on the quality of consumer experience.

The Price-Experience Relationship in Co-Creation

The over-arching dimension of choice in co-creation experiences is
the price-experience relationship—the intersection of price and the co-
creation experience, where consumers judge economic value.

Consider Federal Express. Customers, both shippers and receivers,
can log on and check the progress of packages in real time, viewing the
same information that FedEx employees have. While this system has
reduced the burden on FedEx call centers and trimmed costs, it simultaneously allows for an individual-centric view of interactions. Just

knowing a package's whereabouts can reduce customer anxiety. The transparency of the system gives individuals choices otherwise unavailable, thereby enhancing the co-creation experience and the totality of the price-experience relationship.

FedEx has evolved to allow customers to reroute their packages. It has also accomplished an "inversion of the system"—package recipients can now see all the packages heading their way. If I, as a service manager, know all the product repairs, warranty fixes, and customer returns coming into the dock every day, then I can better coordinate and manage daily internal activities and turnaround projects for customers. In effect, FedEx and both senders and receivers can mutually manage internal efficiencies and quality of customer experiences, further expanding the totality of the price-experience relationship.

Businesses have typically associated prices with costs, setting prices largely based on the company's cost structure. This traditional methodology is becoming increasingly problematic, because it has little meaning to the consumer. After all, when you consider buying a digital camera, what determines its value to you? The cost of producing it? Not really—as a consumer, I may not know or care about the manufacturer's cost structure. What determines its value to me is the quality of the experience I expect to enjoy because of the camera.

This experience, and therefore the associated value, will vary from one consumer to another. A gadget-loving techie may buy the camera just to experiment with new technology—one kind of experience. A parent may buy it to capture her child's first steps, a different experience. A small business owner may buy it to record images of inventory for insurance coverage, still another experience. The cost of producing the cameras may be the same, but the value varies from consumer to consumer.

Traditionally, businesses have also viewed product performance and price-performance relationships through the lens of company think. A classic example is the internal view of the price performance relationship for electronic organizers and handheld computers from *Fortune* 20 companies, prior to the PalmPilot.[10] Palm broke the mold by taking a consumer-centric view: It designed the product so that it integrated into a consumer's life as a "PC to go," with easy synchronization, quick access to information, and literal handiness or "pocketability."

The increasing convergence of features and functions strains the price-experience relationship. Consider Microsoft Office, a bundle of features—Word, PowerPoint, Publisher, and Excel—in one package.

Now, how do I value each of these software programs and its functions? Their value varies tremendously, based on my individual needs, interests, and desires. If I use only 10 percent of the available functions, then why should I pay for the unneeded functions? Price-experience debates increasingly become a function of individual consumers' needs at a point in time, based on the context in which they arise.

When determining a consumer's "willingness to pay," managers conventionally focus on what they can offer customers in isolation from the experiences they desire. For example, look at broadband communications services. Firms with huge infrastructure investments have taken a traditional company-centric, product-centered approach to pricing, where the only logical paradigm is, "Pay me price X for a fixed amount of bandwidth—even though it may be idle much of the time." Predicting demand for bandwidth is not easy, even for the consumer, and so few consumers are committing themselves to large-scale bandwidth purchases that they may not need. Hence, the economic travails of these service providers.

By contrast, a pricing system that recognized the existence of experience-based value would reflect the nature and quality of heterogeneous consumer experiences. Suppose I am launching an important business project that requires interaction with an ad hoc community halfway around the world, and I need five times more bandwidth than what is typically offered in the market, but only for a period of two months. In these circumstances, the unique value for me dramatically increases. I might pay a 20X price premium for two months' worth of 5X bandwidth. The question for bandwidth suppliers is: When we get such a request, are we ready to respond? Can the infrastructure scale up and down to enable unique co-creation experiences on demand? And is the economic framework flexible enough to permit the kind of pricing that reflects the true value of the experience within the specific context? If so, we can then enlarge the economic pie greatly, benefiting everyone in the co-creation process.

Consumers in emerging markets are also straining the price-experience relationship. Consider the costs of treatment for HIV, the virus that causes AIDS. The typical medical cocktail available in the West costs about $10,000 per year per patient, which few patients in most of the developing world can afford. An Indian pharmaceutical firm, Cipla, offered an equivalent solution for about $350 a year.[11] If the consumer experience is comparable, then Cipla's actions put pressure on the cost of treatment for HIV—not just in Africa but around the world, as the news of a totally different price-experience relationship spreads via the Internet and other modes of communication. If I know that I can get a similar HIV cocktail for $350 per year in one part of the world, then it is difficult to convince me to pay $10,000 per year.

Increasingly, the bottom of the pyramid is evolving into a source of innovation in price-experience relationships. India's Aravind Eye Hospital, the world's largest eye care facility, serves about 200,000 patients per year. Sixty percent of its very poor patients pay nothing, while others pay about $15 for cataract surgery.[12] The quality of the surgery and the consumer experience compares favorably to similar care in the United States, which can cost $1,500 or more—and Aravind remains highly profitable. Aravind is now attempting to scale its model in other regions of the world. New business systems such as Aravind's, constructed around radically redefined price-experience relationships, will increasingly go global in many other industries.

Traditional Exchange Versus Co-Creation Experiences

We have identified the basic building blocks of co-creation—dialogue, access, risk assessment, and transparency (DART)—as well as the dimensions of choice in consumer-company interaction that determine the quality of co-creation experiences as seen from the consumer's perspective—experiences across multiple channels and options, transaction experiences, and a compelling price-experience relationship. In the process, we have identified the *quality of interaction* between the consumer and the firm as the critical link in the future of competition.

The emerging reality differs dramatically from the traditional approach to the firm-customer interaction. The differences are summarized in table 3-1. Note that:

- In the traditional approach, the goal of the interaction is value extraction. This occurs in the exchange process, which is the primary source of contact between the firm and the customer. By contrast, in the co-creation approach, the goal of the interaction is twofold: value *creation* as well as value extraction;

- In the traditional approach, the locus of interaction is at the end of the value chain activities. In the co-creation approach, interactions can take place *repeatedly, anywhere, and anytime* in the system;

TABLE 3 - 1

Migrating to Co-Creation Experiences

	Traditional Exchange	Co-Creation Experiences
Goal of Interaction	Extraction of economic value	Co-creation of value through compelling co-creation experiences, as well as extraction of economic value
Locus of Interaction	Once at the end of the value chain	Repeatedly, anywhere, and anytime in the system
Company-Consumer Relationship	Transaction-based	Set of interactions and transactions focused on a series of co-creation experiences
View of Choice	Variety of products and services, features and functionalities, product performance, and operating procedures	Co-creation experience based on interactions across multiple channels, options, transactions, and the price-experience relationship
Pattern of Interaction Between Company and Consumer	Passive, firm-initiated, one-on-one	Active, initiated by either company or consumer, one-on-one or one-to-many
Focus of Quality	Quality of internal processes and company offerings	Quality of consumer-company interactions and co-creation experiences

- And most important, in the traditional approach, the notion of quality is based on what the firm has to offer. In co-creation, it is about consumers co-constructing their *own* experiences.

The dimensions of choice in co-creation experiences suggest the potential richness of the relationship through the quality of interactions between companies and consumers. Business managers can compete in myriad ways by discovering new opportunities through an individual-centric lens of choice in consumer-company interactions, and carefully managing the quality of co-creation experiences. The possibilities are endless, particularly if we gravitate toward innovating "experience environments" that accommodate heterogeneous consumers who seek to interact in a multitude of ways. We explore these possibilities in the next chapter.

Chapter Four

EXPERIENCE INNOVATION

IN CHAPTER 2 we encountered Sumerset, the manufacturer that is transforming the process of buying a houseboat into a richly satisfying, individualized co-creation experience for its customers. The very nature of Sumerset's business dictates that the firm serve a limited number of wealthy, well-educated customers. Can the same process work with mass-marketed products?

In contrast, recall Napster (chapter 3) and the inherent difficulties in dealing with a mass-market phenomenon where the individual consumer is not visible or identifiable. The tensions in co-creating under those circumstances are clear, as well as the tension between company think and consumer think. What if, given the heterogeneity of individuals, we cannot forecast how each consumer will likely approach the co-creation process?

We need a generalizable view of the co-creation process that can accommodate large numbers of consumers of varying interests, skill levels, needs, and desires. We need an *experience environment*—a framework that allows the firm to facilitate a variety of co-creation experiences with millions of consumers.

Experience Environments: The Lego Mindstorms Example

Invented in 1932 by company founder Ole Kirk Christiansen, the traditional Lego system has been a marvelous vehicle for learning through fun.[1] Kids with a Lego set can combine six shapes of interlocking, eight-studded bricks in millions of ways, limited only by their imagination and creativity. Legos are so popular that today there may actually be more Lego bricks than people in the world.

Now, what does a young child value here? The Lego bricks? Or the ability to construct a variety of experiences using the bricks? The Lego brick serves as an artifact around which individuals have experiences. The same consumer can use those Lego bricks to create a new experience every time, and different consumers can have different experiences with the same bricks. Thus, Lego consumers co-create value by interacting with the Lego company *through its experience environment.*

Over the past several years, the rapid convergence of toys, electronics, computers, software, interactive video, and the Web has ushered in new possibilities to captivate a child's imagination. In 1998, influenced by the revolutionary work on children, computers, and learning by Seymour Papert and researchers at MIT, Lego embraced technology convergence with the launch of its Mindstorms Robotics Invention System. Mindstorms combines gears, wheels, motors, sensors, and software to allow users to create intelligent robots using the traditional studded bricks.

Mindstorms contains a device known as RCX, a dedicated, autonomous microcomputer with an infrared link that can execute user-created code sent from a PC. Using the PC as a sandbox of sorts, users can snap together blocks of code, just like the studded Lego bricks, thereby engendering complex robotic actions.

Mindstorms was a huge hit of the 1998 Christmas season, selling a hundred thousand sets at around $200 each.[2] To Lego's surprise, it even rekindled the child in thousands of adults, who made up over half of Mindstorms users. Independent Web sites sprang up where enthusiasts shared ideas and instructions for building countless Lego robots such as sorting machines, intruder alarms, and land rovers.

Lego Mindstorms illustrates a fascinating aspect of the co-creation experience. While the primary interaction in the Sumerset case occurred between the consumer and the firm, here the interactions occur among consumers as well. When an experience environment is sufficiently compelling, *consumer communities* can evolve beyond the firm's control and potentially without the firm's knowledge. Suddenly whole communities of individuals can directly co-create value.

Here's another twist. Markus Noga, a Lego Mindstorms fan, developed a new, unauthorized operating system for the RCX. He dubbed it LegOS—the Lego Operating System—and made it available over the Internet.[3]

How should the Lego company respond to this initiative? It could not accept the liability for an unauthorized OS. If consumers installed LegOS and it damaged the RCX dedicated microprocessor in their Mindstorms systems, they might blame the Lego company. But Lego could not stop its loyal customers from experimenting with the product either.

So what could Lego do to preserve its seventy-year-old reputation? It could sue "customer-inventors" like Noga to cease their contributions—just as the music companies stopped Shawn Fanning and Napster from using their software to distribute music. It could use advertising and public relations to dissuade its customers from using LegOS, warning them that the Lego company could not guarantee the performance of Mindstorms with LegOS installed. Or it could co-opt Noga and his ilk, and make LegOS an "official" Lego product. All of these choices had consequences.

Lego chose none of them. It simply announced that it would not sue anyone for disassembling Lego Mindstorms, for writing new code for the product, or for distributing that code for free. In fact, the company praised its customers' ingenuity, although it did not explicitly endorse Noga's software.[4]

This story raises important issues. Who controls product development and strategy for Lego Mindstorms—the firm or the consumer community? Can customer-inventors override Lego's plans for Mindstorms? Can consumer communities claim intellectual property rights to their enhancements (such as new configurations of Mindstorms)? Can the firm appropriate the benefits without sharing them?

There is both a positive and a negative side here. On the positive side, consumer communities can serve as multipliers for in-house R&D efforts. Managers whose firms have met the preconditions for effective co-creation can augment their creative resource base. On the negative side, enthusiastic but untrained and unrestrained consumers can unwittingly ruin other customers' experiences without liability for quality or safety, thereby tainting the company's reputation. The question is: How can the firm help establish implicit rules of governance for communities such that its negative effects are minimized and its positive effects maximized?

Regardless of a manager's preference, consumer communities will form whenever an experience environment lets them, and they will influence consumer experiences in unpredictable ways. They may alter options and actions, as in health care, where online communities are shaping patient demand for certain treatment modalities. They may serve as product innovators, as with Lego Mindstorms. They may revolutionize distribution channels and marketing alternatives, as with Napster.

More fundamentally, the role of consumer communities evolves and cannot be predicted a priori. As a result, the firm is forced to concentrate on innovating experience environments with consumer communities—environments within which consumers, individually as well as collectively, can co-construct their own experiences. We call this new challenge *experience innovation.*

Innovating Experience Environments

Experience environments are characterized by robustness, the capacity to accommodate a wide range of context-specific experiences of heterogeneous individuals. An experience environment facilitates a total experience for consumers. It includes products and services as well as the various interfaces for individual interactions with the company, including multiple channels, modalities, employees, and communities.

If, as we have argued, value increasingly lies in the co-creation experience, then business leaders must shift the focus of innovation away from products and services and toward robust experience environments capable of facilitating compelling co-creation experiences. The specific experience outcomes, by definition, cannot be detailed a priori. The focus on innovating experience environments, therefore, differs from the traditional focus on innovating products and services.

We can develop a broad specification for designing an experience environment based on our discussion so far. At a minimum, the experience environment must:

- offer opportunities for consumers to co-construct their own experiences on demand, in a specific context of space and time;

- accommodate a heterogeneous group of consumers, from the very sophisticated and active to the very unsophisticated and passive;

- recognize that every consumer (including the active, smart consumer) does not always want to co-create; sometimes they just want to consume passively;

- facilitate new opportunities afforded by the evolution of emerging technologies;

- accommodate the involvement of consumer communities;

- engage the consumer emotionally and intellectually; and

- explicitly recognize both the social and the technical aspects of co-creation experiences.

We recognize that this set of specifications for experience environments may be daunting, especially to those preoccupied with developing new products, increasing product variety, improving processes, increasing market share, and reducing cycle times. Fortunately, the technologies that yield product variety can also help us create experience variety. We must evaluate the potential of these new technologies from a different perspective.

Emerging Technology Capabilities as Experience Enablers

The dramatic flowering of technology capabilities is fueling the potential for robust experience environments. We focus on five of them here to illustrate how they can affect experience innovation: miniaturization, environmental sensing, embedded intelligence, adaptive learning, and networked communication.[5]

Miniaturization

The ability to miniaturize electronics has allowed manufacturers to create smaller, lighter, more portable products. A generation ago, the Sony Walkman freed the consumer to enjoy stereo music whenever and wherever they went. Now the digitization and compression of storage media render a consumer's entire music collection portable. With the miniaturization of storage devices and microprocessors, digital music players are now pocket-sized. The Apple iPod provides instant access to more than five thousand songs in a pocket as well as a user-friendly interface to listen to a particular song. The trend toward miniaturization is permitting such pocket-sized devices to act as telephones, cameras,

Internet tools, game players, and general-purpose computers—sometimes all at once.

Environmental Sensing

Microsensors today can scan the environment, measuring biological, chemical, magnetic, optical, and thermal conditions. For example, in an automobile, micro-electromechanical systems (MEMS) smaller than the width of a human hair can track the vehicle's direction, acceleration, and velocity, and activate air bags in a crash—or help the driver avoid the crash altogether. Another MEMS sensor can detect a significant change in tire pressure and alert the driver, a capability that might have saved lives in accidents involving defective Firestone tires.

With flexible display technologies and electrotextiles, companies are embedding sensors in clothes for medical purposes. For instance, a tiny device worn on the belt of a walker can measure the length of her stride, count the calories burned, and track blood pressure. Woven-in sensors will soon record the heart rate, hydration, and blood sugar of athletes. In time, nanotechnology will move such capabilities to the molecular level.

Embedded Intelligence

A variety of products already contain microprocessors and microchips designed to accomplish specific tasks. Indeed, sales of embedded processors—even excluding those applications that control automobiles, microwave ovens, or can openers—already outnumber sales of PC processors. These chips are becoming increasingly versatile and powerful. For example, Hitachi's "mu-chip" is so thin and tiny that it can be folded or embedded in clothing and paper—and each costs less than fifteen cents.

Or take radio-frequency identification (RFID) tags. A smart RFID tag involves a chip with an antenna. When activated by a reader, it can send and receive information. And unlike bar codes that must be deliberately scanned, an RFID tag need only be present within the range of a reader. Such tags can enable the tracking of individual items, including stolen, missing, or misplaced items through every step in the supply chain. The microprocessors embedded in tags can also sense and store information. For instance, a tag on the carton of a perishable product can report on the temperature inside a shipping container.

Adaptive Learning

Consider TiVo, which serves as an intelligent digital video recorder, among other functions. TiVo stores my personal viewing history as well as those of my spouse and children, analyzes my tastes and interests, and uses the results to evaluate the programming available on my system's channels. TiVo then selects programs that I might like and records them digitally when they are shown—all without my intervention.

Imagine such an adaptive learning system becoming more sophisticated and powerful over time. Why not recommend video entertainment based not only on my preferences and entertainment habits, but also on what other like-minded viewers are currently watching or recommending? Of course, I should be able to exercise my own choice whenever my whims and interests change.

Similar adaptive learning from interactions can provide for real-time, multiuser games accessed through consoles such as the Microsoft X-Box and the Sony PlayStation. Successful firms of the future will understand how to build and tap into embedded intelligence and adaptive learning in interactive communities.

Networked Communication

Technology increasingly allows devices to announce themselves and communicate with one another. For example, interlinked digital music devices can go anywhere—in the car, phone, PDA, PC, home stereo, game console, TV—to create a music collection potentially accessible from multiple locations. Palm Computing, creators of the original PalmPilot, understood the power of networked communication through easy synchronization and portability. Sony is creating the capacity for all its devices to network together, according to how individuals want to interact with them.

Thus, there is a plethora of emerging technology capabilities. But *a new technology capability is meaningful to a consumer only when connected with experiences.* Wireless sensor networks, for instance, can potentially transform how we as individuals and communities interact with everyday objects and create new experience spaces. The matrix in table 4-1 connects emerging technology capabilities with their potential as *experience enablers.* Understanding technology capability and the experience enabler connection is critical to experience innovation. Miniaturization,

TABLE 4 - 1

Technology Capabilities as Experience Enablers

Emerging Technological Capabilities	POTENTIAL CONSUMER EXPERIENCE ENABLERS				
	Self and Remote Diagnostics	Tracking and Monitoring	Connectivity and Interactivity	Mobility and Seamlessness	Continuity and Transformability
Miniaturization					
Environmental Sensing					
Embedded Intelligence					
Networked Communication					
Adaptive Learning Systems					

for example, is meaningful only when it increases customers' personal freedom, simplifies life, or facilitates exciting new experiences. Consider constructing a similar matrix for your business domain, including emerging technology capabilities central to your success.

Making the Transition to Experience Enablers

To illustrate how technology capabilities relate to experience enablers, let us revisit miniaturization. If it is used to make a camera small enough for a patient to swallow so that doctors can get 3-D images of internal organs, then the technology capability is giving rise to the experience-enabler of "self and remote diagnostics." Or consider an adaptive learning system in a reading device. If it helps me to follow news stories as I travel over several days, or access related articles when I'm reading an editorial or op-ed page, it is a potential experience enabler of "mobility and seamlessness."

Or take IBM's concept device, the MetaPad, a computing chameleon with a unique core combination of hardware and software. Attach it to a clever docking station, connected to a keyboard and monitor, and it becomes a Windows XP desktop computer. Slide it into a special hand-held screen and it presents your personal calendar and other data with a Palm interface. Need Linux? No problem. Using the MetaPad is like accessing your desktop PC (enabling continuity) while adding new functions (enabling transformation). Thus, we can also start with the potential experience enablers and augment existing technology capabilities to facilitate them.[6]

Remarkably, the MetaPad conserves and leverages the company's investments: a *single product with the capacity to create a variety of experiences*. In other words, product variety is not necessary for creating experience variety, as conventional product-centered thinking would suggest.

Managers traditionally study how technology can generate product variety and manage technological evolution accordingly. Technology road maps are a staple in most research and development groups. Concepts such as platforms, generations, versions, releases, and upgrades pervade the R&D departments of most high-technology companies. Indeed, that mapping has enabled companies to create the variety and customization of products now taken for granted. But managing the variety of co-creation experiences differs from managing product variety because the firm is ultimately managing the quality of its *interaction* with its consumers: The range of experience transcends that of the company's products and services. We need new tools and approaches such as "experience design," "experience mapping," and "experience prototyping."[7]

But first, we must shift from technology capabilities to experience enablers, a difficult transition for many companies. As managers, even when we make this transition successfully, we must guard against the tendency to view experience enablers from the company's perspective. Falling into company think is easy. To combat this tendency, we suggest that you distinguish between the firm's perspective and the consumer's perspective for each experience enabler. For instance, let us consider the experience enabler known as self and remote diagnostics. Recall the pacemaker example in chapter 1. From the firm's perspective, the focus of diagnostics is on manufacturing the right sensors, building the right network, measuring the right parameters (such as heart rate, muscle contraction, or blood flow), and identifying key values for those parameters. From a consumer point of view, the key questions and concerns can differ: Can I trust the company to monitor me remotely? What other information will the company gather about me? How will it use my information? Will it let me access its information systems? Does this monitoring involve serious risks? Consumers' specific questions will naturally vary, along with the quality of their co-creation experiences. But *trust* is key to consumers—and that is what business leaders must learn to focus on.

Integrating Experience Enablers into Experience Environments

To illustrate how managers can use technology capabilities to create experience enablers and integrate them fully into experience environments, let us consider the fashion company Prada and its first "epicenter" store in New York City. Opened in December 2001, the store is an ongoing experiment designed to enhance the shopping experience through interactive technology.

A key enabling technology for the store is the radio-frequency identification (RFID) tagging system mentioned earlier. Every Prada item has its own RFID tag that gives sales associates immediate access to a rich datastream when scanned by a handheld wireless device. The content includes up-to-the-minute data on every item, such as currently available sizes or colors, so that a sales associate can serve a customer personally and seamlessly, rather than disappear into the stockroom.

The content also includes sketches, video clips, and color swatches, which customers can view on display units throughout the store. Prada customer cards store personal preferences on the company database.

Prada deploys many other in-store technologies to enrich the shopping experience. Each dressing room is a simple square booth with Privalite glass walls that switch from transparent to translucent when a shopper enters. If she wants her companion outside to see how she looks, then she touches a switch to make the walls transparent again. The room allows shoppers to view their selections under various lighting conditions, from daylight to an evening glow. Each room also features a radio-frequency antenna that automatically senses garment tags and links to an interactive touch screen so that the shopper can select alternative sizes, colors, fabrics, and styles, or see the garment in a slow-motion video clip. A video-based "Magic Mirror" allows the shopper to see herself from all angles.

The technical capabilities in the Prada store, created by a consortium of more than twenty firms, are almost as impressive as the deep probing into consumer think that inspired them. The design firm IDEO, collaborating closely with the Office for Metropolitan Architecture (OMA), led the process—with "deep dives," extensive shopping studies, staff interviews, analysis of preferences and patterns revealed by Prada's customer database, and so forth—yielding an environment for co-constructing a transfixing new retail experience, one that "melts into the architecture of the store itself," according to co-CEO Miuccia Prada.[8]

Levers for Experience Innovation

What key tools do companies need to become skilled innovators of experience environments? We have identified four levers: granularity, extensibility, linkage, and evolvability.

Granularity

Granularity is about giving the consumer the ability to interact with experience environments at any desired level of specificity, immersing herself in the experiences over time in whatever way she chooses. From the firm's perspective, it is the ability to design an experience environment based on events such that the consumer interactions can occur at different levels of aggregation and richness.

To achieve a high granularity, managers must deeply understand—indeed, empathize—and continuously experiment with consumers. Let us return to the pacemaker example. How can the engineers at Medtronic understand their customers' experiences without themselves suffering a heart attack?

The design firm IDEO has experimented with this challenge, through experience prototyping and asking such questions as: What is it like to be a defibrillating pacemaker patient? What is it like not knowing when and where a defibrillating shock (strong enough to knock the patient off his feet) may occur? How does this uncertainty affect a patient's everyday life? Besides interacting with pacemaker patients, everyone on the design team received a pager to carry at all times. The pager signal, generated randomly, would represent a defibrillating shock, to which the team member had to respond realistically. The team members then recorded the context under which they received the signal: What were the circumstances? Where were they? Whom were they with? What were they doing? What were their anxieties? How did the event make them feel? How did they communicate their condition to onlookers? How did they seek medical help?[9]

The research team learned several crucial lessons from its explorations, including the importance of warning patients to anticipate and prepare for a shock, the complexities of communicating with bystanders, and the crucial role played by supporters in the patient community and beyond. As this story suggests, focusing on granularity of experiences means immersion in the lives of consumers, capturing their moments of frustration, anxiety, and stress. It also means engaging consumers in dialogue to generate new insights and learning from thematic communities—as consumers do.

Let us consider another example, a small store operated by a local entrepreneur—the cornerstone of retailing in India and in many emerging markets throughout Asia, South America, and Africa. There are more than two hundred thousand such outlets in the Indian grocery sector alone, representing a potentially huge market for information technology devices to automate, accelerate, and track billions of small transactions. But these stores also offer a profound challenge to IT companies because of the specific experiential challenges that entrepreneurial shopkeepers face.

In the United States, firms like IBM have long offered dedicated point-of-sale (POS) systems for automating retail transactions. Increasingly, traditional PC-based POS systems customized for retail applications are more common. However, full-fledged POS systems can cost over $3,000 per retail outlet—far too expensive for emerging-market retail-entrepreneurs. More modest POS alternatives, like electronic cash registers from NCR and Omron, perform basic functions such as billing for less than $1,000 each. Shops that gross over $30,000 a year can afford a POS system, and yet fewer than 4 percent of the stores in India have one. Why? Because most POS systems are designed for the typical U.S. style retail environment—a department store or a convenience store. The Indian shopkeeper's sense of value does not align with that embodied in the design of most POS systems.

TVS Electronics decided to "deconstruct the Indian shopkeeper's experience" to develop a unique solution from the ground up. It first immersed staff in the Indian retail environment to empathize with the Indian shopkeeper's view of the experience. TVS discovered a world very different from the typical U.S. retailer's. Many Indian stores are tiny, noisy, cramped, and dusty. The storefront may jut out into the street, and the store owner may operate behind a counter far too narrow for a conventional POS system. Electric voltage fluctuates throughout the day. Much of the merchandise is neither prepackaged nor bar-coded. Employees are often technically unsophisticated, conduct business in multiple languages, and accommodate idiosyncratic business norms and practices.

TVS responded by working with grocers and shoppers to co-develop an innovative, robust retail system centered on the realities of Indian retailing. TVS designed software and the hardware from the ground up to be intuitive, not just easy to use. For instance, the most frequently sold items are most easily accessible, and the hierarchy of product categories in the system reflects the cognitive approach and language of the user. The TVS system can track a particular household's favorite items, down to (for example) a type of rice or lentil, and can help the shopkeeper jog the consumer's memory for items overlooked. It can print a bill in the consumer's language, facilitating budgeting for the consumer and efficient deliveries for the grocer. The printer and the backup power supply are integrated into a single portable unit whose casing and electronics are nearly immune to dust, voltage fluctuations, and typical user abuse. All this capacity sports a compelling price-experience relationship—affordable monthly payments of about $30 for access to the retail experience environment dubbed "e-shop."[10]

As TVS developed the e-shop environment around a granular understanding of Indian retailing, it essentially expanded the experience space for the retail grocer. "It has given me a new life," says Mariappan, a shopkeeper who participated in the process of innovating this new retail experience environment.

Extensibility

Extensibility involves exploring how technologies, channels, or modes of delivery, can allow consumers to experience established functions in new ways, as well as create entirely new functionalities.

Consider the successful launch of the Starbucks card, a convenient way to pay for drinks and snacks at any Starbucks coffee shop, and a handy gift as well. The card also enables consumers to track their purchase histories at Starbucks. For the business traveler, it can function as a purchasing card, eliminating the need to itemize many small receipts for reimbursement. Unlike prepaid phone cards that come only in fixed spending amounts, consumers can add as much as they want to their cards at a store, on the phone, or on the Web. Consumers can also arrange an automatic reload of the card when it reaches a certain amount or at specific intervals, so that they need never worry about running short. If the card is lost or stolen, it can be canceled with a phone call or via the Web, and the current amount is refunded.

The seamless integration of the Starbucks card with the Web and the many points of sale suggest even more possibilities for consumer experiences. Someday soon, I may be able to order my favorite drink by using my card instead of reciting "a tall, nonfat, no-foam, extra-hot caramel macchiato with light caramel and a dash of vanilla."

Now consider the evolution of one of the world's oldest industries—printing and publishing. New technologies, products, and processes are facilitating the creation of new functionalities that, in turn, are transforming the age-old act of reading.[11] First, with digitization, computers, networking, and the Web, individuals can now access vast, ever-changing sources of textual content that can easily be manipulated, updated, downloaded, printed, and converted into various formats. Millions of people already read electronic versions of their favorite periodicals, accessing digitized content that mimics the paper editions but adds search capabilities.

Technology is obviously opening up an enormous range of ways to expand and enhance the reading experience. Think of the last time you read a story book to a child—a unique human experience that countless adults and children have treasured over the centuries. But now imagine if the storybook could come to life. In effect, this is what the successful LeapPad product does. As the child points to words, characters, and pictures, they talk and sing, offering the child fun facts and ideas, while allowing the child to interact with the book, through learning-oriented games. The technology behind this interactive experience is a tiny mini-cartridge for each book that plugs into the LeapPad console. And with the Mind Station, which hooks to a computer, the LeapPad extends the experience environment with Internet capabilities, providing a never-ending learning experience with a community of other children and parents.

Since introducing the LeapPad in 1999, its manufacturer, LeapFrog, has sold more than five million units at about $45 each; in 2002 its revenues accounted for about a quarter of the $1.7 billion U.S. educational-toy market.[12]

Is LeapPad a toy? A book? An electronic product? A game? A computer? A form of entertainment? A tool for learning? It's potentially all of these. LeapPad offers an experience environment that involves the consumer in a co-creation experience that the company cannot predetermine. The content of this experience is an *emergent* outcome of LeapPad's extensibility.

Linkage

Linkage is the recognition that events connect in multiple ways from a consumer point of view. Therefore, a collection of related events, and not just a single event, affects the quality of the co-creation experience.

Consider the car rental experience. Avis focuses on the customer's entire rental experience, from the moment she reserves a vehicle until she returns her keys at the end of the rental. Avis decomposes the process into numerous events—making reservations, finding the Avis counter, reaching the car, driving it, refueling it, returning it, paying the bill, and so on—and analyzes each step in terms of enhancing the customer's overall experience.[13]

Avis also trains its employees to anticipate customers' needs, seeking new linkages for the consumer experience. Renters with small children are reminded about the availability of car seats; those toting golf clubs get weather reports and maps to local courses; those with extra luggage get special rates on bigger cars. Research showed that stress reduction is a major priority of Avis's traveling customers. In response, the company is opening communications centers in airports where customers can relax, plug in a laptop, check e-mail, or make phone calls, while keeping an eye on the handy display of flight information.

Linkage of events, as in the Avis example, can be further enhanced using the evolving infrastructure for Web services, such as Microsoft's Net initiative. The idea is to create an Internet "cloud" of offerings in which Web services can automatically find one another, negotiate, and link up. Imagine reserving a rental car directly on an airline's Web site that automatically updates your reservation if your flight is delayed or canceled. Imagine finding the gas tank of your rented car close to empty and getting directions to the cheapest open gas station within a mile within seconds of placing a single phone call.

Providing such services requires a multitude of electronic linkages, including voice-recognition and natural-language tools, a location-based service to find nearby open gas stations, and a quick comparison-shopping service to pick one. Yet the resulting consumer experience must feel seamless, fast, and easy. That's the design challenge—and the power—of linkages for consumers.

The consumer can also be a business manager. Suppose you are a manager ready to begin manufacturing a new product. Imagine accessing a manager-centric Web portal where you can order the requisite components, book manufacturing capacity, and arrange for warehousing and distribution. With a mouse click, you create an instant supply chain that dissolves when the job is done. We are taking baby steps in this direction.[14]

Evolvability

Evolvability involves capturing the learning from co-creation experiences and using it to develop experience environments that shape themselves to consumers' needs and preferences, not the other way around.

Let us look at Amazon through the lens of an "experience environment." As a customer, I get recommendations for books, music, and movies based on my tastes, on the selections of those who have purchased the same books I have, on bestseller lists, on reviews by professional critics and fellow Amazon users, and a number of other criteria. Thus, thematic communities are integrated with the experience environment, emerging, morphing, and disappearing as appropriate. One moment, I may link with the community of fans of movies starring former Monty Python member John Cleese; the next, I may link with the community of readers who seek out information on the life and career of Civil War general Robert E. Lee or the leadership philosophy of Mahatma Gandhi.

Amazon continually uses emerging technologies to facilitate new consumer experiences. Customers can now sample a book, including the table of contents, selected chapters, and the front and back covers, just as one might browse in a physical bookstore. Shoppers can also listen to clips of music CDs online, a form of sampling not yet available in many retail music stores. Amazon has also expanded the experience space for consumers by allowing them to buy used products from stores and individuals; Amazon absorbs the underlying risk.

Innovation for evolvability of experiences is not easy. Even as the contexts change for the individual, the experience environment must contain adequate intelligence to maintain continuity while allowing exploration and transformation. This duality requires a deep understanding of the linkages among events that form the basis for experiences.

Let us take a simple example. Suppose I am an unsophisticated investor who has just opened my first brokerage account. When I visit the broker's Web site, I may drown in a complex presentation of investment possibilities: stocks, bonds, mutual funds, real estate trusts, derivatives, options, futures, annuities, and more. Given my background, the site must walk me through the basic investment decision-making process with simplicity and clarity, beginning with fundamentals: Why invest? How do I set my investment objectives? What is a stock? What is a bond?

Fast-forward a year or two. I have bought and traded a few stocks. Now I must learn to analyze my portfolio and understand a range of new concepts, from asset allocation to risk management. My experience of investing has evolved, and the online environment provided by my broker needs to evolve with it. Unfortunately, most Web sites today are static; they cannot learn from the consumer and adapt to the user's shifting needs and interests. The next frontier is the emergence of the "adaptive Web" that can evolve with heterogeneous individuals who seek to co-construct personalized experiences.

The same is true of products, which should learn as much from me as I do from them. *Traditionally, however, most products have evolved more with changes in technology than with changes in the consumer.* We need a new approach to product evolution. Educational software products for children, such as from The Learning Company, suggest one possible pathway. The software co-evolves with the child who uses it. It adjusts the level of difficulty and tasks it offers based on skills the child has previously mastered. It recognizes a child's learning accomplishments before presenting new and more demanding challenges, and reveals new functionalities gradually. Thus, the software can keep the child engaged with fresh and interesting projects rather than being quickly outgrown and discarded like traditional educational toys.

The New Frontier of Experience Innovation

Experience innovation is a new frontier in co-creation, one that requires a seamless integration of imagination, consumer insights, and advanced technology. The challenge of experience innovation is to combine the building blocks of DART (dialogue, access, risk assessment, and transparency) with the dimensions of choice in co-creation experiences (the quality of co-creation experiences across multiple channels and options, the quality of the transaction experience, and the perceived totality of the price-experience relationship) and the levers for experience innovation (granularity, extensibility, linkage, and evolvability) to create a rich new experience space for co-creation.

To illustrate this challenge, let's look at two distinct examples, one drawn from the petroleum industry, the other from investment management.

Consider co-creation of value in oil exploration. Seismic imaging has long been an integral part of the petroleum industry. Oil lies deep underground, trapped in rock pores at high pressures. Because rock is a good conductor of sound, geologists can use sound waves to infer the location of oil deposits. For many years, crude 2-D images that required time-consuming mathematical analysis were the best available. But recent advances in 3-D imaging systems, using sensors and electronic controls developed by firms such as Schlumberger, have changed all that. High-resolution seismic imaging now produces detailed, accurate maps of underground oil fields much faster and cheaper than ever before; in fact, the cost of analyzing a twenty-square-mile area has fallen from more than $8 million in 1980 to less than $50,000 in 2002.[15]

Thanks to another technology called directional drilling, once-inaccessible oil deposits are now within reach. If oil is found underneath an inaccessible piece of land, then a rig placed in a nearby field can reach the oil by boring horizontally for as far as five miles if necessary. This creates a new information technology challenge: How can engineers know exactly where the drill bit is located? The solution: new measurement-while-drilling technology using sophisticated sensors and embedded intelligence that gives drillers and geologists a sense of the terrain ahead. A single drill bit may contain the equivalent of over three Pentium PCs' worth of processing power.

Now link the entire exploration process to the Internet. Geologists and executives from anywhere in the world can click and see what an engineer is seeing somewhere in the Gulf of Mexico, in the North Sea, or in the jungles of Borneo. A networked expert can instruct the rig to notify his PDA or laptop when the hole reaches a depth of 15,000 feet, or when the analysis suggests the presence of oil.

All these technologies complement each other in such a way that they create a new experience environment. Moreover, by combining access, transparency, dialogue, and risk assessment in new ways, the oil companies, their customers, and suppliers can now participate jointly in the value creation process.

Now consider Archipelago, an electronic communications network (ECN) that offers one of the world's most sophisticated systems for finding the best current prices on shares of stock. Using a proprietary execution algorithm and matching engine, Archipelago routes trades at microsecond speeds to find the best price and the greatest liquidity. The Securities and Exchange Commission (SEC) recently cleared Archipelago to operate as a full-fledged stock exchange. Its clients include the world's leading financial institutions, including brokerage firms, investment banks, and market makers.

Creating an enhanced experience environment, as Archipelago is doing, leads to better risk management for investors. Gerald Putnam, the company's chair and CEO, refers to Archipelago as "everything out in the open."[16] Archipelago provides a new level of transparency by opening the trading book, hitherto available only to specialists, to the public. Order execution and routing practices are also fully disclosed. Consequently, customers can know how much stock trading is costing them in real time. Together with decimal pricing, these innovations have helped narrow effective price spreads in the most liquid stocks on NASDAQ and the NYSE by an average of 50 percent and 15 percent, respectively, reducing trading costs and putting tens of millions of dollars back in the pockets of investors.

Archipelago recently launched new online tools, accessible by the public, that facilitate the monitoring of trade execution quality. These tools enable users to compare, contrast, and analyze the quality of trade execution through various exchanges and thereby make more informed choices. Why is this important? Consider a catastrophic stock market event like the fall of Enron on November 28, 2001. On that day, Standard & Poor's announced a downgrade of Enron's debt to junk status, which sent the stock into a frightening downward spiral. Before the NYSE halted trading due to an "order imbalance" (that is, many more sellers of Enron than buyers), ECNs and other alternative venues traded more than ten million shares of Enron as the stock went from $2.60 to $1.10. When the NYSE specialist resumed trading half an hour later, Enron sold at prices discovered by these alternative markets.[17]

The Enron story shows how efficient price discovery through linkage can spread and thereby minimize the risks associated with big shocks to the system. Thanks to linkages between markets in the trading experience space, even a large institutional trader like Merrill Lynch has more choice. Merrill can execute a large client order through an ECN, a specialist, or through its own system, wherever the best price is available. When shocks to the system cause large price swings, these trading alternatives can provide a buffer as well, creating multiple channels for fulfillment and helping clients assimilate events throughout the fulfillment cycle.

Archipelago is an example of experience innovation through technology that not only increases efficiency but also co-creates value through compelling experiences for all stakeholders in the system. By enabling better risk management for clients like Merrill Lynch, Archipelago can co-create value, through better experiences, for thousands of investors, large and small.

Migrating to Experience Innovation

In this chapter, we presented a range of examples from different domains to illustrate the need to migrate to experience innovation. The transition for most firms is from a product/service based, firm-centric view of innovation to an experience-centric co-creation view of innovation. The distinctions between the traditional and new perspectives of innovation are summarized in table 4-2.

The migration to experience innovation is not an easy one. So much of managerial energy in large firms is focused on product innovation.

TABLE 4 - 2

Migrating to Experience Innovation

	Traditional Innovation	Experience Innovation
Innovation Goal	Products and processes	Experience environments
Basis of Value	Product and service offerings	Co-creation experiences
View of Value Creation	Firm creates value; supply push and demand pull for firm's offerings	Value is co-created; individual-centric co-creation of value
Focus of Development	Cost, quality, speed, and modularity	Granularity, extensibility, linkage, and evolvability
View of Technology	Features and functions; technology and systems integration	Enablers of experiences; experience integration
Focus of Infrastructure	Support fulfillment of products and services	Support co-construction of personalized experiences

The internal debate is about the time to develop new features and to phase these functions into new products and services. Increasingly, firms are developing products with multiple application possibilities, so that they can leverage investments in R&D, as well as in the logistics system. Competitive advantage is a result of how well companies do on these dimensions compared with competitors. Managers therefore focus on efficiency in this space. For instance, speeding up feature and product development—the improvements in product cycle time—receives significant senior management attention. Managers may spend time on cost reduction, quality, and creating a platform that allows them to increase the number of applications and spot new segments of opportunity. They tend to be focused on various aspects of making their offerings competitive. They believe that cost, quality, and variety are the primary sources of competitive advantage. This is the point of departure for most managers.[18]

Experience Innovation and Efficiency

Under pressure for cost reduction, most managers focus on efficiency and regard innovation as an attractive distraction. "Do you want efficiency or innovation?" they ask in effect. "I can't give you both." Furthermore, even when managers do focus on innovation, they often become preoccupied with developing an efficient process for innovation. In the end, this invariably forces managers to concentrate on internal, firm-centric competencies rather than on the consumer.

In truth, however, efficiency and innovation are not opposed. They are interconnected. For example, consider efficiency as exemplified in today's hyper-efficient global supply chain system. Implicit in building and operating such a global supply chain is a host of technical and organizational innovations. The sheer logistics of component movement among multiple countries in itself requires innovations in information sharing, component tracking, transaction management, pricing transfers, quality assurance, and global work force management. Underlying all this effort are the innovative IT networks, databases, and applications that support the system. Thus, efficiency at a twenty-first-century level is impossible without innovation.

Conversely, successful innovation must have efficiency embedded in it. Suppose Intel wants to release a new microprocessor. The innovation will not be successful unless Intel applies efficiency criteria, whether in scaling production, reducing costs, or in operating multiple manufacturing facilities around the world. The success of the innovation depends on the operational efficiency with which it is executed.

As managers, we tend to think in terms of opposites—quality versus cost, variety versus mass manufacturing, efficiency versus innovation. Such polarization often misstates reality. As we know by now, a deep commitment to quality can lead to dramatic cost reductions. Mass customization combines variety with large-scale manufacturing. In the same way, efficiency and experience innovation can—indeed *must*—go together. The logic of this is so simple that most of us miss it. We can state it as three simple propositions:

1. Discontinuities are destroying established industry and technology boundaries, thereby increasing the demand for experimentation.

2. Co-creation of value demands "de-risking" experimentation. This demands efficiency in how we leverage resources, experiment in the marketplace, and shape consumer expectations and evolving needs.

3. All experiments may not succeed. When some do, we should be able to scale fast and expand the size of the market. That means

creating systemwide efficiencies in activities, whether in manu-facturing, logistics, channels, customer service, branding, or community management.

We call this approach *efficient experience innovation*. Focus on efficiency, and simultaneously pursue experience innovation and experimentation. The either/or debate is not useful. If we go back to the examples such as Archipelago, oil drilling, or Lego in this chapter, or the Napster, Sumerset, or pacemaker examples from previous chapters, we can see that, in each case, efficiency and experience innovation are mutually embedded. Experience innovation is critical to sustained efficiency, and efficiency is critical to reducing experimentation risk and engaging in experience innovation.

This view of efficiency goes beyond cost reductions in production and fulfillment tasks of the firm—the domain of the traditional value chain. As we move toward co-creation of experiences, we increase the capacity for experimenting and generating insights, reducing risk (in both experimentation and in exploiting a good opportunity), reducing investment (by leveraging resources of the entire company and its enhanced competence base), and reducing time (whether it is for experimentation or for scaling up).

We started this chapter by suggesting that we must innovate experience environments—a new approach to innovation that is neither product-centered nor process-centered, but centered on the co-creation experiences of consumers. Fortunately, today's technical advances allow us to accommodate a variety of experience enablers. We identified the dimensions of experience innovation: granularity, extensibility, linkage, and evolvability. We noted that efficiency and experience innovation are not irreconcilable opposites but two sides of the same coin.

We are now ready to ask the next question: If every individual is unique, how do we innovate experience environments that allow for co-creating *unique value for each individual?* This is the focus of our next chapter.

Chapter Five

EXPERIENCE PERSONALIZATION

I N THE PREVIOUS TWO CHAPTERS, we outlined a progression from the co-creation experience to the innovation of experience environments. To co-create unique value with customers, we must appreciate what constitutes a *personalized* co-creation experience. Further, since this experience may involve more than a single firm or individual, we must understand how multiple firms and communities can function as a network that facilitates these personalized co-creation experiences. Throughout, the individual remains central.

Personalizing the Co-Creation Experience

Remember that the co-creation experience springs from the interaction between a single consumer and an experience environment. If we understand the personalization of interactions, then we can build toward a more personalized co-creation experience.

For example, imagine visiting a museum—the Whitney Museum of Art in New York. Some passersby encounter it as just another building on a certain street corner on New York's Upper East Side. But, for many patrons, it contributes to meaningful experiences both within and beyond the museum walls. Specifically, as a patron, it offers a complex array of elements—art, artifacts, exhibits, catalogues, multimedia devices, tour guides and docents, research materials, gift shops stocked with curios, a museum Web site, and thematic communities that include museum aficionados, staff members, and other art lovers—that I can access to enhance my Whitney experience. Thus, the Whitney Museum provides an implicit experience environment in which I can co-construct my own experience, centered on me, not the Whitney. The museum environment simply enables my experience.[1]

In most museums, the components of the experience environment probably amassed over time, often with little patron-centric planning. In contrast, let's consider a service in another domain that can enable deliberate personalization: the wireless news service. To patronize such a service, I need to create an account on the Web, associate it with a wireless device, and progress through menus that enable me to filter incoming news.

The typical customization process can be difficult. The menu choices may not appear meaningful, forcing me to choose among broad content categories such as "International Business News" rather than specific personal interests like "Semiconductor Industry in Taiwan." The menus may not accommodate shifts in my pattern of news preferences over time. What if I have no interest in news from Russia—except during the six months of my college-age daughter's study-abroad program in St. Petersburg? What if I am unconcerned about the movie industry—except during the runup to the Oscar awards ceremony?

The wireless site of the *Los Angeles Times* is experimenting with adaptive personalization technology to overcome some of these weaknesses. When a new user logs on, the site captures some basic input to provide an acceptable experience. Then, over subsequent encounters, the site's adaptive learning system intensifies the personalization, adjusting quickly to the user's changing interests.

Designing and implementing such a system is a complex task. For example, to gauge my interest in any topic, the system measures how much of a particular item I read. Over a two-week period, if I peruse nine of ten articles about (say) the water treatment industry, the system deduces that I will want further coverage of that topic. But shifting patterns of events often affect behavior in ways that straightforward calculations cannot accurately capture. What if a consumer who skips 162 consecutive stories about the Los Angeles Dodgers' regular-season baseball games reads all four stories about Dodger victories in the National League Championship Series? A team of researchers for the *L.A. Times* project asked that very question. Does the fraction 4/166 reflect that consumer's interest in the Dodgers' subsequent appearance in the World Series? Probably not.[2]

As the *L.A. Times* wireless Web site evolves to meet this complex challenge, the goal is to create an experience environment that accommodates not just the individual, but *how the individual changes in relation to space, time, and events*. Designing an experience environment in which many heterogeneous consumers can enjoy truly personalized co-creation experiences is by no means trivial.

Now let us shift to air transportation. Imagine an Airbus 340 cruising toward New Zealand an hour after takeoff from Hong Kong. Inside one of the plane's four General Electric (GE) engines, tiny bits of insulation are peeling off the surface of the engine's thrust reverser, allowing cold outside air to seep in. The temperature deviation is not large enough to register on the instrument panel.[3]

But a thermocouple in the engine notices the temperature drop. An onboard computer that routinely collects engine readings uploads this data to a satellite, which forwards the data to a GE computer in Ohio. GE employees analyze the anomaly with data from other sensors and the engine's maintenance records, diagnose the loss of insulation, and notify the airline by telephone. Subsequently, mechanics in Auckland order the parts needed to relayer the engine skin.

As little as five years ago, no one would have noticed this small loss of insulation. The problem would have gradually built up until a routine inspection or maintenance procedure finally caught it, at which point the repair would have grounded the equipment for several weeks, disrupted service, and created a seriously negative experience for the airline—GE's customer.

How does this anecdote help us understand the elements of a personalized co-creation experience? Clearly, the *context* of the event is crucial. For example, the aircraft's final destination may determine whether GE's engineers insist that the airline land and service the plane immediately at the nearest airport or wait and fix the problem overnight. Such decisions are *event-driven and context-specific, demanding personalized interaction*.

To participate meaningfully, however, the airline needs access to the same data that GE sees. Dialogue, transparency, and risk assessment all come into play. What about the airline's customers, the passengers on the plane? Any unscheduled stop will obviously affect their travel experience. How transparent should the airline be? If GE, the airline technicians, and the pilots all agree that the risk is minimal and the flight should continue, then should the airline inform passengers of the problem?

Airlines are grappling with these issues today. Delta Air Lines, for example, has rolled out information systems that let passengers access information previously available only to gate agents, such as real-time progress of flights, seating status, and upgrade and standby lists. This transparency can reduce passenger anxiety and gate agent job stress, even though it may sometimes raise more questions, such as, "Why can't I have that remaining seat in first class?"

The above three examples convey the basic dimensions of an experience and its personalization: *events, context, individual involvement, and personal meaning*. The Whitney Museum frees patrons to co-construct their own personal meanings within a flexible experience environment. The *L.A. Times* system learns about customers' involvement and evolves accordingly, attempting to personalize interactions for each consumer within a context of space and time. The airline example underscores the necessity of a network of participants engaged within an event's context. GE engineers, airline flight and maintenance crews, and airport personnel all co-shape the experience of the ultimate consumer—the passenger.

Let us now discuss these key dimensions of a personalized co-creation experience.

Events

Events form the basis for experiences. An event is a change of state in space and time that affects one or more individuals. A football game, a business seminar, a wedding, and a breakfast meeting are events; but so is a series of heart palpitations for a patient with a pacemaker, and so is a boat buyer's phone call to the design engineer about installing cabinets in the houseboat's galley. Your reading this book is an event. So is a leaking gas pipe in an office building basement.

We can disaggregate events into its components or subevents of increasing granularity. For example, a seminar may entail a large-group presentation in the morning, a buffet lunch, and small-group discussions in the afternoon. An NFL football season can be divided into sixteen games: Each game can further be divided into quarters; each quarter, into possessions; and each possession, into plays. Each is a subevent on its own.

People experience events at varying levels of granularity. If I have a marginal interest in sports, I may track Sunday's New York Jets game at a high level of aggregation. However, my Jets-crazy friends may want to analyze all the details of every single replay.

Consider stock price movements. Some investors want to know the overall daily change of the Dow Jones index, whereas others want to know the daily movement of specific stock prices, or even the minute-to-minute fluctuations of a single stock. In a well-designed experience environment, each individual can choose the level of granularity that shapes each experience.

Several businesses have already learned how to provide a variety of offerings, and even stage standardized experiences around these offerings. The next practice is to permit a variety of co-creation experiences, allowing consumers to aggregate and disaggregate events at the level of detail they prefer.

Some event hierarchies (events and subevents) are well-defined by rules. Sports is an example, with its clearly delineated hierarchy of season, game, quarter, possession, and play. In other cases, event hierarchies are not so clearly defined or understood. For instance, health care professionals would have difficulty breaking down the treatment of a patient entering the emergency room into a clear hierarchy of sub-events.

Moreover, event hierarchies shift with contexts. A football fan who joins one of the popular fantasy leagues reconstructs his experience of the sport. He drafts and trades players from various real-life teams, selects starters, and compares their weekly performance with other fans in a thematic community. In this context, the score of Sunday's New York Jets game may not matter, but the yardage gained by running back Curtis Martin might because he belongs to my personal fantasy team, and the members of a subcommunity of New York Jets fans rate Martin's prospects high for the remaining games. Clearly, the interaction among individuals, communities, and the experience environment is critical in providing meaning to events.[4]

Context of Events

Context in space and time is an inherent part of any event and thereby experience. If an event is about *what* happened, then context is about *when* it happened (time) and *where* it happened (space). These dimensions factor into the meaning ascribed to the experience. For example, drinking an ice-cold soda with my children on a summer afternoon at the beach differs from drinking the same soda with my colleagues in a windowless conference room late on a Friday afternoon. Consequently, I will pay a much higher price for the former. Similarly, suffering irregular heartbeats at 9:00 A.M. at home differs from suffering them at midnight somewhere in a hotel in a distant city. As the context changes, so does my experience.

Context also entails the situational circumstance associated with an event and *how* it happens. Companies have moved from providing content to shaping the circumstances of events, as Starbucks has done in its coffee stores. Contextual elements such as store location, interior design, lighting, product options, and recorded music creatively combine to let patrons relax, read, chat with friends, or savor a moment. While the firm stages the broad context through its experience environment, it also provides the scope for individuals to define their own contexts and enjoy different kinds of Starbucks experiences. Some enjoy rearranging the furniture to suit a particular group gathering; others relish the flavor and aroma of specific coffee blends; still others simply like the convivial atmosphere, a social milieu that provides companionship or a place for quiet reflection.[5] Starbucks recognizes that the creative combination of products, employees, and consumer communities shapes the experiences of individuals.

Thus, individuals must be able to bring their own situational context to an experience and co-shape their experiences accordingly. That means the company must have the foresight to understand the heterogeneity of individual experiences and build an infrastructure that enables a variety of individualized experiences.

Context is also about the social and cultural underpinnings of an event. The importance of socio-cultural context becomes obvious when we consider businesses such as event planning—for example, planning a wedding. The event planner has to work in close collaboration with the couple, and in some cases their parents. Every aspect of the wedding—from the church or temple service to the table linen for the dinner—has special meaning for the couple. Needless to say, the couple wants to be deeply involved in making choices. Further, every sub-event can generate a different involvement from each member of the family and their guests. Each one experiences the wedding differently. Given the same sub-event, the emotional involvement of individuals can vary. Moreover, individual and communal preferences—of the groom, bride, best friends, parents, and peers—influence the personal meaning of any sub-event to that individual.

We next discuss the importance of the role of individual involvement and the derivation of personal meaning by an individual in co-constructing a personalized experience.

Individual Involvement

Involvement of the individual in events may take many forms, based on interactions among the individual and various products, channels, services, and company employees, as well as with other individuals in various thematic communities of interest.

When I watch television, the level of my involvement obviously varies. I may simply lie back on the sofa and watch a movie. If the movie bores me, I may even fall asleep before it ends. But if I find a particular movie intriguing, I may want to become more deeply engaged. Interactive products like enhanced CDs, experiential DVDs, and personal video recorders make this possible, opening new gateways to compelling new experiences.

The same can be said of consumer-centric employees in a retail environment (such as the video store manager who notes my enthusiastic reaction to Alfred Hitchcock's *North by Northwest* and recommends I try the Hitchcock-esque *Memento*) or Web sites expressly designed to foster experiences (such as the Netflix site that notes my ratings of favorite movies and offers recommendations for additional films I will probably enjoy). All these elements of traditional business are slowly but surely morphing into *experience channels*, portions of a broader experience environment.

Sony Online Entertainment Inc.'s EverQuest allows thousands of players to enter imaginary worlds where they adopt roles, take on quests, make friends and enemies, and even "die." The available game experiences are so compelling that nearly four hundred thousand subscribers pay about $13 a month to participate.[6] Parlors for aficionados of Ever-Quest and similar Internet-enabled adventure games are popular in South Korea, now one of the world's most wired countries. Microsoft is investing over a billion dollars in a network for massive multiplayer games while forging ahead with its Small Personal Objects Technology (SPOT) initiative, designed to enable everyday products to become smarter.[7] Interactive technologies are increasingly embedded all around us, as we saw in the pacemaker example.

Moreover, individuals enjoy sharing experiences with others, reliving vacations through digital photographs, showing off a brand-new dress, or trading thoughts about the newest Harry Potter adventure. The burgeoning mobile Internet enables new forms of sociotechnical interaction enabling people to participate in thematic communities.

Thematic communities differ from spatially-defined communities. "All of us live in this neighborhood" describes a spatially-defined community. "All of us are breast cancer survivors" or "All of us are Australian wine lovers" are examples of thematic communities. Your company's "executive committee" and its roster of "key customer accounts" are also thematic communities whose participants can shape each other's experiences depending on their community involvement. In large, complex social structures like a corporation, a city, or a nation, sharing among thematic community members promotes informed, effective action. A breast cancer survivor may not be able to single-handedly secure the passage of legislation related to health care insurance, but a large thematic community can decisively lobby for change.

Derivation of Personal Meaning

Personal meaning is about the relevance of an event to the individual and the knowledge, insights, enjoyment, satisfaction, and excitement that emanate from it. Different consumers want different levels of involvement, levels that affect the meaning assigned to the event by each consumer. For example, owners of Harley-Davidson motorcycles are famous for using their bikes to express their own personalities. Connoisseurs spend as much time accessorizing, customizing, decorating, and cleaning their bikes as riding them. If all you want from a motorcycle is a convenient way to travel, you probably won't want to buy a Harley. Those who enjoy the Harley experience to its fullest are those who want to be completely immersed in Harley's environment. Some Harley owners go even further. They belong to the Harley Owners Group (HOG), a close-knit community that holds rallies, shows, and cross-country rides. Beneath the veneer of conversations and activities enjoyed by HOG members lies *shared* personal meanings, which are continuously structured through interactions with other members. Thus, owning a Harley is both a personal and a social statement.[8]

As noted by our colleague, Kerimcan Ozcan, "meaning, in the widest sense, stands for the mental act of signification."[9] The personal meaning of any event is (1) partly subjective, rooted in the ideas, concepts, thoughts, beliefs, and intentions of the individual; (2) partly objective, anchored in the context and consequences of the particular event; and (3) partly relational, deriving from the role that particular event plays within a relevant domain of activities. The derivation of personal meaning is the overarching element of a personalized co-creation experience.

To illustrate, consider the role of line managers. The overall inventory level may mean less to a particular manager than where the inventory is in the world (spatial) and when (temporal). The context of space and time may closely relate to the meaningfulness of information for this line manager. For example, while I may care about overall sales performance, what may create more meaning for me is the answer to the question: in which branches around the world (space) were sales less than 80 percent of forecast (event) last week (time)? A precipitous sales drop in principal markets such as Germany may get immediate attention from me, while a similar drop (in percentage terms) in Chile may not. Another manager may react strongly to even a small sales decline in Chile.

In thinking about the meaning of events, we can't ignore the centrality and importance of the individual. Each manager, for example, has a different perception of what is critical. What is meaningful information to one line manager, in the context of a specific event, and how critical it is, can vary from individual to individual. The same event can evoke different managerial responses at different points in time, even for the same individual manager.

Experience Personalization: The OnStar Example

The four dimensions just described—events, context of events, individual involvement, and derivation of personal meaning—put the individual at the heart of a co-creation experience. This view suggests that *firms can no longer dictate individual experience outcomes*. The challenge is to allow a high degree of personalization of interactions with an experience environment as well as to accommodate heterogeneous consumer interests, knowledge, needs, and desires.

Let us look at the emerging field of telematics, the provision of mobile information and services to auto drivers and passengers. General Motors (GM) launched OnStar to provide safety and emergency services to its customers. As GM has learned about its customers' broader interests and needs, OnStar has steadily evolved. Instead of asking, "How can we use information technology to make driving safer and more secure?" OnStar now asks, "What do consumers desire to experience in their cars? How can information technology improve the driving experience—during a long commute, a cross-country drive, or a round of neighborhood chores?" As the answers expand, OnStar is creating a new space within which consumers can enjoy personalized co-creation experiences that make driving more entertaining, informative, convenient, fun—and safe.[10]

Telematics involves providing wireless connectivity to consumers in their vehicles via satellite to monitoring stations. The OnStar interface is simple: The driver merely presses a button on the dashboard, and a call center operator responds. OnStar can provide a host of location-based services because it can always determine the precise location of the car at any time. Some services focus on safety. When an OnStar subscriber is in an accident, the OnStar service representative dispatches a police car or ambulance to the scene, guided by satellite data.

Other OnStar services, however, are purely experience-extending amenities. For example, an OnStar customer could say, "I'm on the road two hundred miles from home. Is there an Italian restaurant anywhere nearby?" The service rep notes the driver's location, taps a database to locate the nearest Italian restaurant, and can even make reservations.

OnStar can also access the vehicle's internal sensors to monitor vehicle functions and provide assistance when needed. For example, when a consumer locks herself out of her car, OnStar can open the door remotely. When a car's airbag inflates, OnStar can detect the accident and assess its severity. When a car is stolen, OnStar can help the police track it down.

OnStar works because the system addresses the experience space. It focuses on events—a fender-bender, an Italian dinner, a locked-out driver—and respects the time and space context within which events occur. It allows consumers to interact with the system through a simple, flexible interface.

OnStar's current capabilities are quite impressive, but additional experiences are well within OnStar's technological capabilities. Suppose I live in the neighborhood of Pikes Peak, Colorado, and drive a telematics-equipped car. Why can't the telematics service center call or e-mail me with weather, traffic, or emergency alerts? "The National Weather Service has issued a blizzard warning for the Pikes Peak area for tomorrow morning. We recommend you avoid driving. If you must drive to work, then we recommend this alternative route. . . ." Suppose I possess some specific knowledge about the alternative route that the system has not detected. How can I co-develop a route that is best for me?

Telematics systems must also adapt and evolve with me, the consumer, learning about my preferences and offering new services as appropriate. When my telematics system discerns from my past information requests that I listen to Sheryl Crow, and root for the Denver Broncos, it can automatically offer me information on Crow's concert tours, and game highlights. But it must then let me participate, define, and shape what it offers me, so as to suit my desired experiences in a particular context.

The OnStar example also suggests that firms must often invest in new technologies if they want to create experience environments. On-Star has invested heavily in understanding and using wireless telephony, satellite communication, vehicle integration systems, and internal sensors, as well as the technologies to integrate the vehicle diagnostics into public networks, call center operations, and emergency services. The hardware and software requirements and the quality levels needed to deploy OnStar safely as a vehicle-based application are quite impressive, illustrating how emerging technologies, creatively combined, can become experience enablers in a wide variety of businesses.

Finally, notice how the infrastructure for personalized interactions requires a *nodal firm* to orchestrate a large number of suppliers, partners, and consumer communities as an "experience network." A personalized co-creation experience—an "experience of one"—hinges on access to the enhanced competence base of this network, as shown in figure 5-1.

FIGURE 5-1

Experience Personalization

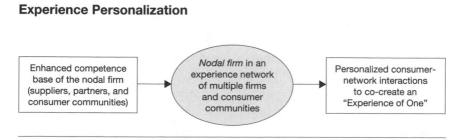

Co-Creating Unique Value:
The Professional Learning Example

Now let's switch to a very different information-intensive industry: university education. In April 2001, the Massachusetts Institute of Technology (MIT) announced a ten-year initiative called OpenCourse-Ware. MIT will spend up to $100 million to create public Web sites for almost all of its two thousand courses and to post materials like lecture notes, problem sets, simulations, and video lectures. Unlike "distance learning" such as Phoenix Online University or the U.K.'s Open University, the MIT approach offers course materials as "ingredients of learning" that participants can combine with teacher-student interaction anywhere—in MIT's own classrooms, at another university, online, or anywhere else in the world.[11]

This example raises an intriguing question: If the specific "content" of an MIT education is free, then where does its value lie? Actually, we know that a university education involves far more than a transfer of information from professors to students. Good professors have always engaged their students in interactive dialogue. Today, just as patients do their homework before visiting their physicians, many students are actually preparing for class, eager to explore new ideas and debate with their professors and classmates. Thus, students are co-shaping their learning experiences more than ever before.

Furthermore, many professors are experimenting with interactive technology as a tool for enabling learning experiences—before or after class and involving not just one-on-one teacher-student dialogues but open discussions among many students in a full-fledged learning community. More than ever, students can tap into the collective competence of their peers.

The advantages of this approach are enormous. Suppose Professor Chips teaches a ninety-minute business class with forty-five students. If he engaged everyone in dialogue during class and spent no time lecturing, then each student would get only two minutes. But if Chips set up a preclass interactive forum, then he could move toward a unique learning experience for each student and free the actual class time for more challenging and student-centric discussions.

Now take this concept a little further. Imagine a learning community that co-creates knowledge around an outline of themes and conceptual threads. Extend the community beyond the college campus to include professionals, engaged alumni, consultants, authors—an assortment of knowledge co-developers participating as a community. Knowledge generation and dissemination become inseparable. The goal of a university as a nodal firm becomes co-creation of intellectual capital, of value to the community at large.

In our own teaching, we've experimented with such personalized learning experiences. We videotaped each class session of one course. Afterward, using a unified multimedia indexing technology that handled video streams, a subset of students reconstructed the class based on their views of the topic, its takeaways, and its challenges. The students created "contextual knowledge capsules," each of which included a specific video segment, the professor's slides on that particular theme, student discussions, and additional resources. Students could use these capsules to enhance their learning experience individually and as a community, and share their favorites with peers who could then add different perspectives on the topic.

Consequently, our students created new course content from their skills, knowledge, and personal learning experiences. The professor simply facilitated a participant-centric learning experience. The result revitalized the idea of continuous, lifelong, community-based learning.

In this kind of multidirectional community dialogue, there are no fixed roles, just *roles of the moment*. The traditional debate among educators as to whether students are customers (buyers of educational services) or products (minds stuffed with knowledge for "sale" to employers) is ultimately pointless, symptomatic of a company-centric view with its traditional roles and boundaries. Students are both customers and products. They are also employees (in their role as institution builders—recruiting new students, for example), and even professors (in their role as teachers).

This vision of education as a truly interactive, personalized, co-creation process elucidates MIT's OpenCourseWare project. How can the university afford to "give away" its intellectual content? The real value of an MIT education lies in the quality of the interaction among all the members of a learning community, not in the information that professors transmit to students. Students value the learning experience—the co-creation of knowledge—and not the underlying products and services.

Migrating to Experience Personalization

We summarize the shift from the traditional customization approach to true experience personalization in table 5-1.

As we have discussed, businesses must now contend with heterogeneity (defined by interaction) that is more complex and subtle than an array of traditional market segments. "Segment-of-one" thinking takes us only part of the way. When managers talk about a segment of one, they see the consumer as a marketing target. We sell to this single customer. We expect him to learn our systems. We may allow him to configure the product from our menu or offer him special discounts. But what we don't do is actively engage the consumer in co-creation. Instead, we tend to fight against co-creation, as the music industry did against Napster.

To illustrate, let us consider "experiential marketing" à la Disney or Ritz Carlton. Yes, they focus on consumer experience, but their consumers are basically treated as passive. Such companies disproportionately influence the nature of the experience, still primarily product-centric, service-centric, and, therefore, company-centric.[12]

TABLE 5 - 1

Migrating to Experience Personalization

	Traditional Customization	Experience Personalization
View of Customization	Segment of one	Experience of one
Focus of Customization	One-off products and services	Personalization of interactions with the experience environment
Approach to Customization	Feature menus, components, costs, speed	Events, context of events, individual involvement, and personal meaning
View of Supply Chain	Fulfillment of a variety of customized products and services through modularity	Facilitating a variety of personalized experiences through heterogeneous interactions
Focus of Infrastructure	Configuration and fulfillment services for build-to-order processes	Infrastructure to support an experience network

Suppose the performers call me up on stage during the Indiana Jones Stunt Spectacular at the Disney-MGM Studios theme park. I switch from audience to actor, riding with Indy over a crocodile-infested river. One could say that I am an active customer participant, or am I really just a human prop in a carefully staged performance? And what about the hundreds of other visitors watching from their seats in the amphitheater? The Stunt Spectacular is not a personalized co-creation experience, but a company-centric staged experience.

Or consider the "Ritz-Carlton experience," a night's stay in a hotel room, potentially with food, beverages, and related services. The focus is clearly on connecting the customer to the company's offerings. Contrast that with OnStar, which focuses on the unique personalized experiences of the consumer at a given point in time, not on the automobile or even on the available services.

Personalizing co-creation experiences also differs from the line of reasoning labeled "customers as innovators." Customers of a firm like General Electric Plastics assume much of the task of developing a custom resin for a specific application. By providing access to tools and a library of compounds, GE shifts effort and risk to its customers. When the process works well, both parties benefit. GE saves development time and reduces its risk, while customers can get what they want with greater speed and accuracy. But as long as the process remains firm-centric and product-centered, it is at best a variant of the dominant logic.[13]

The same applies to the conventional approach to product or service customization. Starting from a traditional firm-centric view of value creation, managers focus on providing products and services to a single customer at low cost. This process leads to mass customization, which combines the benefits of "mass" (large-scale production and marketing and therefore low cost) with those of "customization" (targeting a single customer). The focus on product feature development leads to increased product choice for consumers. On the Web, for example, consumers can customize products and services ranging from business cards and computers to home mortgages and flower arrangements, simply by choosing from a menu of features. But such customization tends to suit the company's supply chain, rather than a consumer's unique desires and preferences.

Personalizing the co-creation experience means fostering individualized experiences. It involves more than just a company's à la carte menu. A personalized co-creation experience reflects how the individual chooses to interact with the experience environment that the firm facilitates. We are suggesting a totally different process—*one that involves individual consumers in personalized co-creation experiences*—a broad challenge that business leaders must face.

Unfolding the Spectrum of Co-Creation Experiences

Let's pause to take stock of where we have been. Our point of departure in this book was the emerging reality of the informed, networked, and active consumer, combined with the convergence of technologies and industries. Driven by these two forces, the consumer is increasingly influencing the firm and the value creation process. The result: the emergence of co-creation of value, which actively combines the traditional roles of the firm and the consumer (summarized in figure 5-2).

FIGURE 5 - 2

Unfolding the Spectrum of Co-Creation Experiences

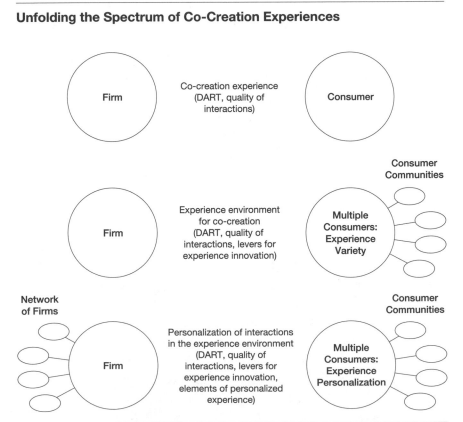

Dialogue, access, risk assessment, and transparency—DART—are the preconditions for an effective co-creation process. We discussed how companies can facilitate a compelling co-creation experience for the individual consumer. We explored the key elements of the co-creation experience and its personalization in chapters 2 through 5.

Now we must ask ourselves: How can we build the *infrastructure* for personalized co-creation experiences? What kind of an *experience network* do we need? What would such a network look like, and how would it function?

We turn to these questions in the next chapter.

Chapter Six

EXPERIENCE NETWORKS

I N THIS CHAPTER, we link the emerging co-creation and experience-oriented view of competition with building an experience network, the infrastructure for effectively co-creating value through personalized experiences. This infrastructure enables managers to *compete on experiences*. Let us consider an example.

Building an Experience Network: The John Deere Example

Farming may seem a traditional and slow moving industry, but farming in the United States today is transforming dramatically, becoming ever more knowledge- and capital-intensive. We do not mean genetically modified seeds or any other infusion of biotechnology into agriculture. Rather, we mean that farm management itself is changing. One company hastening this transformation is Deere & Company, the century-old maker of farm machinery.[1]

Technology is one aspect of Deere's innovative approach to agriculture. Deere is experimenting with global positioning systems (GPS) and biosensors on its combines. Imagine driverless combines and tractors with onboard sensors that can measure the oil content of grain or distinguish between weeds and crops. The benefits are enormous. Farmers can ration herbicide according to soil conditions in a particular area. GPS-guided steering ensures repeatable accuracy, eliminates overtreating of crops, and enables work on hilly terrain, thereby reducing time, fuel, labor, and chemicals costs. There is less stress for field preparation, cultivation, and spraying. Farmers can be more productive, minimizing their costs per acre.

The new technologies can also help the farmer monitor all his equipment, including engine condition and location. By integrating remote diagnostics into the system, Deere can warn farmers of likely equipment failures, avoiding costly surprises during planting or harvesting. The system, dubbed DeereTrax, can adapt to each farmer's unique set of problems, fitting virtually any type of equipment. It can even track smaller machines like pickups and automobiles. Its "geofencing" capabilities let the farmer define zones in which his equipment can operate. If a machine leaves a prescribed zone, it can alert the farmer, potentially foiling theft.

Thus, Deere is making the farmer's life easier and more productive by providing access to vital information through an interactive system. This approach is a major step towards accommodating a wide heterogeneity of farmers' experiences. Furthermore, the system connects farmers with similar problems, creating a thematic community—that is, farmers matched on a variety of factors who share their knowledge. Such dialogue increases the collective expertise of the community, spreading best practices freely and autonomously. The entire system starts to be built around "me, the farmer." *It champions my farm, my farming productivity, and my unique experiences.*

The entire process is farmer-centric. Farmers use not only a product (the Deere combine) but also the knowledge, support services, and peer group access in the Deere network to generate a decent return. With this approach, farmers can make their own definitions and judgments about the price and performance of any new product or service. If they need advice, then they can communicate with fellow farmers who have faced similar problems across the country. The choices are the farmer's, not the company's.

Notice how Deere's approach to agriculture creatively blends the four building blocks of the value co-creation space—dialogue, access, risk, and transparency. Access and transparency are inherent in the system. Dialogue is evolving. Risk assessment may involve not just the farmer community, but also the company, its customers, and its many vendors—from the manufacturers of spare parts to the suppliers of fertilizers, chemicals, and seeds. Assessing business risks requires, at a minimum, data about what end users want and will buy. For example, Americans might accept genetically modified soybeans, but Europeans may not. The farmer who sells produce to an agriprocessor with a significant European operation bears a substantial risk.

Thus, we start with access and transparency, while dialogue and risk assessment evolve over time. The demand for information—access and transparency—inevitably increases as we move toward personalized co-creation experiences.

In the past, companies have viewed themselves as innovating products, not experience environments. The new paradigm puts the individual at the center of the value-creation process, with both employees and technology playing supportive roles. Technology-enabled intelligent products, such as tractors that sense the environment and respond automatically, cater to a given farmer's largely unpredictable needs, accommodating a wide base of experiences across individual farmers.

Thus, Deere and the farmer can interact at *multiple points in the system*, not just at the point of product exchange. Participants have many opportunities to interact and transact, making the farmer's life more productive and even fun.

For example, suppose Deere builds a portfolio of competencies around sensor technologies, such as systems for precisely mapping the application of seeds and fertilizers and the impact on yield of such variables as the oil and humidity content of the crop. This portfolio could transform yield management for a farm. Imagine the information that such a system can produce for identifying and creating new products and services to enhance the farmer's experiences.

More important, Deere is creating a new forum for dialogue with the farmer that eliminates speculation about consumer needs. Instead, Deere and the farmer can co-discover new value for both. Continuous interaction and co-creation of value (using DART), coupled with an intelligent infrastructure oriented toward experiences, can generate insights into new opportunities for value creation.

The Deere example illustrates the possibility of co-creating unique value via an experience network. An experience network does not simply link components, products, or even information, though it incorporates the traditional supply chain. It also sparks communities by connecting suppliers, dealers, and support staff with consumers, and consumers with one another. Firms that contribute intellectual leadership, build coalitions, and forge pathways for products, information, and expertise are *nodal companies*. Nodal companies are like traffic cops, making the rules and allowing for free flow with adequate constraints.

FIGURE 6 - 1a

The Basic Transformation in Co-Creating Value

FROM: FIRM-CENTRIC SUPPLY/DEMAND PERSPECTIVE

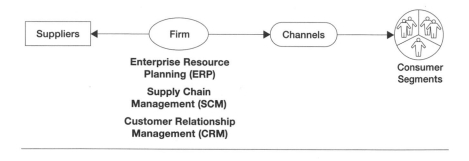

Or, to shift metaphors, they create a sandbox in which all the stake-holders are free to invent their own games, and even modify the infra-structure for their effective participation.

Two simple pictures map Deere's transformation from a firm-centric view of the value creation process (represented by the traditional supply chain system in figure 6-1a) to a co-creation view centered around individuals (represented by the experience network in figure 6-1b). Consider some of the key implications of this basic transformation:

- The firm's task is now to build an experience network such that consumers can easily interact with experience environments to co-construct experiences. The new competitive differentiation may rest in the quality of the experience network that both consumers and the company have access to.

- Nodal firms can create the experience enablers, encompassing both a technical and a social dimension. Such enablers are the heart of an effective experience network.

- The new value-creation paradigm is about managing consumer-to-company-to-consumer links. Acronyms like B2B and B2C miss the point. If we must use an acronym, then let's use I2N2I, which represents the flow from the individual consumer to the nodal firm and its experience network, and then back to the individual.[2]

- Consumer-initiated co-creation experiences can selectively activate the entire supply process, managed by a nodal firm like Deere, which provides the intellectual leadership and influence.

FIGURE 6 - 1b

The Basic Transformation in Co-Creating Value

To: Individual-Centric Experience Perspective

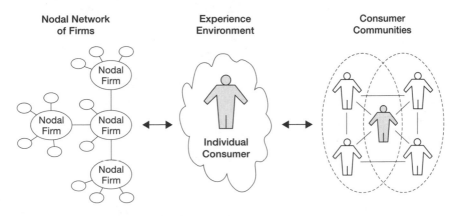

Unique Value to the Individual Consumer Through Personalized Co-Creation Experiences:

- *Consumer-company interaction is the locus of value creation*
- *Individual co-creation experience is the basis for value*
- *Multiple channels are gateways to experiences*
- *Infrastructure must support heterogeneous co-creation experiences*
- *Enhanced network, including consumer communities, is the locus of core competence*

- The traditional supply chain remains important; the physical movement of products and services will not disappear. But the supply chain will morph in some predictable ways. For example, it may no longer be sequential or linear, and different suppliers may join or exit the chain depending on specific consumer preferences.[3]

The Deere example suggests that creating an experience network entails the following:

- A compelling experience environment with *well-integrated experience enablers* that the individual can interact with, coupled with access to a network of firms and consumer communities, to co-construct a unique, personalized experience.

- An orientation around points of consumer-company interaction and the *heterogeneity of experiences*. Firms must be able to facilitate the construction of a different experience for each individual consumer, one that's fulfilling to that consumer in her context of space and time.

- The capacity to adapt and *rapidly reconfigure resources*, accommodating wide swings in consumer demands in the experience space.

- The ability to *selectively activate competencies* required for the co-construction of personalized experiences.

Moving from conventional value chain and fulfillment systems to an effective experience network in one fell swoop is nearly impossible. Instead, it must be accomplished in phases, through experiment-based learning. Following are several examples of such experimentation by firms, as they gradually build effective experience networks.

Social and Technical Enablers of Experiences

In an important sense, building the experience network must start from experience enablers and integrate them into the experience environment. Let's start with the simplest case—where the products on offer do not change, but the consumer experience changes through an experience environment.

For example, packaged cereals and coffee need not change, but my experience of shopping for them can. Consider Tesco, a global food retailing chain that has done a remarkable job of balancing local customization with the cost efficiencies of standardization. Tesco has made it possible for an individual consumer to order groceries online and have them delivered to her home, successfully expanding the scope of the consumer experience by piggybacking on Tesco's existing infrastructure. A Tesco manager said that employees think of their local stores as warehouses, already designed for easy assembly of orders. Thus, Tesco's store picking system leverages the firm's existing infrastructure, letting the company scale up slowly and learn by doing.[4]

But Tesco has had to innovate an experience environment as well. It had to integrate its online and physical operations, linking online shopping to each store's IT system. Tesco has also created experience enablers. For example, if an item ordered online is unavailable, the store picking system suggests an alternative, and this item is placed on top of the order so the consumer can easily accept or reject it upon delivery. The delivery vans are routed optimally within a two-hour window to ensure that perishables stay as fresh as possible. Tesco is a good example of innovation that is not only efficient but also focused on the customer experience.

Companies can use experience networks to help consumers accept new technologies and evolve in their sophistication as experience co-creators. Consider NTT DoCoMo, Japan's dominant mobile operator and a global leader in the fusion of mobile phones with the Internet. DoCoMo, whose name is a play on the Japanese word for "anywhere," has over forty million mobile subscribers. Using its special i-mode phones, consumers can send and receive e-mail, read the news, access weather forecasts and horoscopes, and download special ringing tones and cartoon graphics from more than fifty thousand i-mode-compatible Web sites. Consumers can also use the phones to play music and games, conduct banking and travel transactions, and much more. Thus, i-mode allows consumers to connect with companies and with each other as never before.[5]

DoCoMo illustrates the importance of investing in both technical and social enablers and orienting the consumer-product interface toward co-creating new experiences. DoCoMo continues to up the ante with its investment in 3G "freedom of multimedia access" phones and location-based services. As it builds the network infrastructure, DoCoMo is confronting such crucial questions as:

- How can the DoCoMo experience environment facilitate simplicity, convenience, interactivity, and ease of use, while contending with the inherent limits of the small size of phones?

- How can DoCoMo master the new art of experience design, as opposed to traditional product design?

- How can DoCoMo continue to innovate its experience environment to facilitate social interactions?

Experience networks can shift deeply ingrained behavior—even the mundane practice of paying people. Consider PayPal, a popular method of payment on the Internet, used for person-to-person payments and by more than 1.5 million business Web sites. Acquired by eBay for $1.5 billion, PayPal facilitates payments using e-mail accounts. By 2002, PayPal had more than ten million users, with about thirty thousand joining daily due to "viral growth": If you pay somebody via PayPal, that somebody must have a PayPal account to get paid instantly; otherwise, he waits for a physical check.[6] Since PayPal receives about 1.9 percent of the value of purchases from vendors, merchants who sell through PayPal pay less than they would for credit card transactions. Not surprisingly, the established credit card companies and banks worry about PayPal, which is exposing the limitations of traditional payment methods.

In response to the PayPal challenge, Citigroup (with over 100 million customers) and AOL (over 25 million customers) partnered to announce a new Citigroup Internet payment system for all AOL services. Citigroup has also offered its c2it ("see to it") Web payment service for free. Citigroup can afford to absorb the costs because many of the transactions through c2it involve Citibank credit cards and bank accounts.

New entrants like the PayPal system are sometimes called "disruptive technologies." We prefer the neutral term—*discontinuity*. Technologies don't come labeled as "disruptive." They can disrupt, if not properly managed. It is the *incumbents'* dilemma—discontinuities demand disciplined imagination and innovation. They can herald a great new opportunity. Citi is essentially rallying around the PayPal discontinuity—not just a technology but a momentous institutional change.

The financial services industry, by its very nature, is conservative: Caution, security, and privacy are the key attributes of this industry. But the possibilities engendered by discontinuities are many. Although credit cards account for over half of all Internet transactions, the total is still only 2 to 4 percent of all credit card business, conducted mostly at the point of sale or by telephone. PayPal, in contrast, originated as an e-mail service. Mobile phones are now doubling up as payment mechanisms; so you and I can accept "credit" payments via our phones. Around the world, consumers are increasingly using their cell phones to purchase prepaid phone cards, tickets, text messaging services, fast food, and drinks and to pay newsagents, taxi drivers, relatives, and the like. If mismanaged, this discontinuity can indeed disrupt incumbents in the industry.

An experience network can also change established demand patterns. For example, deregulation is inching the electric power industry toward more competitive generation, transmission, and distribution of electricity. Dynamic pricing by the hour or minute (which telecom companies use) could conceivably cut costs for all parties, but consumers must first change their consumption habits, adjusting the operation of household appliances or shifting the times of day when they use energy.[7]

In this aspect, experience networks need smart control systems to spread some of the intelligence to the points of interaction (consumption) and, simultaneously, to mind the backbone of the network infrastructure. Incumbents will have to invest heavily to retrofit or replace household meters with the embedded intelligence in order to collect real-time usage data and calculate more complicated bills. Moreover, the electric grid must be flexible enough to reconfigure power generation and transmission according to consumption patterns.

The Tesco, DoCoMo, PayPal, and electric power examples illustrate two important issues. First, we must think in terms of *social* enablers, apart from the technical enablers for experience integration. Second, both the social and technical enablers must coalesce seamlessly in the experience environment to facilitate the co-construction of experiences. Moreover, as we develop the experience environments, we must distinguish between the underlying IT and supply chain and logistics infrastructures, and the applications infrastructure that supports the customer interface. The latter is crucial for continuous and flexible co-creation of experiences.

We also must separate the issue of how to enable a variety of experiences at the point of interaction from the intelligence of the infrastructure (where it resides, how it reaches customers, and so on). How much intelligence should we push to products and channels at the periphery of the experience network? How much should remain in the core? Pushing everything to the periphery may mean relinquishing control. We have choices to make concerning how much intelligence is in the product or channel, how much in the network, and how much we should leave to the individual user, remembering that consumers are a heterogeneous lot. We also must have a consistent way of thinking about leveraging infrastructure and resources across multiple businesses. These are issues that companies must address as they build more effective experience networks.

But we must simultaneously recognize that as consumers co-construct experiences, they will *not* honor managerial distinctions between the network and applications, core and periphery, or hardware and software. A consumer-centric view of the experience implies that *high-tech = high-touch in the experience network*. The technical and social enablers of experiences, the experience environment, and the experience network are inextricably linked.

Creating the Social and Technical Infrastructure to Support Heterogeneous Experiences

Experience networks must deal explicitly with the heterogeneity of experiences. There are several approaches to this requirement. The first step is to go from consumer segments to the "experience of one" by explicitly recognizing individuality.

For an example, let us return to the health care industry. The pharmaceutical industry has long relied on the blockbuster approach to drug development, trying to create medications that millions of patients can use uniformly, thereby generating revenues measured in billions of dollars. This approach seeks to minimize the impact of heterogeneity of experiences in favor of uniformity.

But this approach has limitations. Side effects, which characterize virtually every medication, clearly substantiate patient heterogeneity. So do the interactions—sometimes fatal—among the multiple medications that a single patient must take. Yet the clinical trials do not typically encompass heterogeneous populations around the globe.

Ultimately, a physician selects a drug based on patient history, diagnosis, and his own professional judgment. How does this process of choice deal with patient heterogeneity? The conventional approach is basically one of trial and error. The physician prescribes his preferred medication for a given condition and monitors the results. If the drug works, fine. If not, he switches the prescription to a second option. The process continues until an effective medication is found.

Today this indiscriminate process is changing. Take Herceptin, Genentech's breast-cancer treatment that works well—in a small percentage of patients. Herceptin has become successful because these patients can be identified through a diagnostic test. The idea of selectively identifying a product from the available candidates that uniquely suits a given patient, is more efficient and safer than the traditional trial-and-error technique. With new advances in patient screening and gene-based testing techniques, physicians will increasingly be able to determine whether a given drug might work for a specific patient—an example of adapting to consumer heterogeneity.[8]

Companies can recognize and support consumer heterogeneity by allowing individual consumers to work with employees to co-construct their own experiences. To illustrate, let us look at cosmetics, certainly among the most deeply personal products anyone can use.

When you enter a department store, you see an array of cosmetics counters, each of which displays the offerings of a different company—Clinique, Christian Dior, and so on. In theory, the employees behind the counter can work with me to determine my requirements and suggest the most suitable products. But in fact, they tend to push predetermined products—items on sale, for example, or manufacturers' special promotions. Even when the employees genuinely want to facilitate a personalized interaction, their knowledge base may not suffice. In any case, the store's stock limits their offerings.

In contrast, Sephora, the French-based cosmetics store chain, offers a different way of shopping for beauty. A hands-on shopping environment lets me smell, touch, and experience every product, from fragrances and makeup to skin care. I can also choose the desired level of assistance, from minimal guidance to detailed, expert advice. On the Internet, Sephora.com offers access to more than 11,000 beauty products representing more than 230 brands.

Now consider Reflect.com, an experimental venture backed by Procter & Gamble. It allows women to concoct their own beauty products, describing what they want in a lipstick, shampoo, or perfume by responding to visual images and a series of interactive questions. The company then develops and offers appropriate personalized formulas to the consumer.

To develop a personalized fragrance, for example, Reflect.com takes what it calls a "heart and soul" approach. It helps consumers to identify the "heart" or essence of the perfume; then a more in-depth exploration begins, unveiling the possible "soul" of the fragrance. Consumers undergo an interactive visual experience designed to capture both their imagination and their scent preferences. Then the company applies the expertise of many scientists and technologists, and its access to unique fragrance oils and fine ingredients, to prepare three scent variations. Reflect.com shares these with the consumer so that she can smell the fragrances, select one, and name it.

In principle, this personalization process allows women to co-develop their own products.[9] Suppose a customer wants eye cream. Reflect.com asks her to indicate, for example, whether she gets dark circles or puffiness under her eyes, whether she wants smoother skin under her eyes or fewer laugh lines, and whether her eyes are sensitive. Once she completes the interactive questionnaire, Reflect.com's system formulates the product, based on individual consumer input rather than preset programs. If the consumer wants only to minimize dark circles under her eyes, then her eye cream will contain vitamin C but not vitamins A and K, which supposedly reduce wrinkles.

Reflect.com has designed its back-end infrastructure to support the consumer experience. The order goes into a specially built manufacturing facility with access to a flexible supply base; it can turn small lots of raw material orders around in a day. As a result, Reflect.com's productivity on a variable-cost basis is almost the same as if it made fifty thousand units of a given product rather than just a few. As of 2003, consumers have created more than 3.5 million unique products using Reflect.com.

Of course, given consumer heterogeneity, not everyone will want to interact through such a model. As a consumer, I may prefer to sample products, as I can in a Sephora store. I may like the physical ambience of an inviting store and its immersive shopping experience. I may appreciate interacting with a knowledgeable, affable, helpful sales clerk. I may enjoy working with a beauty consultant—an Avon lady—who knows me well. No single experience fits all consumers at all times.

Reflect.com is an ongoing experiment. But with the logistical, manufacturing, and supply chain infrastructure in place, imagine what could happen if we provided the same online capability to competent in-store beauty consultants. Call it a "clicks-*in*-mortar" experience environment. The resulting new capability would allow a wide base of consumers to co-create a personalized experience *in* the store, combining self-help and the consultants' expertise in a unique blend. As the consumer learns the system, the experience environment can evolve in parallel by capturing and integrating the consumer's experiences with the system and the products and services provided.

Some firms are already moving in this direction. REI sells outdoor gear, a very sophisticated and in its own way quite a distinctive business, where you are apt to hear technical discussions concerning everything from the type of ice axe to carry when climbing Mt. Rainier, to the right kind of boots to wear in the Amazon rain forest. REI helps consumers deal with this complexity by providing very detailed product information on the Web, a knowledgeable person with whom to discuss it, and most important, a place to experience it all.

Having started as a catalog operation, REI saw the Internet as a means of providing their customer base with access to a wide assortment of products (over ten thousand items) and of launching new products almost instantly. They also recognized that consumers needed help to sift through the enormous variety of products. The Internet could help consumers make informed choices while shifting the business toward a solutions space centered on consumer lifestyles and activities, from hiking to winter camping to trekking in the desert.

But REI also went further. Understanding that there are multiple ways of producing and delivering any product, REI looked at the Web, the catalog, and the retail store as multiple experience channels that ought to complement one another to create an integrated experience environment.[10]

Now, REI lets you check out a parka in a rain shower, try a pair of boots while scaling a mountain, or test a bike on a rugged dirt road—all *inside* its flagship store in Seattle, Washington. REI provides a staff of very talented and savvy salespeople to share their knowledge; it also lets you consult the REI Web site while in the store. It offers a distinctive experience environment—access to information, specialized knowledge, dialogue, and opportunities to experience the products in a realistic setting within the store. By expanding the experience environment in a meaningful way for consumers, REI has developed the capacity to co-create new forms of value.

REI had to evolve its information infrastructure as it transitioned toward the experience space. Depending upon a context determined by the consumer—not by the company—REI's multitude of experience channels attempt to "wrap around the consumer's finger."

Here's another story. Boris, an avid outdoorsman, wanted to get a roof rack for his automobile. Boris logged on at a kiosk in the REI store. The Web site asked him how he planned to use the roof rack—for a bike, for a boat, for skis?—as well as the make and model of his car. It then generated a complete list of items to install for proper use of the rack. Two of the items were out of stock, and so he ordered those online. The store's cash registers are also Web-enabled. Boris happened to forget an item. The cashier noticed, and she ordered it for him.

REI has also paid as much attention to co-opting employee competence as to co-opting consumer competence. The result is a fascinating blend of the social (employee and consumer experiences, their skills and expertise, their passion for the outdoors, their outdoor activities) with the technical (how products work, troubleshooting techniques, detailed specifications). REI also integrates the physical and online environments from the perspective of consumer think, and gives consumers and employees access to the same integrated environment in support of heterogeneous consumer experiences.

In building its experience network, REI used its "employee consumers" to the fullest. The fact that REI is structured as a business cooperative helps: Employees are both investors in the company and consumers. They are also outdoor enthusiasts; the firm has a policy of hiring sales employees with expertise in various activities ranging from skiing to rowing to climbing. So REI drove the development of the infrastructure from the inside, pulling pieces together from various IT vendors as appropriate but relying on its own staff to drive the Web site and store design processes.

The development of REI's physical presence took place in parallel with the online expansion. In fact, REI's flagship Seattle store, replete with indoor biking trails, climbing structures, and various other interactive testing areas, was opened just after the launch of REI.com.

The REI approach is not common. Imagine visiting a conventional large bookstore. You see an intriguing book review in a magazine on its rack. When you ask for the book at the information desk, you learn that it is not in stock. The typical bookseller's response? "We can order and get you a copy in five to seven days." Thanks, but no thanks. You'll probably forget about the book—or maybe order it online.

This failure to solve problems from the consumer's point of view is not a one-time event. At one time, the major bookstores had in-store terminals that allowed consumers to surf the Web and get e-mail, but not to order a book. Later, they installed terminals that could locate books in the store but, again, not order a book. As the infrastructure evolves, it continues to represent a company-centric view of consumers, oriented around transferring products on offer from the company to the consumer.

By contrast, REI has taken a consumer-centric view, building access, interactivity, and fun into the store and the online experience. The "fun" is both technical and social.

Let us summarize some of the key implications of the Herceptin, Sephora, Reflect.com, and REI examples:

- Creating an experience environment requires that firms explicitly consider the primary goals of that environment as well as the various approaches that can accommodate consumer heterogeneity.

- Firms must also be sensitive to how the infrastructure handles heterogeneity of individual experiences across multiple experience channels. The more combinations of channels provided for consumer access, the richer the experience. But creating a consistent experience across diverse channels is a significant challenge.

• To become experience-centric, firms must rethink the way they analyze their investments. Investment in infrastructure—IT, logistics, manufacturing, and supply chains—must be experience-oriented and leveraged across a wide range of businesses.

Rapid Resource Reconfiguration

The Reflect.com and REI examples also illustrate the complexities of integrating the channel infrastructure with the firm's supply chain, manufacturing operations, and logistics capabilities. We cannot outsource manufacturing or logistics without taking responsibility for ensuring a consistent quality of experience for consumers, even as their needs change. Delivering consistently high quality experiences requires the ability to quickly adjust to shifts in demand—what we call *rapid resource reconfiguration*.

For an example, let us look at the transformation of a very traditional industry—cement—by a Mexican-based company known as Cemex. In the cement industry, consumers (e.g., builders and contractors) demand definite, reliable delivery times. But almost half of these consumers can be expected to change their orders, usually close to the original scheduled delivery time. Under the circumstances, forecasting does not mean much, and a firm like Cemex cannot change the way its customers work and behave. The key challenge is to develop the ability to respond quickly to changes in customer demand.

To tackle this problem, Cemex had to reconceive its operations around giving customers flexibility. That meant that Cemex itself had to become flexible, while continuing to ensure dependable, on-time delivery of cement. To achieve this goal, the company invested early on in CemexNet, a satellite communications system that links all the cement plants, coordinating Cemex's far-flung production facilities. It then installed a logistics system called Dynamic Synchronization of Operations, which uses Global Positioning System (GPS) technology and onboard computers to link the delivery trucks and coordinate them. Like FedEx, it built transparency into its operations, allowing dispatchers to see the location and direction of each truck and obtain information on weather, traffic conditions, inventory, and customers' locations. The result: Trucks can be quickly rerouted to coordinate orders, production plants, and deliveries in response to last-minute changes requested by customers.[11]

On Cemex's online portal, its suppliers, distributors, and customers can check order status and change orders up to the moment of delivery. Customers can specify characteristics such as color, strength, texture, and elasticity, all critical to using ready-mix cement. The access that Cemex managers and customers have to real-time information centered on events is fundamental to the company's rapid response capabilities.

Of course, Cemex took about eight years to build its current infrastructure, starting with the communications network and the IT infrastructure and followed by the logistics infrastructure that enabled its customers to participate in creating value.

For Cemex, rapid resource reconfiguration requires the ability to respond almost instantly to changing customer requirements. Can managers sense changes in customer expectations before they surface directly? Can they amplify those subtle signals and respond ahead of the curve? The clothing retailer Zara, a subsidiary of the Spanish fashion company Inditex, suggests an answer.[12]

While REI uses employees primarily to fulfill consumer needs for information, Zara uses its employees to spot fashion trends. Zara is to European fashion what Gap has been to American casual. To stay ahead of fashion ideas, trends, and tastes, Zara encourages its designers and retail employees to socialize with consumers. They then utilize the company's internal communications network and wireless devices to send real-time information to Zara's commercial group and design center in Spain. If a shop manager sees that customers like a particular garment or a different color or style, then she alerts the company.

Thus, new designs—not just more of what's selling off the racks—materialize continuously. Zara needs as little as two to three weeks to move from a design sketch to a store display of new garments. According to one young Zara shopper, "Fashion is so transient, you just want the look of the moment at a really good price." Zara provides just that by honing its ability to reconfigure its supply chain elements very rapidly. Zara cuts its own raw material; its workshops in Spain do the final sewing and assembly. The chain can replenish store stocks twice a week, minimizing inventory, adjusting quickly to trends, and reducing transportation costs. Slightly higher manufacturing costs are more than offset by savings elsewhere in the system and especially by the increased inventory turns generated by offering cutting-edge fashion.

We see unexpected parallels, then, between the cement industry and the fashion business. The critical ability of the experience network to scale up and down requires the capacity to reconfigure resources effectively and respond quickly. For Cemex, a customer's order or change in plans triggers this reconfiguration. Since calls come in all the time, the process of reconfiguration must be continuous. For Zara, the fashion intelligence of its employees triggers decisions regarding style, designs, fabrics, shapes, colors, and so on. Could Zara involve consumers more directly? Perhaps—but that would require a different set of capabilities, analogous to those of a good Avon beauty consultant or the Reflect.com customized cosmetics system.

The fundamental challenge is integrating the various infrastructure elements to enable a consumer-centric experience network. Once such a network is in place, the company can identify opportunities to co-create new experiences.

Access to Competence

As we discussed earlier, the nodal firm provides the intellectual and technical leadership needed to establish an effective experience network, as well as the incentives that hold participating firms in the network together.

What makes a company that participates in a network into a nodal firm? Sheer size may be a factor. The prospect of working with a very large company is enough incentive for suppliers to join the network around that firm. (We see this force in operation in the networks around General Motors and General Electric, for example.) Alternatively, a nodal firm may start with a new concept of business, as Dell and Cisco did, deliberately building a supply network around it. Or, like Cemex and Zara, a nodal firm may revitalize an existing industry by creating a new market space.

Note that the nodal firm usually does not *own* most of the resources it deploys. As we discussed earlier, people tend to equate access with ownership. We must separate the two. Similarly, we tend to equate *control* with ownership. We must separate these two as well. Managers must find new ways to achieve both access *and* control *without* ownership.

Building an effective experience network requires learning how to access and leverage a broad competence base, drawing on the resources of companies and communities outside your own. The first task is to identify the sources of competence and build them into a network.

For an example, let's consider Li & Fung in the textile business. This Hong Kong–based firm has become a nodal company by accessing a network of 7,500 suppliers in thirty-seven countries. It uses this network to enable retailers like Ann Taylor, Guess, Laura Ashley, and The Limited to rotate their fashions at very short notice—often within three weeks. Li & Fung manages the information in the entire system as well as the relationships with the supplier network to deliver products faster, cheaper, and with less risk.[13]

Here's a glimpse of how the Li & Fung network operates. When an order arrives, Li & Fung uses customized Web sites, e-mail, and other communications methods to work with the customer to fine-tune the specifications. It then creates an optimal "supply chain on demand," finding the right suppliers of raw materials and the right factories to assemble the clothes. Thus, fabric may come from China if only China has the appropriate dye, durable fastenings may come from Korea, and the garment may be sewn in Indonesia. Li & Fung also balances the workload among its portfolio of suppliers in various regions of the world.

As the garment moves through production, a retail customer can make last-minute changes (just like a Cemex customer). In this case, however, the change may impact a global supply base. The customer can alter the design until the fabric is cut, change the color until the fabric is dyed, even cancel the order altogether until the fabric is woven. Li & Fung's competence lies in its deep understanding of the competencies resident in its vast supply network, its mastery of the economics of production, and its ability to create a customized supply chain suited to a customer's specific requirements. Li & Fung illustrates how access to production competence can be a critical element in creating the infrastructure of an experience network.

Another element is access to logistics. Logistics are at the heart of rapid resource configuration. Yet a firm need not build its own logistical infrastructure. Instead, specialist firms can be co-opted. Take United Parcel Service (UPS), the $30 billion delivery company based in Atlanta, Georgia. UPS has become a nodal company in logistics, spending about $1 billion a year on IT tools, including the intelligence-gathering DIAD (Delivery Information Acquisition Device), tracking software, bar-code scanners, and massive data centers. UPS uses these tools to manage nearly 80,000 delivery trucks, 240 planes, and over 360,000 employees in 200 countries while serving more than eight million customers daily and moving fully 6 percent of the U.S. gross domestic product (GDP).[14]

Today, the UPS logistics group offers services that provide visibility into the supply chain. UPS can move inventory, track it, and monitor it at every stage in its journey through the system. The firm also offers such services as inventory maintenance, on-demand delivery of mission-critical spare parts, and even warranty repairs. These and other services are performed in facilities close to airport runways, so companies can provide faster service to their customers.

Yet another key aspect of the experience network is the management of transactions. Specialist firms are emerging in this area as well. CheckFree, for example, is a nodal company that enables more than six million consumers to receive and pay bills electronically. It has contracts with over 250 of the top billers in the United States and facilitates online billing and payment through about 450 consumer service providers, including banks, brokerage firms, and Web portals. CheckFree processes more than two-thirds of the six billion Automated Clearing House (ACH) payments made in the United States each year. In short, CheckFree provides businesses with access to an IT infrastructure not unlike the ATM networks that banks use to provide convenience to their customers.[15]

The Li & Fung, UPS, and CheckFree examples illustrate how emerging specialist firms can facilitate the creation of a globally interconnected experience network. These specialists provide access to a global competence base, thereby enabling small, resource-starved firms to access global markets. With an Internet link, a company anywhere in the world—from Bombay to Boston, from Brussels to Beijing—can now participate in and benefit from the nodal network infrastructure. For example, artisans in Rajasthan, India, are selling their wares online to customers in the United States, delivering table linens and personalized stationery within seven days at one-tenth the cost of U.S. production.

Such Internet-enabled entrepreneurs are inventing a new form of global business: the *micro-multinational*. They need not invest heavily in assets—manufacturing facilities, distribution channels, or logistics systems—around the world. They simply use the services provided by specialty firms like DHL, UPS, and Citibank to manage transactions. Furthermore, they needn't spend an inordinate amount of time, money, and effort on marketing their products and services. Thanks to the Internet, consumer networks are global, and word-of-mouth communication is now on overdrive.

Now that nodal firms are leveraging islands of competencies all around the globe, a new business game is emerging. Rather than traditional resource allocation, this new game is oriented around *resource leverage and reconfiguration*. Nodal firms are increasingly creating new business opportunities by providing other firms with access to their competence base.

Consider Flextronics, a $15 billion firm operating seventy-five factories in twenty-five countries that specializes in high-volume electronic devices. By working with a large number of firms such as Palm (PDAs), Hewlett-Packard (printers), and Cisco (routers), Flextronics develops unique competencies that would be difficult for any one company to develop. Now take, for example, Microsoft. How does a software company get into manufacturing the video game console Xbox? It doesn't. Instead, Microsoft collaborates with Flextronics. With its access to a global supply base of components makers and its significant design and development expertise, Flextronics provides the competence required to effectively participate in the video console business, working along with such secondary suppliers as Intel (microprocessor), nVidia (graph processor), Micron (memory), and Western Digital (hard drives). Hence, one core nodal company like Microsoft can connect with another core nodal firm like Flextronics to jointly create a symbiotic ecosystem rooted in "competence on demand." There is a continuous learning process on both sides, as each nodal firm nurtures and builds its competencies. For Xbox, Flextronics gains access to a wide market base, while Microsoft develops markets downstream.[16]

All these examples show how consumer-centric co-creation of value may involve multiple nodal firms with access to various required competencies, all integrated by a core nodal player. Several nodal companies may exist in a single experience network. But the nodal entity that has a disproportionate identification with the experience space where consumer value is co-created is the core nodal player.

For a business manager, the immediate and fundamental task is to conceive and develop an experience network within which the firm and consumers can co-evolve with their experiences.

Let us go back to Intuit. The company's first significant breakthrough came from recognizing and acting on the centrality of the consumer. Now they are starting to evolve their information infrastructure, thereby expanding the variety of experiences their customers can access. Stephen Bennett, the firm's new chief executive and a former executive at GE Capital, has led Intuit's recent move toward internal networking based on the company's recognition of the centrality of their managers in creating quality experiences. Today, more than a hundred Intuit product managers oversee their staffs on a product-by-product basis, while a business-development team cuts across multiple business lines.

As consumers continue to evolve in their financial sophistication and their comfort in using interactive technologies (PC, mobile device, cell phone), Intuit must continuously innovate new experience linkages. The challenge is to accommodate a wide variety of heterogeneous experiences at points of interaction by providing access to competence for anyone in the experience network and by building the technical and social enablers that will make co-creation easy, profitable, and fun.

Experience Quality Management

As we migrate to an experience network, we must recognize that value lies not just in the variety of experiences that we can accommodate as a firm but in the *quality of co-creation experiences*.

A basic tension is emerging between the Total Quality Management (TQM) of products and processes versus what might be called Experience Quality Management (EQM). Traditional product-oriented TQM taught us to stamp out variation in a bid to control product quality. But EQM means combining heterogeneity—in other words, variability—with quality of execution. The same consumer who demands a unique, personalized experience also demands responsiveness, speed, reliability, and cross-channel consistency in actually experiencing the underlying event satisfactorily.[17] How can we simultaneously meet such seemingly contradictory demands?

The answer lies in the crucial distinction between variability in consumer experiences—access to many alternative channels, products, and services—and variability in the underlying processes. The former is our ally; the latter is our enemy. The trick is in configuring an array of resources so as to create a multitude of possible experiences while maintaining the quality of each of the underlying subprocesses. In other words, the experience network must be designed to accommodate variation in experiences while reducing variation in the quality of the supply processes that are activated to co-construct those experiences.

TABLE 6 - 1

The New Frontier of Experience Quality Management

	Total Quality Management (TQM)	Experience Quality Management (EQM)
View of Quality	Quality is associated with products, services, and processes.	Quality is associated with individual co-creation experiences, and the quality of the infrastructure for enabling experiences. The quality of products, services, and processes are necessary, but not sufficient determinants of the quality of experiences.
Goal	Eliminate known variability in processes; maintain quality across identical products and services.	Accommodate heterogeneity of consumer experiences; variability in experiences with identical products and services.
Methodology	Internal disciplines and processes (e.g., Six Sigma); customer satisfaction surveys.	Co-creation protocols, disciplines, and rules of engagement; DART building blocks of co-creation and experience audits.
Outcomes	Predictable; measured against specs.	Unique as a result of contextual interaction between individual consumers and experience environments.

The new frontier of Experience Quality Management emerging from the shift to experience networks is summarized in table 6-1.

Let's consider a couple of examples. For REI, the channel infrastructure facilitates experiences at the point of interaction. REI accepts variation in consumer experiences and starts with the contextual experience of a specific consumer. To achieve consistent quality for that experience, REI has evolved a robust infrastructure for co-creation, including mechanisms for access, dialogue, and risk reduction (for example, the opportunity to work closely with a knowledgeable sales clerk to find the best mountain bike for a late autumn trip through the Rocky Mountains). Whereas traditional quality tools like TQM and Six Sigma help firms achieve product quality, inventing ways of organizing an effective experience network will help achieve consistent experience quality.

Similarly, Deere is innovating new experience environments and creating new experience space for the farmers who use its new farming systems. But the quality of these new experiences depends on the underlying infrastructure that effectively connects managers, the company's employees, dealers, Deere products and services, and farmers into an experience network.

Migrating to Experience Networks: Key Concepts and Challenges

Following is a summary of some of the key concepts and organizational challenges in building an experience network:

- The company must facilitate the continuous co-creation of experiences at points of interaction, viewing products, distribution channels, technologies, and employees as experience gateways.

- The experience environment should be oriented around the experience space, allowing consumers to initiate experiences on demand.

- Accommodating consumer heterogeneity is crucial. The company must understand its various sources and forms as well as its implications for co-creating unique experiences.

- The experience network should provide consumers with various levels and forms of access, mechanisms for dialogue with the company and other customers, and ways to manage risk.

- The logistics infrastructure should link closely to the experience environment, balancing the consumer's desire for access with the company's desire for control. To win the consumer's trust, a significant level of transparency in the company's information infrastructure is required.

- Managers need the capacity to react quickly and continuously based on events, along with the capacity to reconfigure resources flexibly and quickly.

- All infrastructures have both a technical and a social side. An effective experience network requires both technical and social enablers of experiences.

- The strategic architecture of the experience network is a creative combination of the appropriate technical and social experience enablers along with selective activation of the competence base to facilitate heterogeneous, individual-centric experiences.

Thus, as we have seen, personalization of the co-creation experience needs a robust experience network. The migration from firm-centric supply chains to individual consumer-centric experience networks is summarized in table 6-2.

TABLE 6 - 2

Migrating to Experience Networks

From: Firm-Centric Supply Chains	Motivation for Change	To: Individual-Centric Experience Networks
Consumers are passive recipients of the firm's offerings.	**Consumer-Company Interaction Is the Locus of Value Creation**	Consumers are active co-creators of value.
The firm-consumer inter-action is the locus of value extraction.		The consumer-firm interaction is the locus of co-creation (and co-extraction) of value.
Focus is on managing the quality of products, services, and processes.		Focus is on Experience Quality Management
Products and services are the basis of value. They represent value added by the firm and its supply base.	**Individual Co-Creation Experience Is the Basis of Value**	Individual co-creation experiences are the basis of value. Products and services are a subset of an experience environment.
Channels represent distribution of products from the supply chain. The firm fulfills orders for products.	**Multiple Channels Are Gateways to Experiences**	Channels represent gateways to experiences. Consumers are engaged in personalized co-creation experiences. Nodal firm facilitates co-creation of unique value.
Infrastructure is oriented toward managing assets, processes, resource allocation, and efficiency of the firm.	**Infrastructure Must Support Heterogeneous Co-Creation Experiences**	Infrastructure is oriented toward supporting the experience environment, facilitating DART, access to competence, rapid resource reconfiguration, and efficiency in enabling experiences.
Competence resides in the firm and its suppliers and partners. Supply chains are a predetermined sequence for fulfilling products.	**Enhanced Network Is the Locus of Core Competence**	Competence resides in an enhanced network that includes consumer communities. Selective activation of competencies by nodal firms to co-create unique value.

How does the new framework for value creation and the migration to experience networks change our perspective of the "market"? Is the traditional marketplace still the locus for exchange between the firm and the consumer, and the place where the firm extracts value from the consumer? How does the meaning of a "market" change in light of the new paradigm of co-creation of value? This is the topic we will turn to in our next chapter.

Chapter Seven

THE MARKET AS A FORUM

I N THE NEW co-creation paradigm, the individual consumer is at the heart of co-creation. While firms can create experience environments and build the supporting experience network for a large number of consumers to co-construct their own experiences, firms cannot autonomously create value to be exchanged. What does this mean for the concept of a market?

The Concept of a Market

The word *market* conjures up two distinct images. On the one hand, it is the locus of exchange where a firm trades goods and services to the consumer for money. On the other hand, the market is an aggregation of consumers. Both of these images of the market are challenged by the concept of co-creation of value.

The Traditional Concept of a Market

The traditional concept of a market was company-centric. Consumers were passive, merely someone for companies to sell to. Consequently, firms conceptualized customer-relationship management as targeting customers. Firms focused on the locus of interaction—the market—as the locus of economic value extraction. In this view, the market had distinct and separate roles for the firm and the consumer. Value exchange and extraction were the primary functions performed by the market, which was separated from the value creation process, as shown in figure 7-1.

FIGURE 7 - 1

The Traditional Concept of a Market

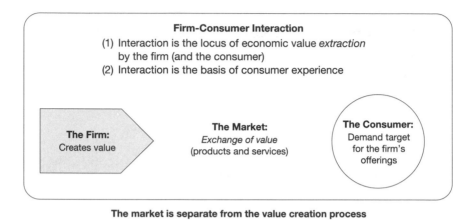

Firm-Consumer Interaction
(1) Interaction is the locus of economic value *extraction*
    by the firm (and the consumer)
(2) Interaction is the basis of consumer experience

The Firm:
Creates value

The Market:
Exchange of value
(products and services)

The Consumer:
Demand target
for the firm's
offerings

The market is separate from the value creation process

Challenges to the Traditional Concept

While companies have focused on their relationships with customers, they have done so through the traditional frame of value creation, resulting in the concept of a market as a target for exchanging the firm's products and services. We have reached the limit of this concept, as in the product-centric notion of "segments of one."[1]

The hunter has become the hunted, as informed, connected, and active consumers increasingly learn that they too can extract value at the traditional point of exchange. Online auctions for hotel rooms and airline reservations are just one example of this growing phenomenon. The popularity of businesses such as eBay suggests that the auction is increasingly serving as the basis for pricing goods and services online. From the customer's perspective, the advantage of the auction process is that prices truly reflect the utility to that customer, at a given point in time, of the goods and services being purchased. That doesn't necessarily mean that prices are lower, only that the customer pays according to her utility rather than according to the company's cost of production.

Traditional pricing won't disappear entirely. In many circumstances, it is the most convenient and appropriate form of pricing. But as customers become more knowledgeable and increasingly aware of their negotiating clout, more businesses—from automakers to cosmetic surgery clinics—will feel pressure to adopt an implicit (if not an explicit) negotiation. An auction is one approach to this negotiation process. Armed with knowledge drawn from today's increasingly transparent business environment, customers are much more willing than in the past to negotiate prices and other transaction terms with companies. We are moving toward a world in which customers can assess their own value to the firm and use this knowledge in negotiation. Managers everywhere must accept the idea that they are now price *takers* as well as price makers.

But more important, as we have discussed throughout, value will increasingly be associated with individual co-creation experiences. An individual consumer's willingness to pay becomes a function of the co-creation experience. As we have emphasized, products and services are *not* the basis of value. Rather, value is embedded in the experiences co-created by the individual in an experience environment that the company co-develops with consumers. Thus, the new framework puts the spotlight squarely on consumer-company interaction as the center of value creation. Because there can be multiple points of interaction anywhere in the system (including the traditional point of exchange), this new framework implies that all the points of consumer-company interaction may become the locus of value creation.

Hence, our view of value co-creation challenges both images of a market: the market as an exchange of product and service offerings and as an aggregation of consumers. Traditional economics focuses squarely on the exchange of products and services between the company and the consumer, placing value extraction by the firm at the point of exchange at the heart of business management. In the co-creation view, all points of interaction between the company and the consumer are opportunities for both value creation and extraction.

Co-creation also challenges the view of the market as an aggregation of consumers who must select from what the firm decides to offer. In the new value creation space, business managers have at least partial control over the experience environment and the networks they build to facilitate co-creation experiences. But they cannot control how individuals go about co-constructing their experiences. The new paradigm therefore forces us to move away from viewing the market as an aggregation of consumers and as a target for the firm's offerings.

The Market as a Forum

In the emerging concept of a market, the focus is on consumer-company interaction—*the roles of the company and the consumer converge.*

The firm and the consumer are both collaborators and competitors—collaborators in co-creating value and competitors for the extraction of economic value. The market as a whole becomes inseparable from the value creation process, as shown in figure 7-2.[2]

Co-creation converts the market into a *forum* where dialogue among the consumer, the firm, consumer communities, and networks of firms can take place. We must view the market as a *space of potential co-creation experiences* in which individual constraints and choices define their willingness to pay for experiences. In short, the market resembles a forum for co-creation experiences.

We have already seen the implications of the changing role of the consumer for the value creation process and the concept of market. *Evolving consumer communities* are an integral part of experience networks for co-creating value. Focusing on points of consumer-company interaction means that companies must address the *heterogeneity of interactions* as never before. Further, companies must innovate compelling experience environments that enable individuals to personalize their interactions. Managers must *co-shape expectations* with consumers. Finally, consumers have a role in *co-shaping experiences* with the firm. Co-shaping expectations and experiences are critical to move to the

FIGURE 7 - 2

The Emerging Concept of a Market

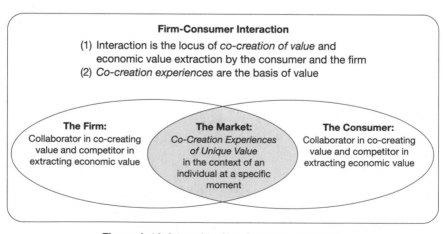

The market is integral to the value creation process

new opportunity space of "experiences of one." We'll now discuss each of these four basic aspects of the market as a forum.

Evolving Communities of Consumers

Traditional industry structures make dialogue between consumers and businesses distant and difficult. Dealers, distributors, and retailers serve as intermediaries between producers and consumers, separating them more than they link them. For example, automobile firms sell luxury cars for $40,000 and up while having little or no direct contact with the consumer. Dealers vary greatly in their understanding of consumers— their aspirations, concerns, and needs. Market research is at best an indirect way to learn about consumers. When there is a dialogue with consumers, it often centers on solving consumer problems, as in help centers. Even more important, because firms target one consumer at a time, the traditional consumer also lacks the ability to communicate with other consumers around the world. Consumers are isolated from each other.

This is now beginning to change. A few progressive firms are starting to recognize that they must engender dialogue with networks of consumers playing active roles in co-creating and co-extracting value— as co-developers, collaborators, partners, investors, competitors, and negotiators. In the coming years, this trend will spread to more and more industries. Connected, involved, and empowered consumers will increasingly engage in dialogue with multiple firms, as well as with other consumers.

This new explosion of dialogue between firms and consumers, and among consumers themselves, creates the opportunity for consumers to become *originators* of dialogue, not dependent on the company. The shift is from firms choosing consumers and learning about them individually, to individual consumers choosing firms and learning about them in their search for value. In the new market-as-forum paradigm, networked consumer communities are a driving force.[3]

In a sense, this is a very natural development. Humans are instinctively inclined to connect with each other and belong to a social network. They want to be unique, but they also want to be connected. (When I buy a Tiger Woods golf shirt, I am expressing my individual sense of style as well as identifying with a worldwide network of "Tigers to be.") The underlying impulse is familiar, but the emergence of more opportunities for consumers to enjoy self-created, externally influenced positions in the marketplace's social fabric is new.

Consider the Hollywood Stock Exchange (HSE), a simulated entertainment stock market where "movie stocks" and "star bonds" are actively traded, their value measured in "Hollywood Dollars" (H$). More than 850,000 traders use the HSE to express their opinions on which movies and stars are hot and which ones are not. When new movies are released, traders predict their four-week box-office take, buying and selling put and call options that reflect their opinions as to which movies will be losers and winners.

HSE members are more than mere movie critics or fans. Their "investment" decisions make entertainment news headlines, and the major studios can't afford to ignore this community in shaping their development and marketing efforts. In many cases, HSE market expectations are stunningly accurate. For example, one month before the release of *The Lord of the Rings: The Fellowship of the Ring* in the fall of 2001, the movie's stock was priced on HSE at H$233.89 million. The actual four-week box-office take was $228.32 million.[4]

It is also important to recognize that consumers influence one another's experiences. Consider the customers of Cisco Systems, the leading maker of computer networking equipment. Recognizing the competence of its customer base, the company created Cisco Connection Online, which provides a suite of interactive, networked services with quick open access to Cisco's information, resources, and systems. This network allows Cisco customers to engage each other in dialogue, helping to solve one another's technical problems and enhancing the "Cisco experience" for everyone.

Also note that consumers belong to multiple reference groups—to social networks of the moment, which change over time and along with the products and services an individual consumes. The same individual can be a part of several reference groups at any one time.

How can a firm continuously learn from a dynamic network of consumers? How can it engage in constant active dialogue with these consumers? How and under what circumstances should it support the development of social communities? These are some of the new issues that emerge in managing interactions with customers within a networked landscape.

Young managers are traditionally raised within a specific industry. They imbibe particular values, learn a certain language, master specific skills. Later, some learn to work with those from other industries and manage collaborative relationships—a continuum from arms-length dealings to joint ventures. Today, all managers are called upon to learn a new set of social skills—one that will enable them to connect with individual consumers and with thematic communities as well.

The Dutch giant Philips Electronics is a case in point. One of the company's products is the Pronto, an intelligent universal remote control. Hackers became interested in tinkering with the Pronto's embedded software, and one of them set up a Web site as a focus for these efforts. Here was a challenge to Philips's control of its own business, to which most companies would have reacted defensively. Instead, Philips chose to cooperate with the hackers. The firm arranged to provide the site with easy access to program files, codes, and other information, and arranged for other manufacturers of audio-video products to post their software code to help people save programming time.

Philips recognized that, by exploring ways to make the Pronto more user-friendly, the hackers were benefiting both consumers and the company. Their efforts lent credence to the brand and strengthened it through their own experiences. Rather than fighting against the self-selecting, independent Pronto hacker community, Philips chose to work with it for the benefit of all.

In the traditional perspective, the market is viewed as *outside* the value chain. In the future, we must gravitate toward folding consumer communities *into* the value creation process. There can now be multiple points of interaction between the firm, its employees, the consumer, and consumer communities anywhere in the system. Thus, rather than being outside the value chain system, the market pervades the entire system.

Heterogeneity of Interactions

We have talked a fair amount about consumer heterogeneity in interactions—the nearly infinite range of variation among individuals and their interactions that makes it so challenging for companies to facilitate truly personalized co-creation experiences for every consumer. Let us take a closer look at some of the dimensions along which this heterogeneity can be viewed.

Sophistication

Consumers vary greatly in their levels of sophistication and domain knowledge. We have already mentioned in this connection the process of filing one's tax return electronically. Those with the technical and financial sophistication to master the protocols involved find the process fast and convenient; for others, it can be a nightmare.

The same is true of the navigation systems in most luxury cars. Depending on the sophistication of the individual consumer, the system may be mastered in anywhere from five minutes to one hour. The fact that not all features are equally relevant or interesting to all consumers makes the problem of personalization even more complicated. The unsophisticated consumer is likely to spend seemingly endless time navigating through features he does not want or care for, desperately seeking some simple but elusive bit of information such as how long he can go before he must fill the gas tank.

The proliferation of products and services that require consumer sophistication and active engagement—from TVs, phones, and cars to household heating, cooling, and alarm systems—means that more and more companies will have to confront an increasing sophistication divide. The challenge: to find ways of creating a space in which *every* consumer can co-construct an experience that fits her own level of sophistication.

Eagerness to Engage in Dialogue

"Virtual consumers" have emerged. For example, a health care insurance provider received inquiries from a small town in Southeast Asia. This firm's operations were primarily restricted to the United States. However, potential Asian consumers accessed the Web page of this firm and sent an email inquiry. The profiles of these consumers were unknown to this firm, but their inquiries could not be totally ignored. They might be an Internet prank, or they might represent a cluster of potential consumers whom the company had not even considered. The question for this firm was how to respond to the inquiry—a very different question from the more conventional debate of how to enter nontraditional (such as Asian) markets.

The rate at which these unsolicited consumer inquiries appear is higher today than ever before. For instance, during the telecom boom of 1996–2000, providers like Lucent Technologies had to contend with battalions of new and unknown entrepreneurs around the globe requesting telecommunications products and services. The only common denominator among several of these potential customers was a desire to invest and participate in the telecommunications revolution, often with limited or no knowledge of the telecom business.

For a management team used to working with a handful of large, highly skilled, and established customers like the Bell operating companies, this proliferation of unsophisticated customers must appear strange. How does one respond to a Thai investor who wants a wireless system set up in six months? Lucent managers at the same time had to deal with AT&T, who wanted all the bells and whistles and was willing to negotiate in excruciating detail the technical nuances of the next generation system.

Tolerance for Irritants

Consumers also vary widely in their tolerance for problems. Take the example of software. Technically minded people—engineers, hackers, computer junkies, and others who love being early adopters—are willing to work with beta versions of software, despite their imperfections. Indeed, they will often pay for the privilege. For such people, the fun and pleasure of the experience may lie in finding the glitches, or in being part of an open source–style effort to improve the software collaboratively. Many others, however, see software simply as a necessity and regard dealing with bugs as needless, frustrating work to be avoided.

Similar differences can be found in many other fields. Some homeowners enjoy tackling all the complex challenges of a self-directed home remodeling job; others want the work designed and managed by professionals with minimal guidance and input. Some travelers like being immersed in native cultures, even if that means some degree of discomfort or inconvenience; others can tolerate only an air-conditioned suite with twenty-four-hour room service. These kinds of differences can profoundly shape an individual's experience with a product or service (to put it mildly).

Willingness to Switch Suppliers and Products

There is always some cost involved in switching from one supplier of a product or service to another. Sometimes the cost is financial: When I change my laptop from one company (or even model) to another, I may have to buy new components and accessories. Sometimes the burden is cognitive: When a new version of the Windows operating system is released, I must invest energy and brain cells in adjusting to the new protocols. Sometimes the toll is emotional: When the physician who treated me for the past decade retires, it takes time for me to become comfortable with the newcomer who assumes his practice.

Costs like these explain why customers sometimes stay with their current suppliers even when they are not completely satisfied. The value frontier where customers perceive enough incremental value to switch to a new source can vary considerably.

Co-Shaping Expectations: Stages of Company Evolution

Companies have evolved through several stages in their practice of managing heterogeneous customers and their expectations. The first and most primitive stage is to assume that the firm cannot actively influence customers' expectations. We call this stage "no focus."

This is followed by the "reactive" stage. Managers who reach this stage have learned to react to the expressed needs of consumers—especially to problems they identify. During the 1990s, many companies that were previously unfocused on consumer expectations reached the reactive stage.

In the third stage, managers become "responsive." A responsive organization does not merely react to customer feedback; it also performs consistently and without complaint, demonstrating through voluntary actions its concern for customer satisfaction. For example, a responsive company might voluntarily recall a defective product or provide a free product upgrade to past customers.

In both the reactive and responsive modes, the firm is still concerned entirely with current products and services. In the fourth, "anticipatory" stage, the company moves beyond this limitation.

Surprisingly few firms engage in the task of anticipating customer needs. We can demonstrate this simply by considering the many obvious gaps in the product and service offerings currently available in the marketplace. For example, a statistically minded manager may know that the United States is home to a large and rapidly increasing aging population. A few notable examples of products and services have been developed in anticipation of their needs, such as Depends undergarments ("diapers for the elderly") and Viagra (a "lifestyle medication" that is especially relevant to the aging). But why is it that no food company is offering a line of tasty meals that the elderly would find easy to prepare, chew, and digest? Why not cars with better access for the elderly, as well as dashboard controls and indicators designed for aging drivers? Why not stylish clothes that are also easy to put on and take off?

One step beyond anticipation is shaping expectations—educating current and potential consumers as to what the world could be like. If only a few companies are doing a good job of anticipating, even fewer have reached the "shaping" stage. Failure to educate consumers about the technologies, products, services, and opportunities of the future has already cost businesses dearly. For example, the failure of companies like Monsanto to fully educate laypeople about the risks and benefits of genetically modified foods led to a massive backlash against the entire concept, especially in Europe and Asia.

Finally, managers must reach the stage of co-shaping expectations. This is not just about the traditional one-way forms of business communication—press releases, publicity stunts, advertising—but about engaging current and potential consumers in dialogue and public debate. It means being open not only to educating customers but to being educated by them as well. When companies reach this stage, their customers aren't merely acquiescent users of products or services. Instead, they become passionate advocates and activists for the company, like Harley and Avon customers, who not only buy and sell products but also advocate the Harley and Avon lifestyles. Likewise, Apple users tend to be fervent missionaries for the products they enjoy.

Let's go back to the movie *Lord of the Rings: The Fellowship of the Ring*. No film in history was released to a larger audience of preprimed, passionate fans—the tens of millions of readers around the world who had been enthralled by the epic novels of J. R. R. Tolkien. These fans were thrilled by the news that a major film was in the works. They were also ready to denounce the movie en masse if it violated their vision of the fantasy realm of Middle Earth.

Wisely, rather than try to shut down or drown out the vast worldwide network of Tolkien fans, New Line Cinema worked to co-opt them. As Gordon Paddison, senior vice president for worldwide interactive marketing, notes, "It would have been arrogant to say, 'We are *Lord of the Rings*, come to us.'"[5] Instead, Paddison treated the most rabid Tolkien followers as early influencers, whose response could make or break the movie. He reached out to the more than four hundred unofficial Tolkien Web sites, giving them insider tips, seeking their feedback on the details of the movie, and offering them access to the production team. With the help of director Peter Jackson, the Web site www.LordoftheRings.net was created, including rough sketches of costume designs, handwritten production notes, and other exclusive content. Millions of fans have visited the Web site. Although Tolkien fans still debate the merits of the movie, nearly all appreciate the respect with which the filmmakers have treated the material—and them.

As New Line's experience suggests, the battle for co-shaping expectations will require the active and evangelical support of customers. Learning how to win that support is a vital new skill for today's managers. Managers now have a critical role in leading, educating, and co-opting customers in the creation of new experience space. Let's consider a couple of examples of managers attempting to do just this.

When John Sculley was the CEO of Apple, he was a great champion of the then-new personal digital assistant (PDA). His proselytizing about the concept helped create awareness and interest about the potential of PDAs. Unfortunately, he oversold the ease of use and simplicity of the early PDA. When introduced, the Apple Newton's performance fell far short of what Sculley promised, leading to massive frustration and annoyance on the part of customers.

By contrast, Jeff Bezos succeeded in making Amazon.com the favorite online retailer of the relatively sophisticated, computer-savvy consumer. He then quickly expanded the company's reach to include a wide variety of consumers with various sophistication levels. Amazon must now deal with heterogeneous interactions from evolving consumer communities, without compromising the quality of the experience for any given customer. For instance, as Amazon has grown, so has the complexity of the customer interface and the consumer-company interaction. Managers must increasingly be sensitive to the consumer's role in co-shaping experiences.

Figure 7-3 puts together the several stages in the development of approaches for managing consumer expectations, as just discussed, while simultaneously catering to heterogeneous experiences in co-creating with consumers.[6]

Co-Shaping Experiences

As shown in figure 7-3, just as the practice of managing expectations evolves through several stages, so does the practice of managing heterogeneous consumer experiences.

In the first and most primitive stage, which we again simply call "no focus," companies provide undifferentiated products. Until recently,

FIGURE 7 - 3

Co-Shaping Expectations and Experiences

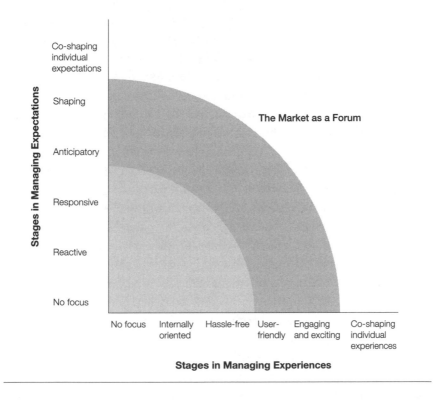

many industries were in this mode. For example, utilities sold telephone services on that basis. Consumers received the same product, had very little say in explaining their preferences (long distance versus local, holidays versus regular days, peak times versus night, priorities on "hot" days such as Mother's Day), and were charged the same price regardless of how they used the product.

Next comes the "internally oriented" stage. Here, products are differentiated, but companies take a view of customer needs and product functions that is based on their own company-centric perspective. Much of today's electronic products entailing significant embedded software (e.g., cellular phones, and TVs) were developed out of this stage. These products boast an extensive set of bundled features, but they are generally designed and organized with the firm's internal needs rather than the customer's preferences in mind.

The third stage entails a "hassle-free" level of performance. Here, product performance starts to become externally oriented, with measures of reliability and durability assuming importance.

The fourth stage is the "user-friendly" stage. Now firms are oriented toward developing products and services that are easy to use, although they may be sophisticated. A classic example of such a product was the Apple computer—with its intuitive icons and pull-down menus, it revolutionized and demystified the personal computer. Almost two decades later, PalmPilot did the same with the PDA—a Newton-style organizer with a portrait orientation but with a small, intuitive, easy-to-use interface that offered instant access and synchronization.

One step beyond the user-friendly stage is "engaging and exciting." Here, a company stages experiences around its offerings, engaging the consumer in immersive experiences. However, companies are still rooted in the traditional company-centric frame of value creation.

Finally, as we saw in chapters 5 and 6, managers will next have to cross the hurdle to "co-shaping individual experiences," involving the consumer in an active dialogue and allowing her to co-construct her own unique experiences. The focus shifts to experience personalization.

Thus, in the market as a forum, the challenge is to understand the actual co-creation experiences of customers and invest in experience enablers that will build and sustain consistently positive co-creation experiences. This paradigm is a new way of creating competitive advantage through technical capabilities and R&D. But it is also a new way of thinking about and creating brands. The value creation process and the brand become inextricably linked.

The Experience *Is* the Brand

The brand has traditionally been a centerpiece of a firm's communication with customers. Companies—especially packaged goods companies like Procter & Gamble and Unilever—communicated a bundle of benefits through their brand positioning. In the battle for market share, product and brand differentiation were carefully orchestrated toward different segments in the product space. The entire advertising industry was created to persuade predetermined groups of consumers by using controlled communications to push an image or a personality associated with a product.[7]

The first crack in this system was the shift in power to distribution channels such as Wal-Mart, Tesco, Ahold, and Carrefour, and the rise of private labels. Later, with the advent of the Internet and the dot-coms, advertisers found that the traditional persuasive techniques that had worked so well in the days of the passive audience were losing their effectiveness, weakening the traditional branding system still further.[8]

Today, the rise of the active consumer has shattered the old company-centric model of brand creation. Advertising has been supplanted as the chief shaper of consumer attitudes by word of mouth, which today's Web-linked consumer communities have put on overdrive. Consumers now have access to the information they need to make informed choices, assess value on their own terms, influence the expectations of other consumers, and decide for themselves how they want to transact with the company. As a result, the power of advertising to create or sustain a product or company image is steadily shrinking.

Communication once flowed almost entirely from companies to consumers. Now consumer feedback is beginning to overwhelm the voice of the company. Active consumer communities are studying, evaluating, and discussing what companies do, and making independent judgments about what they see and hear. More and more companies "have no clothes" like the emperor in the proverbial fairy tale—though many do not recognize it yet.

Nonetheless, most firms are still talking about "owning customers" and "owning customer relationships." This traditional attitude pervades many areas of business, despite the fact that it is increasingly outmoded. For example, the customer-relationship management (CRM) software sold by technology vendors is steeped in a company-centric approach, in which customers are passive "targets" of the firm. In the world of co-creation, where companies must seek not to target customers but to hold dialogues with them, an altogether different kind of communications infrastructure will be needed.

At one time, brands could be created by companies through advertising and other communications. No more. Now, *brands evolve through experiences.*

Consider some of the major survivors of the dot-com decade: Yahoo!, AOL, Amazon, eBay. All are brands that evolved through the personalized experiences of an increasing number of individuals within a social fabric. Individuals legitimized these brands and gave them meaning.

Afterward, the firms used advertising to strengthen and support an already evolving identity, which spread primarily through word of mouth within communities of interest ("viral marketing"). The phenomenon is not entirely new; older firms such as Disney, Harley-Davidson, and Starbucks benefited from a similar kind of experience-based branding. But in the past, this form of brand building was the exception. In the future, companies will have to build brands through individual-centered co-creation of experiences *with* the cooperation of consumer communities, rather than company-centric staging of brands.

Thus, as companies transition toward the new opportunity space, the co-creation experience and the brand become embedded in each other. In the end, *the co-creation experience is the brand*. As long as the company can continue to innovate compelling experience environments, the brand can sustain itself. It lives and dies with experiences.

The fact that the brand is increasingly rooted in an individual's experience strikes at the heart of traditional brand management. An experience is an outcome of the individual's interaction with an experience environment. It is subjective. It will vary from individual to individual. It cannot be predetermined or "pushed" by an advertiser.

What, then, becomes of the company's role in brand management? The new focus must be on fostering a consistent quality of co-creation experience. After all, it is the collective experience of consumers that creates trust and in turn defines the brand. Creating a unified experience across multiple channels, as in banking, bookstores, travel, and a host of other businesses, represents a new challenge to firms that goes to the heart of the issue of trust. The company can't afford to regard the proliferation of channels as merely an opportunity to push products and services to consumers in more ways. If it does, the result is likely to be a set of fragmented and vastly varying experiences for customers. The challenge to managers is one of ensuring a consistent quality of experience across multiple channels, while simultaneously enabling a personalized co-creation experience for each individual.

Migrating to the Market as a Forum

In the market as a forum, the company and consumer converge. The relative roles of the firm and the consumer at a given moment cannot be predicted. Further, we see a constantly shifting pattern of roles for individuals and firms. Rather than predetermined and fixed categories

of players in the system—customers, competitors, suppliers, collaborators, and investors—roles may be temporary and shift as circumstances
change. As we move to the new frontier of co-creating value, we could say
that *Company = Competitor = Partner = Collaborator = Investor = Consumer*.
The common denominator for value is the co-creation experience.

The market as a forum also challenges the conventional economic
view of supply and demand. Traditionally, demand has been viewed
through the lens of what the firm can supply—its products and services.
Demand is conceived and forecast in terms of what the firm can sell at a
particular price. Consequently, a significant managerial preoccupation
is demand forecasting as a basis for organizing supply. Inventories of
finished products reflect lags in demand and excessive supply as well as
errors in forecasting demand. In the auto industry, for example, unsold
inventories of cars in dealer lots, on railroad cars, and on delivery trucks
generally represent over ten weeks' worth of sales.

As the number of SKUs increase and companies offer customers
more choices, the problem of demand forecasting becomes more complex. In response, companies such as Dell Computer have shifted to
producing products only on demand. This approach has significant ap-
peal. It practically eliminates finished goods inventories and allows Dell
to operate with negative working capital, collecting payments from customers before it pays suppliers.

But co-creation of value fundamentally challenges the traditional
distinction between supply and demand. When the experience, along
with the value inherent in it, is co-created, the firm may still produce a
physical product. But the focus shifts to the characteristics of the total
experience environment. Now demand is contextual. Given that customers cannot predict their experiences, co-creation of value may well
imply the death of traditional forecasting. Instead, the focus shifts to
capacity planning, the ability of the experience network to scale up and
down rapidly, and for the system to reconfigure resources in real time
to accommodate shifting consumer desires and personalization of co-
creation experiences. Such a system may be highly demanding, yet it
promises incredible efficiency gains as well.

Thus, the market as a forum challenges the basic tenet of traditional
economic theory: that the firm and the consumers are separate, with
distinct, predetermined roles, and consequently that supply and demand are distinct, but mirrored processes oriented around the exchange of products and services between firms and consumers.

TABLE 7 - 1

Migrating to the Market as a Forum

The Market as a Target	The Market as a Forum
The firm and the consumer are separate, with distinct predetermined roles.	The firm and the consumer converge; the relative "roles of the moment" cannot be predicted.
Supply and demand are matched; price is the clearing mechanism. Demand is forecast for products and services that the firm can supply.	Demand and supply are emergent and contextual. Supply is associated with facilitating a unique consumer experience on demand.
Value is created by the firm in its value chain. Products and services are exchanged with consumers.	Value is co-created at multiple points of interaction. Basis of value is co-creation experience.
Firm disseminates information to consumers.	Consumers and consumer communities can also initiate a dialogue among themselves.
Firm chooses which consumer segments to serve, and the distribution channels to use for its offerings.	Consumer chooses the nodal firm and the experience environment to interact with and co-create value. The nodal firm, its products and services, employees, multiple channels, and consumer communities come together seamlessly to constitute the experience environment for individuals to co-construct their own experiences.
Firms extract consumer surplus. Consumers are "prey," whether as "groups" or "one-to-one." Firms want a 360-degree view of the customer, but remain opaque to customers. Firms want to "own" the customer relationship and lifetime value.	Consumers can extract the firm's surplus. Value is co-extracted. Consumers expect a 360-degree view of the experience that is transparent in the consumer's language. Trust and stickiness emerge from compelling experience outcomes. Consumers are competitors in extracting value.
Companies determine, define, and sustain the brand.	The experience *is* the brand. The brand is co-created and evolves with experiences.

We believe that in time, new approaches and tools consistent with a new *experience-based view of economic theory* will emerge. We have identified and summarized some of the key points of departure in table 7-1.

The new frame of value creation, in which the consumer-company interaction is the locus of co-creation of value, certainly challenges the traditional economic view of the market. It also creates new competitive space for firms and the need for building new strategic capital, the subject of the next chapter.

Chapter Eight

BUILDING NEW
STRATEGIC CAPITAL

L ET'S START by summarizing the key insights presented so far. The
future of competition is being shaped by changes in the meaning
of value, the roles of the consumer and the company, and the nature of
their interactions—changes that are profoundly altering the value creation process.

As we have seen, the most fundamental change is in the nature of
value. Rather than being embedded in the products and services that
the firm offers, value is now centered in the experiences of consumers.
Because these experiences are influenced not only by the firm but also
by individual consumers and consumer communities, value is now co-
created by consumers and the firm. Further, value may be influenced
not just by one firm but also by a network of firms acting together to
create an experience network. Thus, value is both individual-centric
and experience-centric, and is based on the actual co-creation experiences of individual consumers. It cannot be unilaterally determined by
the firm. The market is a forum for co-creation experiences.

We summarize these shifts in perspective in table 8-1.

The Shifting Locus of Core Competencies

The transition outlined in table 8-1 also mirrors the ongoing shift in
the *locus of competence*.

TABLE 8 - 1

The Transformation of the Value Creation Process

	Company and Product-Centric Value Creation	Individual and Experience-Centric Co-Creation of Value
View of Value	Value is associated with a company's offerings. The competitive space is oriented around the firm's products and services.	Value is associated with experiences; products and services facilitate individual and community-mediated experiences. The competitive space is oriented around consumer experiences.
Role of Company	To define and create value for the consumer.	To engage the individual consumer in defining and co-creating unique value.
Role of Consumer	Passive pocket of demand for company-defined offerings and solutions.	Consumer as active player in seeking, creating, and extracting value.
View of Value Creation	Value is created by the firm; consumers have a choice—the variety offered by the firm.	The consumer co-creates value with the firm and other consumers.

The Core Competence of the Corporation

Until about 1990, most managers thought of the corporation as a portfolio of business units. The idea that the diversified firm might also be a portfolio of core competencies was a novel and significant one.

Simply stated, core competencies are unique skills that transcend individual business units, are deeply embedded in the organization, are hard for competitors to imitate, and are seen by customers as creating value. Core competencies are engines of organic growth. Miniaturization at Sony, managing a transient work force at Marriott, and commodity processing and trading at Cargill are examples of core competencies.

As the notion of core competencies gained popularity in the 1990s, managers began to look at the corporation as a portfolio of core competencies, and the unit of analysis shifted from the business unit to the corporation as a whole. Meanwhile, another shift was under way. During the last decade, supply networks *outside* the corporation have become important sources of competence as well.

The Extended Enterprise

Examples of the shift in the locus of competence toward the extended enterprise are all around us. For example, aircraft manufacturers such as Boeing have learned that they can lean on suppliers such as Honeywell not just for components but for subassemblies, modules, and subsystems, all the way up to entire integrated electronic cockpits. As a result, traditional and nontraditional suppliers are ever more closely linked with original equipment manufacturers (OEMs) in product and technology development, often creating joint capabilities that exist only through the combined competencies of two or more firms. For example, with the help of electronics giant Sony, Toyota is accessing know-how on consumer habits and converting that know-how into new hardware and software capabilities. Toyota and Sony recently announced an experimental car that adapts to the consumer's driving habits rather than the other way around.

During the 1990s, the unit of analysis for understanding competence expanded beyond the diversified firm to include the supply base. Thus, privileged access to a global supply base has become a critical factor in resource leverage and value creation.

Consumers as a Source of Competence

If suppliers are a critical part of the competence base available to the firm, why aren't consumers?[1] Today, our understanding of the sources of competence available to managers is expanding yet again to include the collective knowledge available to the whole system—suppliers, manufacturers, partners, *and consumers.*[2]

Consider a few examples:

- Through its InnoCentive initiative, pharmaceutical firm Eli Lilly has accessed the skills of more than eight thousand scientists to solve drug-related scientific problems of varying complexity. Lilly is extending its R&D base by accessing competence outside the company in a process that is carefully controlled by the company.

- Sony has opened up its PlayStation game consoles to the Linux operating system. By providing Linux kits with tools for developing PlayStation applications, Sony is co-opting consumer competence and extending PlayStation as a key platform in the fun space. (Unlike Eli Lilly, which controls its own product development but accepts inputs from scientists outside the enterprise, Sony is engaging consumers directly in the development of its platform.)

- Similarly, Lego Mindstorms is engaging consumers in the innovation process itself. Mindstorms users have developed entire software development environments, such as NQC ("Not Quite C"), as well as custom versions of popular computer languages, including PERL and Java. Coupled with new robotic experiments by consumers, these advances have expanded the possibilities of Mindstorms enormously.

Technological changes are facilitating access to a global network of knowledge. Consider the Research Archives at Los Alamos National Laboratory in New Mexico. They provide anyone in the world with access to scientific research and to a privileged community of scientists transcending economic, social, and geopolitical barriers. Individuals may post their work at any stage, even before it has been peer reviewed. The response has been huge: More than 35,000 new papers are submitted per year, and over two million visitors access the archives each week.[3]

The social infrastructure of the Los Alamos archives is also innovative. In the traditional research process, papers arriving from lesser-known countries and institutions must often overcome subtle and latent bias of the developed world before they are published. Not so with the Los Alamos archives. About two-thirds of the postings are from outside the United States, originating in countries as diverse as Bulgaria, Colombia, Cuba, Ukraine, Iran, India, Romania, Russia, Israel, the Czech Republic, and Zambia. Lubos Motl, an undergraduate physics student from Prague, posted a research paper on string theory that so impressed established string theorists that he ended up in the United States with a scholarship to complete a doctorate. This new level of access and transparency enables multinational collaborative research and fosters intellectual diversity.

Finally, consider Minh Le, a computer game enthusiast who decided to try modifying Half-Life, an action game about a scientist who must shoot his way out of a government lab invaded by mutants—a "death match," in gaming lingo. While small game modifications (or "mods") are commonplace, Minh Le and a loose network of friends transformed Half-Life into a totally new experience, with a new theme (counter-terrorists versus terrorists), cooperative team play, fresh art and sound designs, and a virtual economy where players can earn money to buy better weapons. Called Counter-Strike, this new multiplayer action game has developed a large following, with a peak usage of 90,000 players (as compared with about 1,200 for Half-Life).

To play Counter-Strike, one still must buy Half-Life. Thus, mods like Counter-Strike increase the revenue and customer base of the entire Half-Life family of products. Valve, the software company that makes Half-Life, has bought the rights to Counter-Strike and the $40 million in revenues it generates. According to Gabe Newell, managing director of Valve, "Le's interest in Half-Life has been the best thing that could have happened to the game."[4]

Similar consumer-firm co-creation communities are happening elsewhere in the gaming space. Electronic Arts, which wants to be one of the largest entertainment companies in the world, has encouraged gamers to modify its classic bestseller, the Sims, in which players control characters as they go through their daily lives. More than 30,000 Sims mods are now available. As a result, Electronic Arts had access to a wide pool of creativity and gaming skills as it developed and launched Sims Online, a large-scale forum for social interaction and co-construction of new immersive experiences, as well as a way for Electronic Arts to expand its competence base to include consumer communities.[5]

More and more companies are recognizing that consumers are a powerful source of new competencies. Some companies will want to carefully control the process, as in Eli Lilly's InnoCentive program, or at least maintain quasi-control, as in the Sony example. The Lego, Los Alamos, and Counter-Strike examples are more telling. The implications are simple and profound. The locus of competence must now encompass the entire network, from suppliers to consumers. You can see this transition in figure 8-1.

Most firms are in the midst of the transition from stage 1 to stages 2 and 3. Talking about changing boundaries is easier than making it happen. The first boundaries to break are the internal silos called business units and functional groups. This step is a prerequisite to leveraging the

FIGURE 8 - 1

Sources of Competence

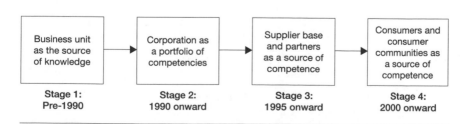

Business unit as the source of knowledge	Corporation as a portfolio of competencies	Supplier base and partners as a source of competence	Consumers and consumer communities as a source of competence
Stage 1: Pre-1990	Stage 2: 1990 onward	Stage 3: 1995 onward	Stage 4: 2000 onward

corporation as a portfolio of competencies. Some believe that working with suppliers and partners may be an easier boundary to cross than the internal ones. But breaking the boundary between the consumer and the company may be the hardest, as it calls for a clear commitment to the building blocks of DART—dialogue, access, risk assessment, and transparency.

The good news is that companies need no longer do everything themselves. Since no single firm can be world-class in everything, managers must learn to creatively leverage the competencies of others, including consumers.

The "not invented here" syndrome is an impediment. Managers simply aren't accustomed to accepting, supporting, and promulgating ideas that come from outside their own departments—or outside the company altogether. But a new approach to management is also necessary. We need a new way of thinking about the skill base of the firm, including both what we own and what we have access to—an approach that is alien to most traditional firms.

In partnership discussions, for example, the first question is often, "Who gets majority ownership?" Somehow, 51 percent is considered a magical number. What we should be discussing instead is the level of access and the appropriate investment for that level of access. The value creation philosophy must be: *Reduce investment, increase impact*. In effect, this increases the resource base of the firm by tapping suppliers, partners, and consumers as resource multipliers. The more effective we are in mobilizing and accessing competencies from these and other sources, the greater the value of those multipliers will be.

Of course, there will always be tensions to be managed. Our suppliers, partners, and consumers are both collaborators and competitors for value. Obviously, suppliers want higher prices, while consumers would like lower prices. Both can and will seek to extract economic value from the shared co-creation experience. We must collaborate to co-create value even as we compete to co-extract economic value.

An image of this changing view of the locus of core competencies is shown in table 8-2.[6]

You may already have benefited enormously from your relationships with suppliers. But is your approach to suppliers one of accessing components cheaper and faster or one of accessing competencies as well? The latter requires you to view suppliers through a different lens. For example, you may have to increase the number of employees who visit with your suppliers. It's important to invest the time, energy, and intel-

TABLE 8 - 2

The Shifting Locus of Core Competencies

	The Firm	Family/Network of Companies	Enhanced Network
Unit of Analysis	The company	The extended enterprise and value network—the company, its suppliers, and its partners	The whole system—the company, suppliers, partners, *and consumers*
Resource Base	What is available within the company	Access to the competence and investment capacity of companies in the network	Access to consumer competence and investment of time and effort from consumers, in addition to the resource base
Basis for Access to Competence	Internal company-specific processes	Privileged access to companies within the network	Infrastructure for active, ongoing dialogue with diverse consumers
Value Added by Managers	Nurture and build competencies	Manage collaborative partnerships	Harness consumer competence, co-create personalized experiences, and co-shape customer expectations
Value Creation	Autonomous	Collaboration	Co-creation
Sources of Managerial Tension	Business unit autonomy versus leveraging core competencies	Partner is both collaborator and competitor for value	Consumer is both collaborator and competitor for value

ligence needed to become familiar with what your suppliers "have in their kitchens."

Regarding customer relationships, you may have been focused on customer-relationship management (CRM) software and other similar tools, whose main purpose is to sell more. That's not a bad thing. But what about focusing on accessing the competence of individual consumers and consumer communities? This will require a shift in the locus of innovation, toward the experience space of consumers.

The Shifting Locus of Innovation

The transformation of the basis of value from products to personalized experiences is an ongoing process. It is a migration in the locus of innovation involving multiple steps: from the traditional product space through the solutions space to the experience space.

The Product Space

The traditional product orientation leads to a particular approach to managing. For example, as managers we spend a lot of time developing technology and product road maps. We describe the features and functions we plan to build and in what sequence. We also spend a lot of time thinking about new technologies and the product features and functions they will support. And we focus on developing suppliers, logistics, manufacturing, load factors, new machine tools, plant modifications, and the like, so as to deliver the new products at an appropriate cost. Thus, innovation in the product space is about cost-effectively reconfiguring the manufacturing and logistics base in the service of product fulfillment.

A major source of tension is the need to match feature sets with customer segments. Internal debates focus on how and when to develop new features and phase them into the system. We also spend a lot of time identifying new applications for existing products so as to leverage investments in R&D and logistics. Competitive advantage is a result of how well we do on the dimensions of cost, efficiency, quality, and variety compared with our competitors.

The Solutions Space

Let's consider how a business changes as it transitions from the product space to the solutions space, using the auto components industry as an example.

Historically, auto suppliers sold a specific component or part to the automakers, who took responsibility for integrating those components into their systems. Now that is changing. Two of the largest auto parts suppliers, Johnson Controls and Lear, have moved from manufacturing components to providing complete systems, taking responsibility for new concepts, design, manufacturing, and delivery. Thus, rather than simply making car seats, Johnson Controls now provides "seating solutions" that may incorporate heating systems, safety restraints, entertainment components, and many other elements. This exemplifies the shift from the product space to the solutions space.

Of course, no single supplier makes all the parts that go into the solution. A tier 1 supplier (like Johnson or Lear) must carefully manage its partnerships with tier 2 and tier 3 suppliers in the newly emerging hierarchy or network of supplier relationships.

What's unique about solutions suppliers is that they add "soft knowledge," based on their accumulated expertise, to the hard components they sell. In the solutions space, it is not just the product features and functions that matter, but soft knowledge as well.

This approach is becoming quite common. The IBM global solutions business, one of the fastest-growing IBM units, is another good example. They sell software and hardware from sources both inside and outside IBM, based not on IBM's capabilities but on the best solution for the customer. They can also finance the solution if desired.[7]

Herman Miller, the furniture company, creates modular furniture solutions through its Miller SQA ("Simple, Quick, and Affordable") initiative, which offers small businesses no-frills, quality furnishings delivered quickly at a reasonable price. Customers can use product configurators to custom-build furniture, choosing fabrics, design styles, wood finishes, and other specifications. Local dealers act as office furnishing consultants, presenting various design options that the customer can view in 3-D. The system then generates an available-to-promise date that is more accurate, and can suggest alternatives for faster delivery.[8]

Once an order is placed, Miller's Supply Net transparently links its many suppliers to its operations, streamlining purchasing, inventory, and production processes, and reducing delivery time. As a result, the order cycle takes about five days to complete versus an industry average of almost two months. The system also allows Miller to manage demand chain volatility downstream, reducing risk on all sides.

The Herman Miller example illustrates the importance of building a consumer-to-company-to-consumer fulfillment capability. The challenge, however, is to deal effectively with customer heterogeneity at the point of interaction. For instance, moving toward "segments of one" in the solutions space may mean giving customers the ability to choose the channel (phone, Internet, person-to-person) they want to use in dealing with the company rather than imposing the company's preference.

Migrating to the solutions space is a natural evolution for many businesses, one that often happens semiconsciously rather than as a result of a deliberate effort to transform the business. Thus, many companies give away their soft knowledge rather than price it appropriately. As one manager put it, "We still have a box mentality. We do all the systems integration work, but we only get paid for boxes."

This conflict is a source of tension for many companies. Customers increasingly demand solutions but are often willing to pay only for products. Managers must recognize and live with this tension. Because the additional work and cost of the solutions space is shifting upstream to suppliers, firms cannot afford to do it all themselves. Thus, competing in the solutions space will lead companies to further access the competencies and investments of others. It will also lead to the emergence of specialized vendors that enable firms to leverage scale.

On the positive side, the solutions space may create a new layer of barriers to imitation. The soft knowledge involved in stitching together a supply base and the competencies that suppliers provide can be hard to duplicate, creating a level of competitive insulation from which companies can benefit.

The Experience Space

The migration from the solutions space to the personalized experience space, which we have discussed in this book, is far more challenging for most companies. One reason is that it demands that they rethink the meaning of *differentiation*.

When coupled with DART, the personalized experience space forces managers to "differentiate differently." Focusing on heterogeneous consumer experiences assumes managers can continually reconfigure resources, interact with consumer communities, accept dynamic pricing, innovate around the context of the consumer, and be sensitive to the linkages and evolvability of the experiences of every consumer, one experience at a time. These new capabilities depend on the nature of the infrastructure that is available for managers to recognize emerging problems with consumers as well as new opportunities to serve. Thus, we must create both *an infrastructure for experiences and a methodology for managers* to actively engage customers and consumer communities around the world.

The transformation from solutions space to experience space demands explicit choices by senior management. It's not easy—but the competitive advantages that result are immense. The trend toward value creation through managing the experience space will ripple through the entire business system. If you lead the transformation in your industry, you will seize a distinct advantage over your competitors.

The New Competitive Space

By focusing on the two core drivers—the shifting locus of competencies and the shifting locus of innovation—we can derive a new view of the competitive space (figure 8-2), which includes the emerging experience space.

Many firms today are still in the product space. They focus on the competencies available to them within the firm, and they compete on the quality, cost, and delivery of products and services. At the same time, many firms are rapidly developing outside sources for components and subsystems, building global supply chains, and moving toward the solutions space. In the end, all firms will have to gravitate toward the experience co-creation space. The question is—how fast?

Customers are also evolving. Some of your customers may still operate with a product perspective. Others may expect more from you—they are seeking solutions. And some would go even further and expect

FIGURE 8-2

The New Competitive Space

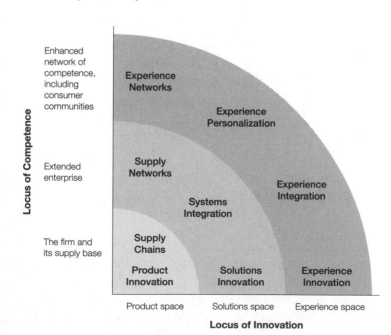

to create a unique, personalized experience. Your company's evolution will occur in parallel with that of your customers.

For some firms, the migration from the product space to the solutions space has been painless—a gradual, almost imperceptible evolution. The migration to the experience space will be different. The preconditions for co-creation, including DART and the focus on building an experience environment, aren't easy to incorporate into a traditional managerial system. Neither are the implications of co-creation for R&D, business development, marketing, accounting, logistics, pricing, branding, and other familiar business practices.

Yet, sometimes improvements to an existing system will not do; you must simply discard what you know. For generations, sailing ships were gradually improved by adding and redesigning sails, refining hull designs, modernizing navigation systems, and so on. But the development of the steamship rendered most of those incremental improvements worthless. We still have sailboats, but they are no longer economically viable for commercial transportation anywhere in the developed world.

The moral is clear. There comes a time when investing in improving the efficiency of the current model is inappropriate. At some point we must create a new model. The emerging model of value co-creation is such a turning point. The question for you as a manager is simply this: Are you going to keep trying to add more sails to your boat—or build a steamship?

We hope you want to build a steamship. We believe the new competitive space, as we have described it, demands it. We suggest that managers "fold in the future of competition," starting with the experience co-creation space. Extrapolating existing capabilities from the product or solutions space will not get us there. In short, managers must build *new strategic capital*—a new theory of how to compete on experiences and build new capabilities consistent with that theory.

Building New Strategic Capital

New strategic capital is about challenging the traditional approach to competition and value creation. It entails new ways to think about opportunities, access competence, leverage and reconfigure resources, engage the whole organization, and compete to co-create value based on experiences.

The current capabilities of companies—including your company—reflect an implicit theory of how to compete, based on the traditional system of value creation. For example, managers who believe that cost is a basis for creating competitive advantage will tend to build infrastructures to manage costs effectively. Sure enough, for the last one hundred years, cost reduction and efficiency have been central themes in strategy. From the Colt revolver to the Model T assembly line at Ford, standardization of components, vertical integration, and process efficiencies have been at the heart of effective management. Later, the pressure to create differentiated products forced managers to devise new ways to manage costs: process reengineering, outsourcing, modularity, use of common platforms, and embedded software. The desire for economies of scale drove expansion into national, regional, and global markets. All these strategic approaches were based on the cost imperative—one of the fundamental assumptions of the traditional view of value.

In a similar way, every major initiative in your firm and in your industry is based on a critical, if implicit, assumption about value creation. For example, anticipatory pricing based on the firm's "experience curve" (with its expected cost reductions over time) dominated the early years of the semiconductor industry. Understanding the connection between the often implicit theory of competition and value creation, and the underlying infrastructure and behaviors, is crucial for successful management around a turning point.

We are clearly experiencing such a turning point, as exemplified by the new competitive space. The ideas in this book collectively embody an emerging theory of the meaning of value and the value creation process. By implication, they also direct our attention to *new sources of competitive advantage*. So managers today should step back from their daily responsibilities and problems and ask: What does the new view of value creation mean for us as managers? And how will it affect the way we compete?

The need for new strategic capital is fairly obvious. But building it, in a world of co-creation, will require several challenging steps.

Building Bridges Between Managers and Consumers

Despite decades of sincere effort by companies to understand customers and become customer-focused, managers and consumers remain deeply disconnected. The reasons are clear. There are few opportunities for managers in large organizations to understand and viscerally experience the business as their consumers do. Infrequent and planned visits to key customers do not provide a meaningful perspective on how consumers experience the business. The irritating long waits we've all experienced when using call centers are a good example. Metrics such as how many questions were resolved and how soon do not capture the consumer's true feelings.

Consumer experiences are a distant reality for most managers—especially senior managers. Furthermore, like consumers, managers are a heterogeneous lot who react differently to similar stimuli. Though IT systems assume that all managers at a given level need similar information, the reality is that *every manager has a unique approach to managing*. This can contribute to significant variance in "feel" for the consumer experience among managers.

Because frontline employees are closest to the customers, they are most likely to understand customer concerns. In an airline, a hotel, a retail store, a financial services firm, a utility, or a government agency, the people closest to the customer experience are the call center operators, the salespeople, and the service representatives. What voice do they have in determining policy? How often do call center operators or salespeople on the floor get asked about customer experiences? A few firms have systems in place to capture the voices of frontline employees. But how often do senior managers share that experience directly?

To build new strategic capital, companies will need to bridge the gap between managers and consumers. This is the subject of chapter 9.

Facilitating Rapid Knowledge Creation

Because the co-creation process presents an evolving and continuously changing milieu, managers must continuously rethink their actions. More important, they must act and react in real time. Creating a culture of rapid knowledge creation and consensus building around opportunities becomes a necessity.

Such a culture of rapid consensus building requires both a technical and a social infrastructure. The technical infrastructure can facilitate access and transparency to information. But the social infrastructure can provide access and transparency to employee knowledge. Firms must ensure that open dialogue, access, risk assessment, and transparency (DART) are as deeply embedded in internal management as in the co-creation of customer experiences.

To build the new strategic capital, businesses must create the pre-conditions for rapid knowledge creation. A "managerial experience environment" is an integral part of this process. This is the subject of chapter 10.

Strategy as Discovery

Traditionally, strategy has been thought of as mastery of the game of competition and its rules. The fact that firms could follow existing strategies suggested that the game was known and the rules for winning were clear. Tools such as industry analysis and value chain analysis were built on the assumption that the goal of the strategist was to position the firm within the framework of a known game.

For over thirty years, this was an appropriate way to approach strategy. But starting around 1990, the game of competition started to change. Major discontinuities, such as deregulation and the convergence of industries and technologies, rendered old ways of competing less and less relevant. How should a utility or an airline compete post deregulation? In the past, the new game was knowable. The manager of a utility firm could look at other industries and understand what competition meant. Utilities went through wrenching processes of change—but whatever the process, whether it was deverticalization (separating power generation from power transmission and distribution), market segmentation, or globalization, there were analogs in other industries that had previously undergone such changes. While new to utilities, the new game was known to strategists and managers in other industries and therefore inherently knowable by all.

What we are witnessing today is *not* more of the same. How should a computer equipment maker or a health care provider compete in the coalescing "fun space" or "wellness space" where traditional industries and products commingle? What does a product or service mean in the fun or wellness space? How should one compete in a networked world where intelligence resides in software or on the Internet rather than in a hardwired motherboard or physical device? How does one compete when consumers are no longer passive recipients of products and services? How does one cope when the very meaning of value starts to shift? How do companies engage consumers as co-creators of value? How do firms differentiate themselves in a world of co-creation? These are some of the new questions that the old rules of the game don't answer.

Co-creation of value suggests that managers must rethink the meaning of resources and how access to resources is obtained. As we have seen, consumers represent a resource base. So do employees at all levels, as well as partners and other participants in experience networks. Gaining privileged and timely access to these resources requires managers to explicitly consider ways in which they can manage relationships in the networks. Managing the infrastructure of the network, with its continual friction between collaboration and competition, value creation and value extraction, can be a source of competitive advantage. In this book, we have described the contours of the evolving new game, with new rules and new strategies for you to invent. The evolution has just begun. Therefore we cannot fully anticipate, understand, or describe its end point. We can only list the basic elements of change that seem clear from today's perspective—especially the forces that will drive the new game of co-creation of unique value. Under the new circumstances, strategy is not a game with knowable rules and finite options. Today the goal of the strategist is to navigate through fog effectively. Strategy making today calls for a new spirit of discovery, involving experimentation, analysis, consolidation of gains, and further experimentation. This is the subject of chapter 11.

Building New Capabilities for the Future

The new frontier of co-creation of unique value, centered on personalized co-creation experiences, challenges a wide variety of cherished managerial practices, from R&D, market research, and advertising to manufacturing and logistics. No single functional discipline will remain unscathed. However, some will be subject to more change than others—and none more than the management of human resources.

Managers must begin by evaluating how their traditional approaches to functions help or hinder the co-creation of value and the new form of competition. Companies will also have to attend to infrastructure capabilities as they migrate to the new frontier. As firms build the new capacity to compete, the opportunity space of co-creation of value will demand that they govern differently as well. Governance in an era of co-creation, with so many moving parts and so many inherent and apparent conflicts, will emerge as a dominant new challenge. Building *functional, infrastructure, and governance capabilities* for the future is the subject of chapter 12, which concludes this book.

In the next chapter, we will look at the changing role of the manager in co-creating value. But before we proceed, we urge you to reflect as a manager on the challenges and opportunities the new competitive space presents for your own organization. What are the constituents of the strategic capital that your organization must create? What are the new capabilities that will be required to build that steamship? This will help put the following chapters in perspective.

Chapter Nine

MANAGER AS CONSUMER

MANAGING the co-creation of unique value demands a new capability: the ability for managers to relate to consumer interactions with the experience network. Managers must increasingly experience and understand the business *as consumers do*, and not merely as an abstraction of numbers and charts.[1]

How can managers of large and mid-sized companies achieve the kind of visceral understanding of the business that a mom-and-pop store owner has? How can line managers feel and share the consumer's concerns, desires, and aspirations? How can they make their experience of the business, on a real-time, continuous basis, approximate to the experience of consumers?

In the emergent world of co-creation, we consider every employee who has the ability to directly influence the consumer experience, and facilitate the co-creation of value, to be a *line manager*. Companies must build an information infrastructure that allows all managers, especially line managers, to experience the business as the consumer does, thereby achieving a new level of *personal effectiveness*.

Creating an Infrastructure for Real-Time Experience Quality Management: The ER Example

Let us consider the example of an emergency room in a busy downtown hospital to illustrate the managerial experience space. It's not uncommon for about 40 percent of a hospital's patients to enter the system through the emergency room. From a managerial perspective, it's critical to be very efficient in moving patients through the ER as fast as possible without compromising the level of care. But in an emergency room, demand is random and unpredictable. There are no predetermined sequences of procedures that can be followed. The need depends on the nature of the problem; a gunshot wound, a heart attack, and a broken arm are all different. But they all require the services of multiple doctors, medical staff, and technicians, as well as the physical movement of the patient through various stages of examination, testing, and treatment.

Yes, real-life emergency rooms look as crazy and chaotic as they do in TV medical dramas. The progress of the patient, the status of various tests, and the availability of rooms are tracked on bits of paper, in PCs, and on whiteboards posted in the clinic. Often the patient is too sick to talk, and friends or relatives anxiously wait outside, demanding information and answers from harried hospital employees.

Imagine that you are a manager of the ER. How do you know what is happening at any given point in time? Historical analysis of two-day-old data will not help you solve problems as they are happening, much less improve the quality of current patient experience. Improving patient care, on a real time basis requires managers to answer *specific questions:* Are patients waiting too long at a given station? Do the doctors, nurses, and technicians have access to the resources they need? Are ER capacities being fully utilized? Is there a long line for X-ray?

Further, how do managers at different levels—from the chief nurse, the head of the emergency services unit, to a vice president of the hospital, experience the business as patients, patients' families, technicians, doctors, and the interns experience it? Is the patient "Hilda Schmidt" waiting for more than forty-five minutes of service? How do we begin to understand her co-creation experience with the hospital's experience network?

And how do you as a line manager respond in real time? For instance, as a head nurse, how do you respond when two night-shift nurses call in sick—just as a massive fire across town fills the ER with victims of smoke inhalation and burns? And suppose you are the head of the emergency unit. Can you provide the level of required staffing without compromising the quality of care for other existing patients in the hospital?

Meanwhile, a VP in the hospital, a couple of steps removed from the ER, has some questions of his own. What is the average waiting time for a patient to receive care? Where are the bottlenecks? On arrival and registration? Waiting for a doctor, for a room, for tests? And who is paying for the care? Are insurance reimbursement rates rising or falling? Is the ER a profitable center for the hospital, or is it incurring chronic losses? Why?

The goal of the information system is not to substitute the nurse, technician, or the doctor, but to provide them with a system that aids the amplification of weak signals based on the real-time experiences of consumers (patients). This means the construction of information in the context of a specific co-creation experience. A manager's personal effectiveness in such a situation depends on his capacity to generate hypotheses around the problems encountered by a patient and develop actions in real-time.

To make this happen, the information system must start with *events*—a patient arrival, a registration process, a visit to an X-ray room—as well as their metrics—time spent in the waiting room, time required to make a diagnosis, and overall length of stay. This event-centric information must be available to the line manager in real time and within its context of space and time. For example: "Patients are waiting forty-five minutes for X-rays on Wednesday mornings," or "Bed assignments are taking longer than thirty minutes."

As a manager, I should be able to construct the experience from different perspectives, such as an overloaded doctor, an anxious patient or a beleaguered technician. I should also be able to connect with others involved in providing services within the system and create "appropriate practices" by collaborating in real time to solve new problems. Just as it is critical for consumers to be able to interact with consumer communities, managers should also be able to communicate with practice communities to co-construct new knowledge and co-create better consumer experiences.

As a manager, I should be able to experience consumer-company interactions as they are happening, and understand and evaluate their implications. Real-time information without context has little value for me as a manager. Learning from experiences requires that the event-centric information system enables me to reconstruct events. Real-time intervention is different from the analysis of specific experiences after the fact to search for patterns, formulate hypotheses, and codify the learning. For managers to become co-creators, they should have the capability for real time intervention as well as after the fact analysis.

Such capabilities must be available to every manager in the ER. That includes all of the employees involved in creating a good customer (patient) experience, including doctors, nurses, lab technicians, the clerk at the registration counter, and the ward assistants who transport patients and deliver supplies.

In today's ER, do line managers have access to all of the capabilities we've suggested? Usually they do not—not for technological reasons, but because our management systems have not yet caught up with the changing locus of value creation—*the various points of consumer-company interaction*. The question is: How do we get the managerial equivalent of embedded intelligence, as when a smart product, like the pacemaker, interacts with the consumer? Thus, companies must facilitate managerial learning and action, through *co-evolution* with consumer experiences, at *all* points of company-consumer interaction.

Providing Managers with "Embedded Intelligence" at Points of Company-Consumer Interaction

To illustrate, let's consider the needs of a field technician for Bell Canada, a telecom firm that is experimenting with employee-consumer interaction. A Bell Canada field technician "wears" an array of devices, including a small computer with an attached input medium, a flat-panel display screen, and the ubiquitous cell phone. Through these devices, technical and human intelligence of the firm is available to the technician at the customer's site. For example, the technician can print out an up-to-the-minute bill, much like the attendant who accepts your rental car return at the airport. The technician can also access work orders. And just as Cemex grafts taxi-like dispatch services in routing their cement trucks to changing customer orders, here Bell Canada employees can be routed to troubleshoot sudden disruptions or an emerging service problem. Further, once the technician is at work—for example, analyzing storm damage to a relay box atop a telephone pole—he can access technical diagrams that will help him understand and fix the problem.[2]

As this experiment unfolds, new capabilities will be developed and tested in response to new situations, each situation unfolding in its own idiosyncratic context in space and time. Imagine each technician being able to access the expertise of other technicians and employees in the company. The employee becomes a co-creator of knowledge that is contextualized around specific service events. We can also imagine in certain instances where other line managers may want to intervene and experience a service event with a customer. Advances in wearable computing and mobile communications will continue to offer new possibilities here. As Bell Canada evolves its information infrastructure, it will co-create unique consumer experiences and productivity gains simultaneously. The point is that all businesses must build managerial environments within which individual line managers can learn and act more effectively. Managers learn from one another, from customers, from suppliers, and from broader communities of interest and expertise. Technology must support this learning process.

The generation of new knowledge in a systematic fashion around events is indeed a significant managerial challenge. It requires coming to terms with the "learning disabilities" that mark the social infrastructures of so many organizations. For communities of practice to flourish, we must understand how managers want to interact with each other and with the technical infrastructure. And to make this happen, we must employ the same DART building blocks that are so crucial in the co-creation of consumer experiences: dialogue, access, risk assessment, and transparency.

Manager as Consumer: The Requirements

Three basic requirements must be met if managers are to share the experiences of consumers and others who play an important role in co-creation:

- Managers must get as much real-time event-centric data as possible regarding consumer experiences.

- Managers must understand and intervene selectively in individual consumer events even as they manage the overall operation. "How did we do with Hilda Schmidt today?" is just as important as "How did we do around the world this week?"

- Managers must be able to respond quickly by mobilizing and reconfiguring resources as needed.

In short, to co-create value effectively, managers must have the capacity for *agility*. Agility is the ability to act fast—to improve the cycle time for managerial action. It's a capability that has become more important than ever. Traditionally, the cost of managerial lag time has been additional spending on capital and missed profit opportunities. For example, when managers are unable to react promptly to sales declines, the result is inventory buildup. Conversely, when managers cannot scale their operations fast enough to respond to sales increases, the result is lost sales. In today's margin-squeezed, highly competitive environment, firms are increasingly unable to pay the price for managerial lag time. What are the building blocks of business agility? How does the managerial context affect the quest for agility? And can our existing information infrastructure support agility?[3]

We believe that agility depends above all on the readiness of line managers to respond quickly to changes on demand. And it is important to recognize that line managers, like consumers, are a *heterogeneous* lot. No two managers react the same way to similar events. Therefore, business agility is largely a function of the capacity of the managerial environment to respond to the needs of heterogeneous line managers.

Building the Managerial Environment

How, then, do we build a managerial environment that will meet the varied needs of heterogeneous line managers? Here are some of the key considerations.

Rapid Resource Reconfiguration

As we saw in chapter 6, experience quality management (EQM) requires flexibility in resource reconfiguration (as exemplified in the operations of companies like Cemex, Zara, REI, and Reflect.com). Obviously, this capability affects logistical and manufacturing infrastructures. It may also involve shifting inventories from one location to another, scaling up production, reassigning salespeople, stopping or redesigning communications programs or selling across business units. It requires the ability to co-create value by collaborating *internally* in the organization, as well as with suppliers, and customers.

The ability to reduce the cycle time for managerial reaction to changing conditions hinges on the capacity to recognize the nature of problems associated with events at points of company-consumer interaction, and to develop a consensus among all the affected stakeholders for action. That means being able as a manager to access information in context.

Access to Information in Context

In order to act, managers need information. But information without context is of little value. Context is defined by a specific concern or question that requires action.

Consider a global sales manager. She may want to know all of her company's branches where sales were less than 80 percent of forecast last week. Here, the context has three dimensions: the topic (sales versus forecast), time (last week), and space (branches around the world). The manager might also like to know what promotional programs were run in those markets by her firm and by its principal competitors. Finally, she may also want to know whether the sales/forecast discrepancy was a one-time event or part of a continuing trend.

As this example illustrates, the agile manager needs access to information that can help answer an array of constantly changing questions, some clearly formulated and others rather vague. Our sales manager in this case may be wondering, "Have back-to-school promotions by our biggest competitor produced sales declines for us in specific markets? Does unseasonably cold weather account for the problem? Or do long-term trends, such as demographic shifts, play a major role?"

Thus, the need for contextual knowledge transcends mere transactional data. We must be able to seamlessly interweave transactional and nontransactional data so as to answer new questions as they arise. Developing this capability in a firm is fraught with technical and social challenges.

Consider the case of the natural-history museum "industry." Around the world, there are over three billion animal, insect, and plant specimens in natural history museum collections. Nearly all of these museums are digitizing their collection records and making them available online. Some museums in the United States, Canada, and Mexico have agreed to share data using the XML format. Integrated access to these databases can facilitate research into the global biodiversity of species.[4]

Now imagine that I'm a museum curator (that is, a manager) who has been asked to help set up an exhibit on Asian long-horned beetles that have been destroying trees in Chicago. This request creates the managerial context for me. The networked databases connecting many natural-history museums provide a rich array of resources quickly and easily. But in order to develop an interactive exhibit that models the beetle's ecosystem, I need answers to several specific questions that the databases may not be able to provide directly. I know there are some knowledgeable sources in-house and significant expertise in other museums, and I want to access this expertise to develop context-specific knowledge as quickly as possible. Thus, to make this process work to its full potential, another element must be added to the managerial environment.

Capacity to Create New Knowledge and Insights

Getting access to information in context is necessary but not sufficient for true agility. Managers also need the ability to interact with the information system on their terms, posing new questions and generating new hypotheses. This raises the question: How do we create an information infrastructure that can aid "managerial intuition" and provide the capacity to test ideas as they emerge?

Furthermore, in a large firm, a single line manager seldom acts alone. She usually must depend on a host of colleagues across multiple locations. She must interact with other managers, access their skills and expertise, work with them to draw conclusions regarding the risks inherent in the problem, and build a consensus on both diagnosis and action.

All of this demands an information system that can navigate through a maze of databases and applications in search of answers to questions whose formulation may be imprecise, or "fuzzy." In the world of information systems, responding to fuzzy queries is far from a simple matter. For example, answering the sales/forecast question in a global firm that has grown through acquisitions and mergers may require access to twenty-five different databases and applications. And line managers are unlikely to pursue the emerging questions and develop new hypotheses if the system is unable to provide real-time responses. No one wants to communicate an evolving thought or a tentative question to an analyst and wait three days for the results. So the central question is: How can line managers use the system to create new knowledge *for themselves* so they can act fast in response to challenges?

When managerial collaboration and consensus building include those outside the firm's boundaries (such as critical customers or suppliers), the problem widens. The museum curator must work with a knowledge base beyond her own institution's boundaries. How do we create a basis for dialogue that effectively taps the skills and insights of several groups or organizations, each with its own goals, values, and interests? For co-creation of experiences, line managers must have access to information within the firm, often to the entire network, including that of consumers.

Recognizing Managerial Heterogeneity

As we have noted, managers are a heterogeneous lot. They differ in how they access information, how they develop insights, and how they build consensus for action. Yet in developing information systems for managerial use, IT groups tend to ignore or minimize the problems these differences create. For example, the information needs of sales managers (a functionally and hierarchically defined group) are usually treated as monolithic—even though, in reality, the needs of Sales Manager Rajid may be quite different from those of Sales Manager Chen.

When IT groups try to accommodate variations in needs, they usually do so by building a large variety of features and functions into the system. (Remember product variety?) Unfortunately, this approach often increases the complexity of the system without improving its ability to meet complex managerial demands.

"Individualization" here is different from catering to a specific user group or customizing an application at the level of the organization. It's about being sensitive to the "context of the moment" and to how individual managers want to access, visualize, and use information. It's about giving managers the capacity to collaborate and co-create value in the experience network with suppliers, partners, and consumers.

To achieve true individualization, it's important to understand the basic sources of managerial heterogeneity.

Sophistication and Domain Knowledge

Because managers differ in their levels of sophistication and domain knowledge, the same information system may take one manager an hour to learn but another two days. Furthermore, while the sophisticated manager can access the features she wants and be pleased, a less sophisticated manager may spend endless time navigating through features he does not want, feeling increasingly frustrated and alienated. Obviously, IT systems that require active engagement by managers must accommodate heterogeneity in sophistication and domain knowledge if they are to be effective.

Willingness to Operate in Real Time

Let us go back to Cemex. Its corporate philosophy, spearheaded by chief executive Lorenzo Zambrano, involves tightly controlled managerial standards for operations worldwide. At Cemex's manufacturing facilities, quality control reports are generated automatically by machines that extract samples from the production line, analyze them, and report the results to a computer network accessible by managers. This also means that Zambrano can use the network to check sales figures or kiln temperatures, and ask managers to explain their units' performance. Suddenly, the pressure for managers to stay on top has been significantly increased.

When these changes were first implemented, there was resistance among some of Cemex's managers, especially those not willing to operate closer to real time. But others began to strive for improvements. Today, anyone who becomes a Cemex manager understands the real-time pressures and must be prepared to deal with them.

Propensity and Need for Dialogue

For managers to co-create value, they must have the capacity for engaging in dialogue around the context of specific events. In turn, this means they must have access to knowledge, including communities of best and new practices. Furthermore, the system must accommodate contextual demands for dialogue that will vary across individuals and from one project to another.

For example, managers and key suppliers at Harley-Davidson have access to a collaborative environment, called Ride that facilitates dialogue around design and development. But the ways in which individual employees engage in dialogue will vary by context. When developing the electronic fuel-injected (EFI) engine for the V-Rod bike, Harley engineers and managers had to collaborate with key supplier Delphi Automotive and with European firms, including Porsche and Magneti Marelli. Later, when Delphi's initial attempts to adapt an automotive-based system to a motorcycle did not succeed, the team had to redesign the system from the ground up—which meant trusting the development of a critical component to an outsider. Thus, the need for dialogue increased dramatically as the project unfolded.[5]

Willingness to Experiment

Individual managers vary in their willingness to experiment, due in part to their varying responses to the trade-off between efficiency and innovation. Managers have traditionally focused on increasing the efficiency of transactions and business processes. But agility requires willingness to experiment as well, which generally reduces efficiency (at least in the short run). Whether and how a particular manager trades efficiency for experimentation depends on the context for managerial action.

Ultimately, efficiency and innovation must both be accommodated. The development of the EFI engine for the Harley V-Rod certainly called for experimentation. Engineers within and outside the firm needed real-time access to plans, files, pictures, and audio and video clips, as well as the ability to create new knowledge continuously. But the co-experimentation process and the positive experiences it created fostered a new level of trust that in turn catalyzed new efficiencies in product development.

Risk Preferences

Often overlooked in discussions of managerial choices are the personal risk preferences of managers. Let's return to the sales/forecast example. Should the company alter its production schedules if last week's sales were less than 90 percent of forecast in a small market, such as Chile? Or should the firm stay the course, assuming that one week's decline will be balanced by another week's increase? The Chilean blip may serve as an action trigger for some managers, but not for others.

Capabilities of the Managerial Environment

Having recognized the importance of designing a management environment capable of responding to heterogeneous managerial behaviors, we can now identify some of the key capabilities that a real-time information infrastructure should provide.

Consistency of Decentralized Action

Clearly, managers are not all the same. They do not respond to problems the same way. Managers must have autonomy and must be able to personalize their actions. But the actions of managers at various levels in the firm must be consistent with the overall direction of the company. Thus, the interactivity needs to strike a balance between personalization and consistency.

Visualization of Experiences

Managers must have a visceral understanding of the customer experience—a "gut" sense of customer reality. Simply reading a written report rarely conveys this sense. Information systems should also provide video and audio inputs, preferably integrated with textual data, and ideally be able to capture, in real time, the nature of the activities taking place in a specific location.

This kind of rich, multisensory information enables managers to refine and clarify their questions about the activities they control. The emergency room manager should have access to video and audio files that let him say, "I see a problem at nurse's station two—the main computer used to access patient records is down. How is it being addressed? Is the problem persistent, or will it affect the quality of care only this morning?"

We are reminded of Tom Cruise's character in Steven Spielberg's 2002 movie, *Minority Report*. His job is to prevent crimes before they happen. He must examine and rapidly reconstruct events (in this case, crimes) in space and time, search for patterns, formulate hypotheses, and act quickly. As a manager, imagine if you could reconstruct consumer experiences the way you want so you could respond to opportunities and problems effectively. This effort is about discovery and action. Unlike Tom Cruise in the movie *Minority Report*, managers need to do this in real time, as when consumers are co-constructing their own experiences. This capability would allow managers to experience the business in real time, by participating in the consumer experience at the point of interaction.

Aggregation and Disaggregation of Events and Metrics

Managers must have access to information at varying levels of granularity. Suppose the emergency room is having problems getting X-ray results quickly for patients with orthopedic injuries. If I am an ER manager, I need the ability to disaggregate that event into its components to identify whether the problem is in the management of the X-ray room, in the handling of films, or in the subsequent information flows. The solution to the problem will be very different depending on which is the case. By contrast, if I am a hospital VP, I may not be interested in that level of detail. I may simply want to focus on improving overall throughput, and data about average overall patient hours in the ER may be granular enough for that purpose.

One System, Multiple Experiences

Different managers in the same organization will have different information needs. For example, their level of interactivity with other managers and the levers of action they can initiate will likely be different. The choices around building four new emergency rooms are different from those involved in assigning a nurse to the stroke patient who was just wheeled in. Accordingly, managers should be able to access differing perspectives on the same event.

However, it's also critical to enable a common event context. Remember, the same manager may be involved in different roles at different times. One day, she may be focusing on day-to-day operations; the next day, resource optimization; the day after that, resource allocation and planning. Thus, the system must provide continuity and consistency while also permitting the manager to shift focus at will, calling up varying sets and styles of information as her changing roles demand.

Ability to Ask New and Nonroutine Questions

One of the most important activities of any manager is asking new, nonroutine questions. These will often be stated in vague form, supported as much by intuition and hunches as by hard data. Unfortunately, most traditional information systems are geared toward answering known questions presented in standardized forms.

For example, it is easy to do a traditional analysis of forecast and actual activities, including a breakdown of the discrepancies between the two. These are important inputs. But seldom does such analysis provide new insights. Managers must be able to ask more tentative, *hypothesis-generating* questions: Do we get more emergency patients during the Christmas holidays? If so, do they suffer especially from strokes? Are they old or of all ages? Are they predominantly from poor neighborhoods, or does this phenomenon cut across all income levels? Are we losing business because patients with less-critical conditions get tired of waiting for care and go somewhere else?

The well-crafted information system must be able to generate answers to these hypothetical questions. It should also enable the manager to collaborate with others who may have to act on this hypothesis or who may have a different perspective on it. Collaboration in rapidly building a consensus around a hypothesis is a critical capability and a crucial step in building new knowledge.

We think of the manager's ability to be experience-centric as consisting of three levels (see figure 9-1). At level 1, where the co-creation experience occurs, she asks the most interesting, intuitive questions, which usually have no clear answers. This is the hypothesis generation stage. Here the line manager must develop an understanding of the context of co-creation experiences. She must develop a consensus among the immediate managerial community for action. Dialogue and transparency are critical, since all members of the cohort must have access to the same information that led to the hypothesis in the first place. This level entails *experience quality management*. It is where the most variability in managerial action is.

If the hypothesis pans out and the problem persists, it can move to the level of *business activity monitoring*, as in the use of tools to monitor

FIGURE 9 - 1

Experience-Centric Information Systems

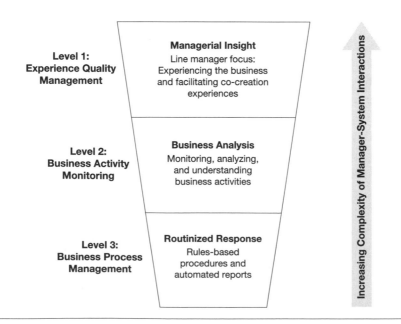

call center activities. Further refinements can move the discovery process to a level of process automation, routine analysis, and reporting. This third level is conventional *business process management*.[6]

The problem with most information systems is that they are designed from company-centric business processes (level 3), rather than being centered on the individual line manager (level 1). A line manager cannot manage business activities through the lens of consumer experience without the company developing the requisite level 1 capabilities. For a line manager to become experience-centric, she must have the ability to understand the context of events underlying a co-creation experience, capture her own interpretations and business implications associated with a specific event, and create actionable insights. In most companies today, level 1 gets the least attention and level 3 the most. Some companies have recognized the importance of level 2 (i.e., monitoring, analyzing, and understanding the business activities to be measured) for creating more effective rules-based and automated processes in level 3. These companies must further recognize the importance of level 1 for building more effective business activity monitoring capabilities that enable line managers to enhance the *quality of co-creation experiences*. Thus, for companies to become experience-centric, their information systems must be centered on line managers and enhancing their personal effectiveness in co-creating value.

Co-Evolution: Enabling Managers to Evolve with Consumer Experiences

The goal of the manager who experiences the business in real time is *zero latency*. As a manager, I may not be pleased with a long delay in the emergency room after a patient complains; I certainly will not be satisfied to read in a report at the end of the month that 40 percent of patients waited thirty minutes or longer before seeing a doctor. I want to act *when* the patient is having a problem.

Therefore, companies must identify the key elements of the co-creation experience (call it *experience-centered domain knowledge*) and build systems that enable individual managers to evolve with consumer experiences:

- *Personalized alerts*—Managers need personalized alerts when events happen, so they can act. For instance, in the ER example, a manager may not tolerate having 10 percent of patients waiting longer than ten minutes at any station. Another manager may set different standards, and should receive alerts that fit her criteria.

- *Contextual information*—Managers need access to and presentation of information within their own contexts to enable more effective decision making.

- *Real-time collaboration*—Managers must be enabled to develop and test hypotheses, to collaborate with others in real time, and to build consensus around a proven hypothesis and an action plan.

- *Rapid reconfiguration of resources*—Managers must have the ability to flexibly re-configure resources on demand, oriented around co-creation experiences.

- *Real-time monitoring*—Managers must have the ability to monitor business activities and track the results of corrective actions immediately after they've been put in place.

- *Experience-based operating rules and procedures*—Business rules and standard operating procedures in most companies have evolved from an internal company-centric view of efficiency and interactions with customers. To become an experience-centric company, line managers must have the ability to evolve new rules and procedures that simultaneously enhance revenue-creating opportunities—through a focus on co-creation experiences that consumers are willing to pay for—while also simultaneously boosting efficiency by reducing costs that do not disproportionately contribute to compelling customer experiences.

The message is clear. To embrace the co-creation of value paradigm, we must build an information infrastructure that recognizes the centrality of the managerial experience. We must treat managers as consumers. Like consumers, managers should be able to personalize the way they want to experience the business, with a focus on co-creating value. The environment of the individual manager is a subset of a broader culture of co-creation that embraces an entire network, starting with the individual firm. Thus, the managerial environment is part of a larger "knowledge environment," the subject of the next chapter.

Chapter Ten

RAPID KNOWLEDGE CREATION

K NOWLEDGE ENVIRONMENTS for managers resemble experience environments for consumers. Innovation in knowledge environments must reflect the granularity of managerial experiences, just as innovation in experience environments must reflect the depth of consumer experiences. Figure 10-1 summarizes the consumer and manager perspectives of co-creation.

To co-create value continually, we must continually co-create new knowledge. The opportunities to do so range from solving a particular problem (say, reducing the recharge time for a battery pack in a particular cell phone configuration) to identifying major emerging opportunities (such as the explosive growth market for cell phones in China and India). To make this happen, we must create knowledge environments that facilitate discovery and action in the new competitive space.

The Concept of a Knowledge Environment

When heterogeneous customers interact with a firm, they will make demands that cannot be predicted. This is an inherent challenge in the co-creation of value. When a customer says to a frontline employee, "Help me solve this problem," the question is posed not just to that employee but to the entire organization. How can that employee access the knowledge base of his peers around the world to help that customer? How can the organization combine the experience and the skills of its employees to co-create new knowledge? To meet these challenges, the firm

FIGURE 10 - 1

Convergence of Company and Consumer: The Co-Creation Environment

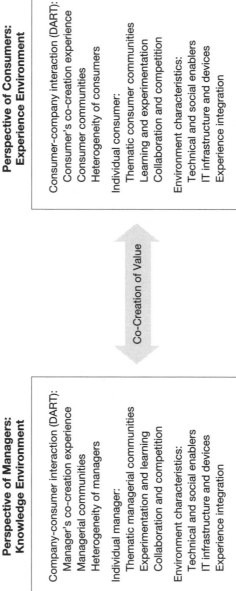

must develop an environment where knowledge can be co-created and shared continuously.[1]

Capacity to create new knowledge rapidly has two critical dimensions: the ability of the individual manager to generate new insights, and the ability to share these insights with others so that consensus can be built on how to act. Thus, an interactive, collaborative environment that enhances managers' capacity to access knowledge for specific contexts is key to managerial agility.

Knowledge environments call for building new social and technical information infrastructures. The tools of the technical infrastructure must allow for the social infrastructure to evolve.

The first step is to open the knowledge environment not just to the top management but to a very large part of the corporate population—up to fifty thousand workers at a large global company like General Motors. Of course, this goes against the grain. Managers are accustomed to being protective of information access. It's a habitual way of thinking that must change. Some employees may misuse the privilege of access; others may fail to use it. That doesn't matter. If a large number of people are given access to information, many will choose to explore it. As they discover the freedom to communicate with others in their practice communities, best practices from around the world can spread. And as the socialization of sharing and learning expands, vertical and geographic boundaries can break down.

New communities will gradually form across the geographical divides both within and across businesses. As a result, opportunities that transcend current organizational limitations can emerge. For example, consider such questions as these: How does a company provide its global customers a global warranty? (If a consumer buys a camcorder in Miami, how can it be serviced in Peru?) How does an organization share its customer databases? (If a consumer buys a laptop, is he a likely customer for a digital camera?)

In several global companies today, these simple questions have no quick answers—but they soon will. The emergence of "knowledge threads" that cut across multiple vertical and horizontal boundaries is where the real value lies in co-creating knowledge around consumer experiences.

What are the main characteristics of a powerful knowledge environment? Because competence is widely distributed throughout the network, the direction and intensity of knowledge and information flows cannot be predetermined. Patterns will emerge over time, subject to continual change. Thus, managers must strive to facilitate the flow rather than manage it and provide access to competence on demand rather than develop predetermined structures for access.

The Power of the Knowledge Environment: The Buckman Labs Example

Consider Buckman Laboratories, a $300 million specialty chemicals company based in Memphis, Tennessee, with around thirteen hundred employees in over a hundred countries. Buckman produces more than a thousand different specialty chemicals in eight factories around the world. It competes in a variety of businesses, from pulp and paper processing and water treatment to leather, agriculture, and personal care. Like a typical multinational corporation (MNC), Buckman operates in a large number of countries, with multiple businesses. Unlike a typical MNC, it is small, enjoying a competitive edge due to its ability to apply the power of *all* its employees to every customer experience. And central to this capability is its global knowledge sharing network called K'Netix, which is integral to Buckman's information infrastructure.[2]

Here's a story that illustrates a typical application of K'Netix. A managing director for Buckman Labs in Singapore—let's call her Mary—has been asked to propose a pitch-control program to an Indonesian pulp mill. Pitch is a chemical released from wood in the pulping and refining processes; its composition depends on the characteristics of the tree from which the wood is obtained and other environmental factors. If pitch is not separated from the pulp, it affects paper quality and can cause problems in paper mill operations. Thus, developing an effective pitch-control program is an important and complex aspect of paper mill management.

Mary logs into K'Netix and asks for an update on recent pitch-control approaches around the world. Three hours later, she gets a response from Memphis that refers to a master's thesis by an Indonesian student in the United States on pitch control of tropical hardwoods, and offers some specific suggestions on Buckman chemicals that might be appropriate for this application. About an hour later, a Canadian manager sends a note about his experience in solving the pitch problem in British Columbia. Later Mary receives data from Sweden, New Zealand, Spain, and France, followed by an offer of technical expertise and scientific advice from the company's central R&D group. In all, Mary receives eleven postings from six countries, forming several conversational threads that enable each participant to learn something new. The net result: The contextual knowledge that was created helps Mary secure a $6 million order from the Indonesian mill.[3] This would be interesting enough if the Buckman network included only the firm's technical experts. But everyone at the company has access to the same system, right down to frontline employees.

Now consider another story. One of Buckman's paper customers in Michigan realized that the peroxide it was adding to remove ink from old magazines was no longer working. A Buckman sales manager presented this problem to the knowledge network. Within two days, salespeople from Belgium and Finland identified a likely cause: Bacteria in the paper slurry was producing an enzyme that broke down the peroxide. The sales manager recommended a chemical to control the bacteria, and the problem was solved.[4] Now imagine how that customer feels about doing business with Buckman. With the company and the customer co-creating knowledge, a new level of trust and value can emerge.

Building a Knowledge Environment

The Buckman example helps us identify some of the critical premises and requirements underlying the concept of the knowledge environment:

- Competitive discontinuities put a premium on new knowledge creation.

- Globalization puts a premium on access to competence across the firm, since redundancy of effort in multiple locations increases costs without improving the quality of the customer experience.

- Knowledge is different from information. Knowledge, like experience, is *inherent in the individual* and cannot be separated from the individual.

- The creation of new knowledge requires that individuals have access to competence, not just to databases. The knowledge environment is as much about people as about technology.

- The social and technical enablers for knowledge creation must recognize the heterogeneity of managers and employees in the knowledge-creation process.

- The knowledge environment must be woven into the culture of the organization. Just as knowledge is associated with the individual, the knowledge environment must become identified with the organization, as in the case of Buckman Labs.

Knowledge environments evolve over time. We must create mechanisms that can enable the emergence of knowledge threads and facilitate the rapid creation of new knowledge. Such mechanisms, or "knowledge catalysts," are critical for integrating the information infrastructure, typically designed for managing explicit information (structured and unstructured data) into an effective environment for rapid knowledge creation.

Just as experience enablers focus the technological capabilities on creating a compelling experience environment for consumers (as we discussed in chapter 4), knowledge catalysts focus the information infrastructure on creating a personally effective knowledge environment for managers.

Let us now look more closely at some of these premises, their requirements, and the organizational implications.

Catalyzing Tacit Knowledge Versus Managing Explicit Information

To clarify the distinction between knowledge and information, let's consider a museum that has received an extraordinary new collection, such as the Benny collection of Indian miniatures at the San Diego Museum of Art. This acquisition creates a special challenge in knowledge creation. Museum employees must identify, categorize, store, display, and otherwise process a collection of art that is unfamiliar to them. The art may arrive with basic information on provenance, value, and history. But the staff must facilitate a context, providing meaning and perspective to the collection. Only individuals can provide this contextual background. The individual's interpretation of the art is by definition personal, as the individual interacts with the available information and his own prior knowledge.

As this example illustrates, knowledge, by its very nature, is *tacit*. Despite the talk about "knowledge management," we argue that knowledge *cannot* be managed as such. It cannot be catalogued in databases or other repositories. Knowledge is inherent in the individual, and emerges at the intersection of the individual and a particular situational context.[5]

What *can* be managed is the explicit information that results from continuously generating knowledge in the context of specific problems. But change the problem, and the individual may be needed again for recontextualization, to generate the *new* knowledge that fits the new problem.

Creating Access to Competence for Knowledge Creation

Let's continue with the preceding museum example. A curator charged with designing a new exhibit must make many decisions, including which artworks to display, how to group them, how to identify and explain them through signs or catalogs, how to create the right ambience for visitors, and how to convey a point of view about the exhibit as a whole. Progressive museums that have embraced new display technologies have additional choices in creating immersive experiences.

What is crucial here is that museum personnel have access to competence *through individuals* not only from within the organization, but also from museums worldwide for creating new knowledge—particularly when the exhibit includes artifacts of a type that the museum is relatively unfamiliar with. Today the Internet is facilitating such global consultations among curators and experts. Now that collections can be made available online (including descriptions, images, research notes, and other supporting materials), curators can create virtual exhibits, generate and evaluate ideas, and gather comments and impressions from experts around the world (including art lovers)—all before opening the "real" exhibit in a physical gallery.[6]

Co-Constructing and Codifying Knowledge

As knowledge is created continuously, the information associated with a person's knowledge can be codified and made more explicit—for instance, by writing down the influence of enzymes in peroxide breakdown in paper slurry, as in the Buckman example.

Codifying tacit knowledge *into* explicit information is often challenging. For example, in planning a space shuttle mission, NASA must convert all the tacit knowledge held by the scientists in developing experiments for the mission into explicit information. The goals of the experiments must be made unambiguous. Every testing procedure and troubleshooting algorithm must be documented. Astronauts who are responsible for experiments must be trained. It often takes years to perfect the experiments and train multiple people to document all the related knowledge.

While the time, cost, and caliber of people needed for the NASA approach may make it inappropriate for general adoption, for most managers, the challenge is not to codify *all* tacit knowledge into explicit information, but to creatively balance the two. As with the notion of efficient experience innovation, discussed in chapter 4, we must learn to engage in efficient knowledge creation by focusing as much on innovating the knowledge environment as on gaining efficiencies through codification—thereby enabling individual employees to co-construct new knowledge in a particular context, and simultaneously codify the information to develop the new routines.

Harmonizing Multiple Streams of Knowledge

The convergence of industries and technologies is putting additional pressure on knowledge creation and the capacity to cope with tacit, human-embedded knowledge. The ability to harmonize multiple streams of knowledge becomes critical. For example, the personal-care products industry today must work with the pharmaceutical industry as creams, shampoos, and soaps take on pharmaceutical functions, such as products for wrinkle reduction (e.g., Retinol), hair growth (e.g., Rogaine), or healthy living (e.g., herbal supplements). Biotech increasingly needs large-scale computing, and the automotive industry realizes that a car is becoming a "computer on wheels" with remote communication capabilities.

From a knowledge creation standpoint, this means that *intellectual diversity* (e.g., managing chemical, software, and electronics engineers in a single team) is as great a management challenge as managing race, gender, and age diversity. Take microelectronics, for example. To reproduce circuit patterns on a silicon wafer, the wafer is typically coated with a thin film of an ultraviolet-sensitive polymer known as photoresist, using solvents such as glycol ethers that are harmful pollutants. The use of polymers that dissolve in liquid carbon dioxide can produce coatings that are both thin and harmless, reducing environmental risk. But the creation of such a polymer requires a technical understanding of how the lower surface tension and viscosity of liquid carbon dioxide enables it to spread thinly over the silicon wafer. That means not only harmonizing knowledge about surface tension and viscosity, but also getting multiple experts to collectively create new understanding.[7]

Further, as the solvents evaporate after they are spread, which is important to controlling film thickness, people doing experiments on the interface between liquid and gaseous carbon dioxide must be brought together, along with scientific theorists, to co-construct the new knowledge. Thus, we have to learn how to create access to individual competence, overcome the intellectual barriers that separate multiple technical disciplines, and manage intellectual diversity. These are the challenges in harmonizing multiple streams of knowledge.

Engaging the Total Organization

To be effective, a knowledge environment must engage the total organization, including multiple levels, functions, and geographies. Its social infrastructure must have no boundaries. The goal: the creation of thematic, task-oriented practice communities.

For a glimpse at engaging the total organization, let's return to Buckman Labs. Buckman Labs did not always have its current intense focus on customers. Prior to 1978, when Bob Buckman became chairman and CEO, it was centered on products. Its work force was replete with technical talent, most boasting doctoral degrees, who viewed their mandate as narrowly focused on the creation of new chemicals.

Furthermore, the firm's managerial structure was strictly hierarchical—in the words of Bob Buckman, a "command and control" approach. Realizing that this approach was slowing the company's response to market changes, in the early 1980s Buckman began to champion a focus on customers. The locus of innovation was still the product, but innovation would now be customer-driven. The company also began to recruit and train a large sales force.[8]

In the late eighties, Buckman Labs sensed that its strategic space was changing rapidly. Discontinuities like globalization of the customer base, deregulation in certain customer industries, and the existence of large emerging markets were creating global opportunities. But to be competitive in this expanded arena, the firm had to reinvent itself. Buckman Labs began sending their scientists to visit customer sites, gather best practices, and feed their insights back to R&D. But the process was slow and painful.

In the early nineties, Bob Buckman had an epiphany. For two weeks he was stuck in bed, having ruptured his back in an accident. He used this time of isolation to formulate a new corporate philosophy—one that put individual employees at the center of a knowledge-sharing environment, with customers at the top of the organization (conceived as an inverted pyramid). Buckman describes that moment of insight as a turning point in the company's history.

Buckman went on to list the qualities he sought in the new knowledge-sharing environment. It should

- be easy to use.

- be available twenty-four hours a day, seven days a week.

- permit people to talk to one another directly, with minimal distortion.

- give everyone access to the company's knowledge base.

- allow everyone to contribute knowledge to the system.

- allow communication in any language preferred by the user.

- continuously capture new knowledge from questions and answers in the system.

Buckman's vision implied a broad-based cultural transformation, turning the company upside down in terms of managerial control and inside out in terms of customer focus. Like the epiphany that led Bill Gates to bet Microsoft on the power of the Internet, Buckman's intent exemplified what strategy is all about: the *continuous search and discovery of new fundamental bases for competitive advantage*.

Note, too, that Buckman's experiment in knowledge sharing was launched pre-Internet. The lesson: Technology per se is only important insofar as it affects the ability of a manager or employee to get work done. More important than the technology of knowledge sharing is the social commitment that the company makes to the underlying concept and a corporate culture that supports it.

In early 1992, Buckman appointed Victor Baillargeon, an organic chemist in his mid-thirties, to create a rudimentary knowledge sharing system. Baillargeon had spent some time as Buckman's assistant researching theories of knowledge sharing. Starting with the notion of an easy-to-access, ubiquitous network that would work reliably with a single phone call, Baillargeon selected CompuServe as the technology platform, since it offered e-mail access to public network services and the ability to create private bulletin boards for internal use. These bulletin boards could serve as the basis for the "transparent forum" for knowledge transfer that Buckman sought. Each salesperson was given an IBM Thinkpad 720 with a modem. Baillargeon launched K'Netix with seven technical forums, and initially served as the interlocutor for the company's conversations.

In the beginning, it was rank-and-file Buckman employees who jump-started the process of knowledge sharing. After all, they had the most to gain. Every time a question was answered or a problem was solved via the network, the employee who had participated in it gained effectiveness and power.

As the virus of knowledge sharing spread, managers realized that they were being somewhat left out. They were losing control of the flow of information, and in some cases their employees were better informed than they were. Bob Buckman personally pushed the managers to accept the new regime. Rather than feel threatened, he urged them to shift their role toward being mentors of their employees. He also served as chief corporate cheerleader for knowledge sharing, compiling weekly statistics that detailed employee use of the network, and using this data to remind people to participate In 1994, he took the system's 150 most frequent users to a resort in Arizona for a special treat. The fact that the firm's "best knowledge sharers" were rewarded sparked further participation.

Buckman also made it clear that refusal to participate would damage careers. Employees, he said, were being paid to represent and serve their customers. The new K'Netix system made everyone's contributions transparent. Those who had something intelligent to say now had a forum in which to say it. Those who did not would soon become obvious. And the latter should understand that the company's best opportunities would no longer be available to them.

Obviously, Buckman Labs has had to spend money to create and support its knowledge environment. Is it possible to calculate the return on this investment? Bob Buckman practically dismissed this question. He considers the knowledge network to be the central nervous system of the company, and as such inseparable from its soul. He acknowledges that about 4 percent of company revenues were spent on the network. This spending produces some tangible benefits that can be quantified, such as improved speed of response to customer inquiries (down from as much as three weeks to six hours). Other benefits are harder to measure; for example, some customers say that Buckman's knowledge environment was a critical factor in selecting them as a supplier.

In the strictest sense, precisely measuring the benefits and total costs of the Buckman system is impossible. But, clearly, few of Buckman's employees, managers, customers, and suppliers who have experienced its power would want to return to operating without it.

Over time, the knowledge-sharing system at Buckman Labs has developed and evolved. Today, managers can create a technical conversation focused around the problems and needs of a particular customer— an unusual and important capability. The network also fosters internal dialogue by way of online discussions on issues such as compensation. To hold transparent debates about topics like these among company employees would not be possible without a culture in which implicit trust is strong—another indication of the importance of the social infrastructure in the creation of a powerful knowledge environment.

Co-Evolving the Knowledge Environment

With a knowledge environment in place, the challenge is to learn from it continuously, in order to nudge its evolution in the appropriate directions. You can probably tell that Bob Buckman was guided primarily by intuition in the early stages of developing his firm's knowledge environment. Buckman Labs' new CEO Steve Buckman and knowledge strategist Melissie Rumizen have been working on aligning its evolution with Buckman's overarching purpose and goals, as the company has grown.

K'Netix now combines e-mail, bulletin boards, virtual conference rooms, libraries, and electronic forums. Each forum uses a common structure, featuring "knowledge catalysts" to facilitate co-construction of new knowledge—for example, threaded conversations, as seen from the employee's perspective (similar to experience enablers from the consumer's perspective, discussed in chapter 4). The threaded discussions are indexed by topic, author, and date and contain questions, responses, and field observations. A forum specialist and subject experts take the lead in guiding discussions and assuring the integrity and quality of advice. Subject experts also serve as section leaders, answering requests and preparing weekly summaries. They extract the threads, edit, summarize, assign keywords, consolidate the insights, and organize, validate, and verify the information before transferring it to an evolving repository of interconnected "knowledge bases" supplemented by external information sources.

The knowledge bases have multiple forms, ranging from relatively loosely organized expertise possessed by knowledge workers to highly organized and more structured knowledge bases. The system is customer-centric, semistructured, and dynamic, yet flexible, interconnected, and continuously evolving. The evolution is both organic and guided. There is a rapid exchange of knowledge between individuals separated by time and space. The key is that the system enables individuals to bring their contexts of space and time while drawing on the collective knowledge and insights gleaned on a global basis. Buckman Labs also has regional forums that continue to evolve as they build local language capabilities (including European, Latin American, and Asian languages).

Thus, thanks to the evolving K'Netix, Buckman employees have unfettered access to competence, experience, and resources from over a hundred countries around the world. Frontline employees can serve customers while specialized groups capture and codify useful knowledge. Buckman's IT group maintains the technical infrastructure, while the social infrastructure is maintained by personnel from the knowledge sharing group, associates, product development managers, research librarians, and many others.

What we like here is the equal support for both frontline and IT employees. Too often, initiatives are user-hostile and counterintuitive, making it hard for employees to interact with the system. The knowledge environment is not about the technology per se, but is a process that's woven into the cultural fabric of the organization. Both the social and technical aspects of the information infrastructure are critical to building an effective knowledge environment.

The knowledge-sharing culture has become deeply embedded at Buckman. Increasingly, its capacity for *new knowledge creation* will become widespread as well. Both are now part of the pulse of the organization. Everyone is expected to read the forums on a regular basis and become contributors to the process. Compliance becomes the norm, rather than the exception. The Buckman example suggests that collaborative, peer-to-peer, co-construction of knowledge can unlock imagination and ideas on a scale and scope as never before. It breaks the tendency for expertise to be self-designated.

In a sense, new knowledge creation is the death of "experts," but not of expertise. As the Buckman example shows, employees have skills and capabilities that cannot be captured in vitae and databases. To tap those hidden resources, we need knowledge environments that facilitate transparent dialogue and enable thematic communities to flourish.

Enabling a Global Knowledge Environment: The BP Example

We chose the Buckman example to illustrate the concept of a well-knit knowledge environment oriented around the interactions between employees and customers, and the power of tapping into the tacit knowledge of the total organization. But can this process work in a typical large multinational corporation? We believe it can, provided we build the requisite infrastructure to enable a global knowledge environment around individual managers as well as the interactions between managers and the experience network.

To illustrate, consider British Petroleum (BP), a large, global organization with a knowledge and expertise directory called Connect. BP has systematized the process by which individuals can create their own Web pages and links to others. The result is a corporate "yellow pages" of knowledge workers and the subnetworks they are associated with—for example, the drilling learning network, the refinery operations managers network, the green operations network, and the engineering authorities' network. It started with technical staff and has evolved to include over 20,000 knowledge workers and more than 250 subnetworks. What's important, however, is not the particular tools of implementation, but the fact that it is *centered around individuals as knowledge workers.* Thus, as one manager suggests, Connect can help answer a question like, "Who knows about deep water drilling, speaks fluent Russian, and is currently in southwest London?"[9]

Now consider an event like drilling a deep water-well in a precise location and time. Such events cut across projects and require the participation of individuals with specific expertise. At BP there are tools such as "Peer Assist" that enable managers to learn *before* doing. Peer Assist enables a project team to address a specific challenge by acquiring knowledge from outside the team, identifying possible approaches and new lines of inquiry, and promoting the sharing of knowledge with each other. These tools are an example of knowledge catalysts that facilitate selective access to competence.

There are other tools that facilitate "learning *in* doing." This includes the "after action review," a U.S. Army technique that involves asking probing questions after any important event: What was supposed to happen? What did happen? Is there a difference? Are there any anomalies? What can we learn from these anomalies? Imagine the power of managerial access to the answers to such questions, ideally in real time.

As we discussed in chapter 9, managers must be able to aggregate and disaggregate events with ease, providing the desired level of granularity. They also must be able to examine linkages between events (for example, via correlations of incidents). The important point here is that *the manager sets the context* for examining these linkages. Is there a pattern? Is there any commonality to the discrepancy? The goal is to formulate and test hypotheses quickly in the context of the business situation. The concept of a knowledge environment implies that we must recognize a triggering event, and the same event can evoke different responses in managers. How one manager wants to approach, visualize, examine, and re-construct events, generate hypotheses, make choices, and initiate appropriate courses of action will be different from another colleague's approach.

The knowledge environment is also where *the manager, as consumer, interacts with the experience network* to co-create value. As with the consumer co-creation experience, the managerial involvement with multiple channels required for project implementation, evaluation of price-experience relationships (e.g., in stitching together a portfolio of services for a project), and the transaction experience (e.g., with contractors), all condition the ability for managers to co-create value effectively.

The knowledge environment must embody the DART building blocks for value co-creation. For example, each BP network has a performance contract (including a budget) between the network and a senior leader who acts as a sponsor and advisor. The network is open to employees and contractors, including engineers, scientists, and technicians. All of the subnetworks are transparent, and every knowledge worker can use Connect. There are huge gains in on-site productivity when offsite engineers can access drilling and seismic data.

Transparency also allows knowledge to be created on the fly during a project, and for participants to engage in an internal dialogue. For instance, BP created its Highly Immersive Visualization Environment (HIVE), built around fifteen highly sophisticated 3-D-imaging rooms where decisions on whether to drill at a particular site can now be made in hours instead of weeks. In this environment, geoscientists and engineers can engage in a dialogue around a common "virtual" site. In one instance, this dialogue enabled BP to recognize that eighteen rather than twenty wells could suffice, saving $60 million. When they included facilities engineers in the dialogue, another $30 million was trimmed from the cost of the surface facility. The individuals involved could also engage in risk assessment—for instance, certain routes were less hazardous and more cost effective within this particular deepwater environment. In all, the geologists, geophysicists, reservoir engineers, pipeline engineers, and drilling and facilities engineers reduced the total project costs by as much as 10 percent.[10]

What is interesting here is that the infrastructure and the DART building blocks help integrate the existing set of informal organizational networks and associated latent expertise in an explicit, transparent manner. Thus, knowledge and value are co-created more rapidly and efficiently.

In the new competitive space (recall figure 8-2), the broad challenge for organizations is to scale the locus of the knowledge environment to collaborate across the enhanced competence base (including consumers), while simultaneously orienting the creation of new knowledge around consumer-company interactions.

In the next chapter we will focus on the specific challenge of collaborating to co-create value in the new competitive space. But first, we must consider the following question: If knowledge environments are so critical for co-creating value, why is creating them not a higher priority? In other words, what are the impediments to creating knowledge environments, especially within a large organization?

Impediments to Creating a Knowledge Environment

In most corporations, there are many social and technical impediments to creating a seamless knowledge environment, of which the history of the organization is often the single most important.

Consider, for example, the difficulty of forging international links in large global organizations like General Motors and Ford. For over seventy-five years, the Ford and GM units in Europe and North America have led independent lives. Self-sufficient and resource rich, they grew in response to regional market opportunities and problems. Managers saw their careers as regional and were loyal to the regional organization. In this context, global strategy is hard to come by. Seventy-five years of extreme decentralization (coupled with geographic separation) have created a genetic code that is hard to change.

In other cases, constant merger and acquisition activities lead to multiple subcultures within the corporation. The acquired firms want to protect their cultures and resist sharing information across their borders. Unless a clear and concerted effort is made to create a shared culture, attempts to create a seamless knowledge environment are likely to be thwarted.

In still other cases, the problem is the lack of a technical infrastructure enabling managers to access and share information and expertise. Lower-level managers often have no way to break out of the silos in which they are trapped. Poor infrastructure for communication reinforces the walls of organizational separation.

We could add to the litany of problems, but every established organization will have its unique impediments. Top managers must hunt down these impediments and eliminate them one at a time, as in the Buckman example. And in a large, well-established, multinational firm, this must be done globally, as in the BP example.

The Challenge to Management

To discuss the challenge to management in creating effective knowledge and managerial environments, let us return to the BP example. BP is organized in a flat, decentralized structure. Each of its more than 120 business units is led by a general manager who signs an annual performance contract that sets out specific financial, environmental, and other results-oriented goals. These general managers work directly with a small group of operating executives who oversee the corporate portfolio with the CEO. In 1997, when project director Kent Greenes launched the virtual network for sharing knowledge across all the BP business units, BP had come to realize that a global corporation was not just about units dispersed in a geographic fashion. In effect, it had to reconceive itself as a portfolio of competencies.[11]

Note that BP and Buckman Labs both feature flat, decentralized organizational structures. As noted by BP's then-CEO John Browne, the de-layering of the organization was critical for BP, as it opened up an implicit impetus for lateral communication, as opposed to communication up and down a hierarchical ladder.

Oil exploration is an expensive, capital-intensive business; it takes billions of dollars to locate and develop a large oil field. Thus, the pressures to be efficient and accelerate project completion are enormous. BP used an intranet to connect managers in the various business units with one another, enabling them to share questions and information just as Buckman employees do. Thus, when a BP geologist working off the coast of Norway devised a more efficient way to find oil by changing the position of drill heads, he posted information on the new process on the intranet. Within a day, a BP engineer working on a well in Trinidad saw the posting, requested details via e-mail, and ultimately adapted the same technique to save five days of drilling and about $600,000. In this example, knowledge sharing led to savings through increased operational efficiency. In other cases, capital efficiency has been improved—for example, through improved project selection and investment allocation. In one project in the Gulf of Mexico, BP saved $45 million.[12]

Now, suppose BP wants to tap expertise from various sources both inside and *outside* the company in evaluating a new major offshore site. This event requires the creation of a robust, high-bandwidth, intensive, scalable network infrastructure specifically for the project. (Call it *infrastructure on demand*.) The convergence of telecoms, IT, managed applications services, and, more recently, Web services is allowing companies to create virtual collaborative communications networks that can scale on demand.

We can see the impact of such a technical, networked infrastructure on BP's knowledge sharing. But even more crucial is the social infrastructure. Chris Collison, BP's then Knowledge Architect, puts it very well: "The best medium for knowledge is the human brain, and the best networking protocol is conversation." In a company the size of BP, Chris says, there's a potential for millions of ten-minute conversations. Thus the emphasis of the IT infrastructure is on generating connections, so as to uncover "new ways to access BP's most valuable reservoir—one million person-years of experience."[13]

In addition to facilitating connections, the infrastructure must provide a common language, processes, and protocols for knowledge sharing. This may require the development of *hybrid knowledge* that cuts across intellectual divides. How do you get people who are trained as software engineers to work with chemical engineers? How do you get mathematicians to work in a bank? Joint development often requires harmonizing multiple intellectual disciplines. BP tackles this challenge by organizing around large site-specific projects, leveraging project expertise across oil and gas exploration or across refining and marketing.

Building the Infrastructure for a Knowledge Environment

We are now in a position to outline the key conceptual building blocks for creating an effective and powerful knowledge environment. First, here are some key insights that companies must internalize when seeking to create the *social* infrastructure for knowledge co-creation (you can add your own insights to the list):

- Individuals are at the heart of the process. Thus, the starting point must be respect for individuals and their uniqueness.

- Meritocracy must rule—not hierarchy. The focus must be on discovering and mobilizing expertise, regardless of job descriptions or titles.

- Knowledge must be organized around communities of practice, not administrative or organizational silos.

- Companies must use a "Velcro system" of management—painless and continual combining and disengaging of talent based on tasks and skills. Rigid structures must not impede access to competence from various organizational units.

- Contributions must be recognized across organizational boundaries—both vertical and horizontal.

- The DART building blocks—dialogue, access, risk assessment, and transparency—must serve as the basis of knowledge co-creation among employees/managers and the entire competence base, including customers.

Then, to create the *technical* infrastructure:

- Information from multiple, heterogeneous, and legacy databases—all parts of established firms—must be readily and seamlessly available.

- Multiple data types—audio, video, images, text, statistics—must also be available in a seamless fashion.

- Navigation must be easy enough that busy line managers can explore databases themselves rather than delegate the task to analysts.

- The data interface must be easy and intuitive.

- The infrastructure must facilitate not just hypothesis testing but also hypothesis generation.

- The infrastructure must facilitate the sharing of information from multiple sources, and nurture and protect knowledge threads that connect managers.

- It must be possible to revisit data, add new information, and continuously generate new insights.

We now describe seven necessary foundational layers for the knowledge environment infrastructure, as shown in figure 10-2. Let's examine them in turn.

FIGURE 10 - 2

The Seven Layers of a Knowledge Environment

Layer 7:	Co-creating value Creating next practices
Layer 6:	Facilitating discovery Incorporating diverse insights
Layer 5:	Mobilizing action teams Creating new initiatives
Layer 4:	Leveraging sources of competence Ease of access, visibility, and dialogue
Layer 3:	Using information Extracting contextual knowledge
Layer 2:	Information sharing Knowing best practices within the firm
Layer 1:	Training and development Building the skill base

Layer 1: Training and Development

Strategic transformation must start with providing new skills and new perspectives to the total organization. Many companies recognize this need, but shy away from providing adequate training and teaching because they find traditional classroom-based approaches too expensive and time-consuming. Fortunately, new Internet-based technologies can make training the whole organization quick and affordable.

Knowledge that emerges from Buckman-style forums can also be used for training purposes. Imagine posing real-world problems in such forums and allowing employees to discuss the problems among themselves and with mentors. Breakout sessions among participants could tap into the community of practice within the company. Through such a program, a community of practice can be transformed into a learning community.

Layer 2: Information Sharing

Crystallizing organizational know-how into "know-why"—that is, a theory of *why* the best practices work—takes time. Managers must share this "know-why." Thus, effective information sharing goes beyond capturing and indexing information to include synthesis of the underlying concepts.

Layer 3: Using Information

Knowing best practices does not automatically translate into an ability to act. Managers must also be able to extract contextual knowledge so that best practices can be "recontextualized" as necessary. McDonald's must understand that "beef extract" is unacceptable in India. Disney must know that the French have a different view of work culture. Even within a country, the competitive context could be different across businesses. For example, in India, shampoo is sold in a single serve package—a sachet—for consumers at the lower end of the economic spectrum. This very popular packaging format makes shampoo affordable to the poor. However, for the same consumers, a single serve package in a sachet may be inappropriate for certain indigenous cooking oils. In other words, there should be mechanisms for gaining and sharing deep local knowledge as well as broader best-practice concepts.

Layer 4: Leveraging Sources of Competence

The system must encourage managers at various levels to access knowledge—not only explicit information (text, audio, video files) but also tacit knowledge (embedded in people). How does General Motors know what it knows? Further, how does GM know what it does *not* know, but what its enhanced network knows? More specifically, how does a GM engineer in Michigan get access to the transmission expertise of a Fiat engineer in Milan or a Daewoo engineer in South Korea? An effective knowledge environment creates systems that provide such access, as in the BP example.

The visibility of talent is also critical. The backgrounds, interests, and accomplishments of people must be accessible to the relevant practice communities. Thus, all of GM's transmission engineers around the world ought to know one another and view themselves collectively as a practice community engaged in active dialogue.

Layer 5: Mobilizing Action Teams

Carefully selected projects and initiatives can become carriers of learning within the firm, and even forces for the ultimate transformation of the business. But selecting and mobilizing the members of an action team requires extensive knowledge about the talent pool available, project priorities, and personal traits.

Managers must also control experimental projects with rigor and self-discipline. Too often companies waste valuable resources on pilot projects, supporting unproductive initiatives too long while underfunding the most promising ones. James McNerney, the CEO of 3M, launched a new approach in this area, built around the use of a database that tracks R&D spending in great detail. The database facilitates continuous debate about which opportunities deserve continued (or expanded) support and which should be killed.

Intel is experimenting with another interesting approach, spending part of its $4 billion R&D budget to support a series of twenty- to thirty-person "lablets" adjacent to top universities that are focused on promising embryonic technology.[14] In a similar vein, IBM's new Emerging Business Group plans to offer startup firms access to IBM's extensive IT research, to encourage them to build new technologies on top of IBM's software and services platforms. In both cases, there is huge potential for two-way knowledge sharing and learning.

Layer 6: Facilitating Discovery

While action teams can create multiple projects, the broad perspective of the emerging competitive space requires a methodology for incorporating diverse sets of inputs (including customer reactions) into low-cost action projects, as we saw in the BP example earlier in this chapter. New insights can arise from an active dialogue with customers.

Layer 7: Co-Creating Value

The firm that engages in true value co-creation goes beyond the creation of action teams or the development of insights, to a consistent set of actions that are based on a new consensus about how to compete. Besides consumer-company interactions, it must focus on interactions among employees and between the manager and the experience network. The company must recognize the heterogeneity of these interactions. The good news is that a variety of contextual knowledge, across domains, can be generated. However, implicit norms and protocols must be established to control process variation in how the information is codified to develop the new routines. In other words, we must think about total EQM (Experience Quality Management) based on the quality of managerial/employee interactions with the knowledge environment, in addition to the quality of consumer interactions with the experience environment (the EQM approach discussed in chapter 6). In other words, we must pay as much attention to building the infrastructure to support the managerial side of co-creation of value, as the consumer side.

At the highest level, the process of value co-creation includes the development of strategy itself. Strategy as a process of discovery is the subject of the next chapter.

Chapter Eleven

STRATEGY AS DISCOVERY

A LTHOUGH the co-creation of value paradigm implies a different view of strategy, we have so far chosen not to focus on the strategy-making process and the meaning of strategy. However, now that we have discussed the criticality of line managers and the need to build a manager-centric environment for rapid knowledge creation, we can outline the new strategy framework.

The traditional view of strategy is that firms can shape industry evolution and customer expectations more or less autonomously, subject only to the actions of competitors. The new paradigm recognizes that industry evolution is influenced by the actions of consumers and consumer communities as well. As we saw in the Lego, Napster, and other examples, consumer communities can have a significant influence on strategy options. So can the firms that jointly constitute the experience network.

In the world of co-creation, while a firm's strategic direction (or strategic intent) may be obvious, strategy is a process of continuous experimentation, risk reduction, time compression, and minimizing investment while maximizing market impact. Strategy must be a process of innovation and discovery. No single firm can unilaterally do all the above.

The good news is that this process of discovery allows us to be more creative—but only if we are willing to challenge many of the traditional assumptions about strategy.

The Changing View of Resources

The most basic task of a strategist is to recognize opportunities and allocate resources. Traditionally, assessing the resources available within the firm and creating a fit between resources and goals was the starting point of strategy analysis. This began to change during the early 1990s, with the concept of "strategy as stretch." Rather than seeking a strategic fit between the company's goals and its resources, the idea was to capture the essence of entrepreneurship by emulating the model of a start-up, deliberately creating a misfit between resources and aspirations. This was to be accomplished not by reducing resources, but by raising aspirations. The need to leverage resources, including accumulated intellectual capital—core competencies—was a logical extension of the concept of strategy as stretch. The approach to strategy development, as a result, changed in many firms.

In the mid 1990s, resources available through others, such as joint venture partners and suppliers, began to enter the debate among leading strategists. The goal was now to gain a disproportionate advantage by accessing resources available to the firm from the supplier and partner network.

Co-creation of value pushes the perspective on resources further. Why should the resources available to managers be limited to what is available within the firm and its supplier network? Why not access the knowledge base of the consumer communities as well? Organizing to access resources from the extended network (suppliers, partners, and consumer communities)—including competencies, knowledge, infrastructure, and investment capacity—can significantly expand the notion of available resources.

Thus, a focus on control and ownership of resources is giving way to the importance of *accessing and leveraging resources* through unique methodologies for collaborating with customers and suppliers. As we saw in chapter 6, Li & Fung may not own any of the nodes (suppliers) in its extended network, but it influences resource allocation within that network. The goal of the nodal company is not to own resources but to influence how resources are allocated by providing intellectual leadership for the entire network.

The co-creation process also challenges the assumption that only the firm's aspirations matter. As we have seen, every participant in the experience network collaborates in value creation—and competes in value extraction. This results in constant tension in the strategy development process, especially when the various units and individuals in the network must collectively execute that strategy. The key issue is this: How much transparency is needed for effective collaboration for value co-creation versus active competition for co-extracting economic value? The balancing act between collaborating and competing is delicate—and crucial.

Collaboration and Strategy

Without active collaboration to co-create value, the experience network will obviously collapse. But collaboration is not easy or natural for most managers. Therefore, strategists must understand the dynamics of collaboration—its advantages and limits.

First, what *is* collaboration? Despite the widespread use of the term, its definition is often unclear. Collaboration is used to refer to many types of joint activities, from periodic information sharing to complex, multiyear development and marketing projects. The examples cited in this book represent a wide variation in collaborative activities, from Intuit to Archipelago, from DoCoMo to Zara, from Li & Fung to Microsoft.

Nonetheless, there appears to be general agreement that collaboration is inherently necessary and good. More to the point, firms cannot co-create value without an active collaboration agenda. But to develop such an agenda, managers must be able to answer five key questions.

1. Why collaborate? What competitive demands make collaboration necessary?

2. What does it take to succeed in collaboration?

3. How do collaborative modes differ in method and purpose?

4. What are the costs and benefits of collaboration? Who bears the costs? Who enjoys the benefits?

5. What kind of information infrastructures do complex collaborative arrangements require?

Let us begin by addressing the *why* of collaboration. There are several important business issues whose successful resolution in today's environment demands collaboration.

Improved Cycle Time and Cost Reduction

Succeeding in the new competitive space requires both speedier managerial reactions and higher levels of efficiency. Collaboration can help companies achieve both. For example, working with suppliers in a transparent environment can reduce frictional losses in the system, as information becomes a substitute for investments in inventory.

Achieving Scale and Scope

In many large, diversified firms, autonomous business units underleverage the size and scope of their operations. Should the separate divisions of General Motors have a common development platform? If they don't, how great is the waste of resources due to redundancy in development? Should financial institutions provide a common statement of accounts to customers who have a credit card, savings account, checking account, mortgage, auto loan, and life insurance with the same institution? If they don't, how many opportunities for streamlined service (as well as cross-marketing) will be lost? Collaboration both within the diversified firm (across business units) and with outside companies can provide the leverage needed to reduce these kinds of losses.

Access to Knowledge

When industry boundaries and technological boundaries morph, as is happening in digital imaging, gene therapy, and many other fields today, managers must learn to harmonize old and new knowledge. A traditional cosmetics firm that suddenly needs expertise in areas like genetics and biochemistry that are not part of its integral skill base can get access to knowledge through collaborative arrangements.

Investment Leverage

The resources—talent and capital—required to compete in some fields may be greater than those available to a single firm. Combining talent and capital provided by two or more collaborating firms can multiply the power of those investments beyond what any single company could achieve.

Method for Change

A traditional firm can find in a collaborative partner a role model for change and a method for infusing a new culture. For example, managers at a large, established firm can absorb lessons of agility and speed through collaboration with a smaller firm.

Partitioning Risk

The best approach to a new competitive space is often difficult to discern. Multiple experiments may be needed before the market opportunity is obvious. Partitioning risk by accessing knowledge from others at low cost may allow for multiple experiments.

DESPITE the many good reasons to collaborate, most organizations fail to take full advantage of their opportunities to do so. Why?

The fundamental reason is that collaboration is *not* natural. Exercising autonomy is. Collaboration requires two or more units (within or outside the firm) to work together. In most cases, the frictional costs outweigh the obvious benefits. These costs include managerial time and effort, issues such as cross charges and transfer prices, concerns about priorities and deliveries, incompatibility of IT systems and strategies, and other administrative headaches. These costs of collaboration are immediate, while the benefits at best represent the potential.

Furthermore, the difficulties are accentuated by the common practice of linking compensation to short-term unit performance. Thus the natural tendency of managers to feather their own nests is further reinforced. While collaboration may in the long run improve efficiencies and increase profits, in the short run such gains are often elusive.

It takes a clear, strong demand for collaboration to overcome these obstacles. For example, when Wal-Mart is dealing with a large supplier like 3M, it wants a single contact point. This requirement provided the necessary motivation for 3M to reconfigure its resources and processes to form a common account management team based on collaboration among many 3M divisions. Strong leadership from top management, coupled with performance incentives, can also increase the level of internal collaboration, as General Electric, for instance, has demonstrated over the years.

Collaboration as Co-Creation

Various modes of collaboration, distinguished by different levels of intensity and prerequisites, can be articulated as shown in figure 11-1.

FIGURE 11 - 1

Collaboration as Co-Creation of Value

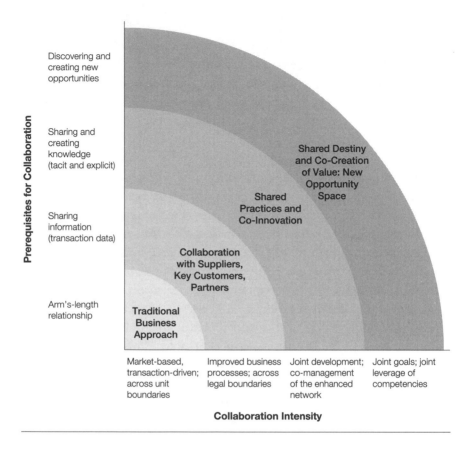

Market-based, transaction-driven; across unit boundaries — Improved business processes; across legal boundaries — Joint development; co-management of the enhanced network — Joint goals; joint leverage of competencies

Collaboration Intensity

This taxonomy allows us to assess the forms of collaboration needed to co-create value in the emerging competitive space.[1]

Beginning with traditional arm's-length, market-based transactions, most firms have learned the benefits of working closely with suppliers and key customers in a network. Such collaboration improves costs and response times, increases sales and marketing opportunities, and can enhance customer satisfaction. However, reaping the full benefits of this level of collaboration requires information sharing. And while firms may willingly share order management information, aggregated sales and marketing data, and sales forecasts, they are often reluctant to share individual customer data, cost structures by product or service line, and financial and resource allocation data. The greater level of information sharing requires a greater level of trust as well as special incentives, which are more likely to exist as firms move beyond improved business processes toward shared work and co-development.

Most current discussion of the value of collaboration focuses on multiparty business processes in which both the tasks and the modalities of collaboration are clear. As we move up the collaboration intensity continuum, the tasks and modalities become more complex—but the ability to co-create value also increases. For instance, as a firm moves toward co-development, both within the firm and with other firms, the management of shared tasks, joint goals, and resource leverage becomes increasingly complex, leading to debates about ownership of intellectual property, risk/reward trade-offs, and responsibility for deliverables.

To assess their collaborative capacities, firms must critically evaluate their experiences with different modes of collaboration and identify needed improvements in both the technical and social infrastructures. In-depth case studies of collaboration and co-creation experiences are an excellent way to do this. Note that appropriate improvements in the technical infrastructure can facilitate improvements in the social infrastructure.

Our review of the varying modalities of collaboration yields several basic conclusions:

- The sharing of clearly defined business processes across multiple businesses is the simplest and most basic form of collaboration— but it generates only a small portion of the potential for value creation that collaboration can offer.

- The collaborative capacities of a management team will vary as the intensity of collaboration changes.

- Firms need a variety of collaborative modes to satisfy their multiple needs in the emerging competitive space.

- Significant changes in technical and social infrastructures are required to co-create and co-extract value in different collaborative modes.

The Risks and Costs of Collaboration

Needless to say, the risks and costs of collaboration are just as real as the benefits. Here are a handful of key questions managers must debate in order to better assess and manage the inherent risks.

What Information Should Be Shared?

As we have noted, many companies that are willing to collaborate in creating a supplier network believe they must be wary of sharing too much information. One reason is the fear that competitors will somehow get their hands on this information. The typical reaction is to construct "Chinese walls" designed to prevent such leakage. But before launching such a leakage-control effort, consider: What is the real likelihood that information will be revealed to competitors? How can we balance the risks associated with disclosure of critical information with the benefits gained from operating in a totally transparent environment? On the other hand, will information leak anyway in a networked society? Should we even attempt to control it? Consider that a good strategy in the emerging co-creation view is no secret, if viewed as the ability to discover and de-risk the "next" practices.

Supply Chain Volatility—Who Pays the Price?

Increasing volatility in the demand for products and services is exerting new pressures on supplier networks. As a supplier, should I incorporate my own corrections to the forecasts supplied by the nodal player? If I do—or even if I don't—who will pay the price for the resulting costs of over- or under-supply? Although information transfer may be instantaneous, the capacity to react and to control inventory levels, given a complex set of product configurations, may not be. One way to deal with this problem is to co-locate operations, thereby reducing logistical difficulties and costs. But this raises new questions about the vulnerability of relationships in a global supply chain.

Who Extracts the Value from the New Efficiencies?

The fact that global supply chains increase systemwide efficiency is obvious. In many cases, the nodal company—the GM, GE, or Dell—is in a position to extract a disproportionate amount of the incremental value created. Does the risk/return profile look equally attractive to members of the supply chain, especially during a business downturn? How can arrangements be structured so that every participant in the network has a fair opportunity to benefit from the new value it helps create?

Who Bears the Burden of Learning Multiple Systems?

Most suppliers who are part of multiple supply chains must conform to the IT system requirements of several nodal players. Even within a single large nodal firm, like GM, various divisions may have different IT platforms, placing yet more demands on suppliers. How does a supplier manage the costs of operating multiple systems? Must we create industrywide standards or an open systems approach to reduce the costs for smaller participants in the supply chain?

Who Owns Intellectual Property That Is Co-Created Through Collaboration?

As we move to joint product/service development efforts between companies, the issue of ownership of intellectual property can become quite troublesome. Each collaborative interaction creates its own dynamic, usually involving tacit critical knowledge. How does one measure and reward an individual firm's contribution to the jointly developed knowledge? Even within a single firm, debates about cross charges and transfer prices can slow collaboration across units; the complexity and intensity of these debates is multiplied when numerous separate legal entities are involved.

Who Bears the Costs of Creating IT Capabilities?

Most established firms have multiple legacy IT systems. When entering a new collaborative phase, such firms often undertake costly, time-consuming "data purification" projects. These programs may be a necessary part of building the infrastructure for collaboration. But they tend to be poorly conceived and planned, since managers rarely have a clear and accurate sense of how their current systems are working. How should the huge costs of developing and executing such projects be shared?

Building the New Capacity to Collaborate and Compete

As we move up the value co-creation continuum, building the capacity to collaborate is, in essence, creating the capacity to compete—itself a more important dimension of strategy than any specific competitive move. As we have seen, co-creation requires constant adjustments and adaptation to the evolving dynamics among consumers, suppliers, and companies. Since managers cannot predict or control specific experiences, they can only create an experience environment. The capacity to co-create and co-extract value, therefore, is a measure of strategy. It should include at least the following basic elements:

- *The ability to provide a compelling view of the opportunity, so that the firm can be the nodal firm.* The nodal firm must provide an intellectual agenda that will make other firms want to be part of the system. Thus, intellectual leadership is a prerequisite for building access to the competence base and investment capacity of the network.

- *An infrastructure that spans the network and can selectively activate any combination of firms.* Firms may move from a passive to an active state at any time, depending on the co-creation status of specific consumers. Thus, a critical managerial task is maintaining active connections even with companies that are not continually active players. The ability to selectively activate competence on demand becomes essential.

- *An information infrastructure within the experience network that is transparent and operates in real time.* Contextual information access is critical for quick response and zero latency.

- *A managerial mind-set and skill set that enables participants to access competence and build consensus rapidly within the experience network.* The knowledge environment must allow for "actionable insights," facilitating rapid experimentation, debriefing, consolidating, scaling, and moving forward.

A measure of the capacity to compete is continuous innovation. This doesn't necessarily mean major breakthroughs. Instead, it may mean a wide variety of small changes, adaptations, and fresh nuances that co-create new value for consumers. This ongoing change in the field will not only reveal new opportunities but also create a continuous and evolving instability in the marketplace.

We consider this instability a *good* thing—contrary to the assumptions of traditional strategists.[2] They generally crave steady states and well-known games, which are easy to understand, describe, and support with resources. But as F. A. von Hayek suggested over four decades ago, competition is about destabilizing industry structures.[3] And an evolving game will always be full of surprises. When resource availability, capacity for leverage, and the value creation process are all in flux, strategy is an exercise in *continuous adaptation.* Speed of reaction time, therefore, is a critical strategic tool.

Under the circumstances, a manager may wonder, "If we are constantly adjusting and adapting, what does strategy mean? Aren't we supposed to know where we are going?"

Yes, management must have a point of view and a clear sense of direction. But within that broad framework, continuous smaller adjustments are necessary. It's like starting a cross-country drive from Omaha, Nebraska, by saying, "We are driving north to Toronto, not south to Miami." But on any single day of driving, we will adjust our speed, stop for food and fuel, detour around traffic jams or road repairs, and perhaps make an unexpected side trip to visit an enticing local attraction.

Of course, without a clear idea of where we are going—north to Toronto—such adjustments would make no sense. We need a long-term goal—a clear and well-articulated point of view that serves as the anchor around which continuous adjustments and adaptations can be made. Effective strategy encompasses both.

The Critical Role of Management in Co-Creating Value

In the emerging co-creation environment, the role of top management is very critical. A company's leadership must

- invest in developing the capacity to compete on experiences.
- develop and articulate a clear point of view about the future.
- reinforce the mind-set and skill set of managers.
- foster internal collaboration.
- support and nurture the knowledge environment.

However, the co-creation of value is impossible without the active involvement of line managers at all levels. Understanding the roles of all members of the experience network, and acting in real time in response to the changing demands of co-creators is the role of line managers. They must

- have a deep understanding of the broad direction, or strategic intent, of the company.
- understand the relationship between their specific jobs and the company's strategic intent.
- continually monitor the experiences of customers, suppliers, employees, and all other participants in the co-creation network.
- continually adjust their actions as demanded by changes in the environment.

The frontline manager is the driver who will take our car to Toronto. In fact, every employee who interacts with customers—from the call center operator to the service mechanic, from the sales representative to the logistics manager, from the billing clerk to the product developer—has the same responsibility: to facilitate a compelling co-creation experience for the customer. *Co-creation energizes the whole organization.* Therefore, strategy is the capacity to engage the whole organization— to ensure that every member of the organization shares in a common vision, while having the ability to act in a decentralized and autonomous fashion in real time.

Co-Creation and the New View of Strategy

We summarize the differences between the traditional approach to strategy and the emerging approach in table 11-1.

TABLE 11 - 1

The Transformation of Strategy

	Traditional Firm-Centric View	New Co-Creation View
Goal of Strategy	Positioning a firm in a given industry space	Discovering new sources of value and new opportunities
View of Resources	Fixed; firm-centered	Expandable; available on demand; centered on enhanced network
Critical Resources	Financial and physical assets	Talent, knowledge in the network, infrastructure for dialogue in the enhanced network
Industry Perspective	Search for stability and equilibrium	Coping with instability and disequilibrium
Responsibility for Strategy	Top management	Organization-wide; critical role for line managers
Strategy Development	Analytical	Analytical and organizational
Top Management Role	Resource allocation	Access to competence; resource leverage, and allocation
Time Perspective	Long-term	Long-term and short-term
Execution	Dichotomy between strategy formulation and implementation	Continuous discovery, active learning and adaptation, within broad long-term direction (strategic intent)

In the new strategy framework, the distinction between strategy formulation and implementation disappears. There is no handoff between thinking and acting. Management is no longer like conducting the performance of a fixed musical score by an orchestra; instead, it's more like a jazz improvisation (as our esteemed colleague Karl Weick puts it).[4]

The changing view of strategy and value creation demands a new capacity to govern and compete. We must reexamine every functional skill in the organization and ask: Are the assumptions behind this function and its management consistent with the requirements of a co-creation view of strategy, and a focus on co-creation experiences as the basis for value? What new capabilities does the organization need? This process of self-examination and the functional, infrastructure, and governance capabilities required for co-creating value is the topic of our concluding chapter.

Chapter Twelve

BUILDING NEW CAPABILITIES
FOR THE FUTURE

W E STARTED THIS BOOK by outlining the challenges to the traditional thinking about value creation. As the co-creation paradigm gains momentum, practically every traditional function within the firm will change. Every manager must make a bigger commitment to learning—and perhaps equally important, to selectively forgetting some of the old assumptions that underlie traditional business practices.

The examples in this book illustrate many of the ways in which the key business functions are already evolving and were chosen to help you see, think, and plan differently. But you must *act* differently as well. This chapter enumerates the key functional transitions that businesses will face. Only you as a manager know how your company's idiosyncrasies will inhibit its ability to transform. So we suggest that you use this chapter as the basis for developing your managerial agenda.

Product Design and Development

In the traditional value chain, companies use product variety to help cope with a heterogeneous consumer base. The game is a specifications war focusing on quality, fit, finish, or features. In the new value co-creation space, the basis for product development changes dramatically; the challenge shifts from meeting a different set of specs to developing unique ways to co-create value with consumers.

This challenge is tough, especially because overcoming company think is hard. The trained professional, socialized as an engineer, production manager, accountant, business analyst, or service representative, does not readily think and feel as a consumer would. Only by experiencing the business as consumers do, and gaining a deep understanding through the lens of consumer experience, can managers and employees truly resonate with and share the consumer's dreams, desires, and aspirations.

Experience Design

Think of the product as an artifact around which consumers have experiences. Or as an evolving interface between two equal problem solvers, the consumer and the firm. Product design must incorporate the problem-solving skills and behaviors of *both* sides to facilitate the co-construction of an individualized experience. It opens up or forecloses future capabilities, and introduces or eliminates constraints on both the consumer and the firm. Therefore, engaging the product development team in exploring how consumer experiences evolve can profoundly affect product and service design.

Consider the Vietnam Veterans Memorial in the Mall in Washington, D.C. Architect Maya Lin decided to list the names of the American soldiers chronologically. Some people lobbied for a more conventional alphabetical listing, but Lin pointed out that dozens of similar names (e.g., "Smiths") would appear together. Imagine six or eight consecutive "Robert Smiths." Which engraving represents *my* Robert?

A chronological arrangement put the human losses into the historical context of time, rendering a far more moving monument. But when families of the war casualties visited the memorial wall, they often could not locate their loved ones because they could not remember the exact dates. Families became frustrated and angry. Now, an alphabetical index stands in book form near the wall to solve the interface problem.[1]

In contrast, consider something many families consume several hours a day: television. People around the world now have dozens, even hundreds of available channels. Yet millions still have trouble finding something worth watching. New interactive systems like TiVo and satellite TV provide an alphabetical index, which works when I know what I'm looking for, like the name of the show or its genre. Half a century after the very first broadcast, why has no one developed an equally effective, simple means of locating a program that might actually entertain me?

Evolvability

In the era of co-creation, companies must design products not for final use (however defined) but for *evolvability*, thus enabling future modifications and extensions based on consumers' changing needs and the firm's changing capabilities. For instance, whenever possible, products should contain enough embedded intelligence to recognize an individual consumer's patterns of use and evolve accordingly, like the most-used features of menu-based interfaces floating to the top, or revealing more sophisticated product functionality as the user evolves. Certain video games already perform in this fashion; why not televisions, mobile phones, kitchen appliances, cameras, or light fixtures?

Pricing, Accounting, and Billing

All adaptive, dynamic, and variable pricing methods—what we might call *heterogeneous pricing*—base prices on experiences, not on a company-centric set of product specifications or on the firm's costs.

Consider auto insurance. OnStar-style telematics enable insurance companies to ascertain not only a car's make and model but also its owner's driving history, risk factors of the current trip, and even its location and speed at any time. Analysis of such data could yield a fair premium for insurance coverage on a per-trip basis. Progressive Insurance and other firms are already experimenting with similar concepts.

Heterogeneous pricing will also alter accounting and billing systems. Designed to reflect stable business models and fixed assets, traditional accounting reinforces the belief that maximizing the use of physical assets leads to profitability. It cannot reflect the need to reconfigure resources constantly (thereby shifting budget categories), allocate scarce capital (including talent not located on the balance sheet), or adopt the auction pricing model (which bears no direct relation to costs). To run daily operations, managers can no longer use traditional accounting models, though legally required for public reporting. Instead, they need critical new tools like flexible program-oriented budgeting (rather than budgeting driven by administrative categories), contribution thinking, and real-time cash flow analyses.

Closely associated with heterogeneous pricing is microbilling, increasingly one of the major infrastructure capabilities needed to compete in the new experience space. Telephone utilities have always had powerful, by-the-minute accounting and billing systems; other firms must create similar systems. Auction pricing and personalized product and service bundles create further levels of billing complexity.

Billing systems are also repositories of embedded customer information as well as part of the customer interface—which is to say, a social instrument. For all these reasons, billing must no longer be treated as an obscure, back-room operation but as a potentially valuable tool for enabling a personalized experience and extracting economic value from it.

Channel Management

In many established organizations, the traditional channel structure is a major impediment to personalized experiences. For example, the auto dealerships have long resisted the sale of cars on the Web by Ford and General Motors. Similarly, the brokers at traditional financial services firms like Merrill Lynch and Aetna weren't eager to allow for trading stocks or buying insurance via the Internet, and traditional travel agents opposed the migration of their industry to the Net. The tensions are understandable—and very real.

Established firms and traditional channel partners, locked in the traditional frame of value creation, have found it difficult to implement a multichannel experience environment—necessary to create a variety of consumer experiences through channel choice. The predictable result: industry newcomers like Expedia.com and E*TRADE have taken the lead in exploiting new opportunities.

The need to view multiple channels not just as a cost-saving mechanism but as an integral part of the experience environment suggests that businesses must develop new information capabilities. For example, how does a bank keep track of every customer encounter, whether via ATM, PC, telephone, mail, or in person? If different channel interactions provide different experiences and therefore differing levels of customer value, should the bank treat them the same? How do the pricing and billing systems differentiate among these multiple experiences? Should banks attempt to migrate their customers to lower-cost channels, or adapt to accommodate a customer's preferred modality? Few traditional organizations currently have the infrastructure capabilities to answer these questions effectively.

Brands and Brand Management

Think of some well known global brands: Sony, Honda, IBM, Hewlett-Packard, Dell, Disney, Nokia, General Electric, Toshiba, and Virgin. What do they all have in common?

They are all corporate brand names. Sony, for example, is the over-arching brand of the whole company, linked to product and unit brands such as Walkman, PlayStation, Sony Music, and the Sony Trinitron that made Sony televisions famous. The hierarchy in building brand equity at Sony is explicit. It consists of the broad company (Sony) promise (which includes innovation and quality), and a category of offerings under that umbrella (e.g., Walkman, PlayStation) with very specific product descriptors identifying particular products. With the multitudinous product choices available to consumers, as well as the many financial choices open to investors, the company itself is emerging as a center of brand equity, an anchor for value in a sea of discontinuities.

As companies orient themselves toward experiences, what is the value anchor?[2] We believe it is a consistent quality of co-creation experience across multiple channels and multiple events in the experience environment. The experience *is* the brand—not firm-centric, one-way communication as in advertising, public relations, and image manipulation.

For brand management, the focus on individual-specific experience implies a subjective notion of brand definition, one that the company cannot directly manage. Instead, firms must shift to managing experience environments, working with consumers and consumer communities. Brand managers must now facilitate new experiences and create new points of interaction, letting consumers connect the dots as they choose.

Marketing, Sales, and Service

The rules of engagement between the firm and the consumer are changing dramatically as the new paradigm gathers force. Table 12-1 contrasts the evolution of company-consumer interaction with the emerging co-creation view.[3]

In the traditional view, consumers are passive demand targets for a company's offerings. They are akin to prey, while marketers act as hunters with binoculars trying to get a better view of their quarry. Even expressions like "front-office" reflect this company-centric view of pulling consumer marketing information into the business system.

TABLE 12 - 1

The Evolution and Transformation of the Company-Consumer Interaction

	CONSUMERS AS PASSIVE AUDIENCE			CONSUMERS AS CO-CREATORS
	Persuading Predetermined Groups of Buyers	Transacting with Buyers	Lifetime Bonds with Buyers	Co-Creating Unique Value with Consumers
Time Frame	1970s, early 1980s	Late 1980s and early 1990s	1990s	Beyond 2000
Role of the Consumer and Concept of the Market	Consumers are "outside the firm"; they are seen as passive buyers with a predetermined role of consumption. Consumers are a target for exchanging the firm's offerings.			Consumers are part of the enhanced network of competencies; they co-create (and co-extract) value. They are collaborators, co-developers, and competitors. The market is a forum for co-creation experiences.
Managerial View of Consumers	The consumer is an average statistic; groups of buyers are predetermined by company.	The consumer is an individual statistic in a transaction, anywhere from a database record to an individually addressable entity.	The consumer is a person; cultivate trust and relationships.	The consumer is not only a person whose individual identity must be respected, but is also embedded in thematic communities and part of an emergent social and cultural fabric.

	CONSUMERS AS PASSIVE AUDIENCE			CONSUMERS AS CO-CREATORS
	Persuading Predetermined Groups of Buyers	Transacting with Buyers	Lifetime Bonds with Buyers	Co-Creating Unique Value with Consumers
Time Frame	1970s, early 1980s	Late 1980s and early 1990s	1990s	Beyond 2000
Company's Interaction with Consumers and Development of Products and Services	Traditional market research and inquiries. Preconfigured products and services are created without much feedback.	Shift from selling to helping consumers via help desks, call centers, and customer service programs. Identify problems from customers, then redesign products and services based or feedback. Cross-sell and bundle pre-configured products and services.	Providing for consumers through observation of users. Identify solutions from lead users, then reconfigure products and services based on deep understanding of customers. Customize products and services from preconfigured menu of features.	Consumers are co-creators of value. Dialogue, access, risk assessment, and transparency are building blocks of co-creation of value. Products and services are part of an experience environment in which individual consumers co-construct their own experiences. Experience environments are designed for evolvability of experiences. Companies and lead consumers co-shape expectations and market acceptance of experience environments.
Purpose and Flow of Communication	Gaining access to and targeting predetermined groups; firm-to-group access; one-way communication.	Database marketing; firm-to-individual access; two-way communication.	Relationship marketing; two-way access and communication.	Active dialogue with consumers (and thematic communities) to co-shape individual expectations and co-construct personalized experiences. Multiway access and network communication.

Market research, including focus groups, statistical modeling, video ethnography, and other techniques were developed in an effort to get a better understanding of consumers, identify trends, assess consumer desires and preferences, and evaluate the relative strength of competitors' positions. Firms have also organized consumers into segments that they hope will enable them to efficiently address consumer needs and deliver goods and services. Within this framework, the ultimate in customer segmentation is one-to-one marketing, which is touted as a source of competitive advantage.

While debates rage about the adequacy of our marketing methodology, the underlying vision of consumers as prey is rarely questioned. But what if the consumers were to turn the tables? What if consumers were to start investigating companies, products, and potential experiences in a systematic way? Is it sufficient for companies to "sense and respond" to customer demands? Do managers need market foresight—besides market insight? Must they learn to anticipate and lead, and further, to co-shape expectations and experiences in the market as a forum?

Consumers now subject the industry's value system to scrutiny, analysis, and evaluation. Consequently, companies can no longer unilaterally feed products to passive consumers. Active consumers participate in communities and access information resources comparable to—or even better than—those within the company. Consumers can choose the firms they want to have a relationship with based on their own views of how value should be created for them. The hunter becomes the hunted.

In the new market-as-a-forum, direct connections with consumers and consumer communities are critical. Consumer shifts are best understood by being there, co-creating with them. Firms must learn as much as possible about the customer through rich dialogue that evolves with the sophistication of consumers. The information infrastructure must be centered around the consumer and encourage active participation in all aspects of the co-creation experience, including information search, configuration of products and services, fulfillment, and consumption. Co-creation is about more than co-marketing or engaging consumers as co-sales agents. It's about developing methods to attain a visceral understanding of co-creation experiences so that companies can shape consumer expectations and experiences along with their customers.

Customer-Relationship Management

In recent years, a major focus of information technology has been on automating marketing, sales, and service delivery using so-called customer-relationship management (CRM) software. The emphasis has been on reducing costs, streamlining processes, eliminating delays, and improving efficiency.

This emphasis must change. We must develop new CRM capabilities based on questions such as the following:[4]

- How can we design systems that take a consumer experience-centric perspective?

- How can we build a platform for ongoing, active, multiparty dialogue between the company and its communities of consumers?

- How can we keep consumers excited and actively engaged in co-creation?

- How can we interact effectively with competent consumers who will increasingly recognize and leverage their own value to the company?

- How can we develop systems that can respond to fuzzy queries in the consumer's own language?

- How can our systems accommodate a wide base of heterogeneous consumers?

- How can we develop customer service responses that recognize and reward the heterogeneous competencies of consumers?

In the new CRM, transaction efficiency must coexist with experience-centric relationship flexibility. The John Deere example is a case in point. The enhanced Deere network and experience infrastructure does more than just enable the firm to develop services. It helps to change the consumer's entire relationship with Deere. For example, traditional selling of agricultural equipment has always centered on product push: "Buy this combine and we'll give you a good deal." Now the farmer has data on his specific needs that enable Deere and the consumer to co-develop ideas on how productivity can be boosted, effort reduced, and returns increased. Mutual transparency works to the benefit of both customer and company.

Customer service is also changing. Fixing problems promptly is no longer the highest standard. Remote diagnostics and repair, often without any direct customer intervention, is now possible in many industries, from John Deere combines to Medtronic defibrillators, from Otis elevators to GE aircraft engines. A newly robust IT infrastructure makes this change possible.

Thus, building the infrastructure for co-creation experiences will be a fundamental task for businesses over the coming decades.

Manufacturing, Logistics, and Supply Chain Management

The trend toward reconfiguring and recontextualizing the entire manufacturing, supply chain, and logistics systems around points of consumer interaction is already in progress. Honda, for example, has invested in flexible global manufacturing. Each Honda factory can make several models and switch among them easily using software-enabled robots, eliminating the time-consuming and costly plant retooling formerly required when a new model went into production. Meanwhile, rival automaker Toyota has cracked the code for taking orders on the Web and delivering a customized car within a week.

If the goal is to enable heterogeneous co-creation experiences and let consumers co-construct their own experiences, then the entire supply chain will obviously change. How do we create a system that can build to order, easily scale up and down, change configurations constantly, selectively activate competencies, and co-create unique value at low cost? How do we migrate from firm-centric supply chains to the new frontier of consumer-centric experience networks? This is the broad challenge all businesses now face.

The experience environment must be built with an event-centric perspective that allows customers to initiate experiences on demand. The logistics infrastructure must be tied closely to the experience environment. The physical product and information flows must be event-centric and visible within the organization. We must recognize that infrastructures for manufacturing, logistics, and supply chain management have both a technical and a social side. Firms must creatively integrate the appropriate technical and social enablers into the infrastructure underlying the experience network. (We discussed the infrastructure capabilities for experience networks in chapter 6.)

The only further point we'll make here is that large emerging markets such as Brazil, China, and India already have a sort of low-cost logistics infrastructure in place: individualized delivery to homes by bicycle, pedicarts, bullock carts, camels, donkeys, and the like. What is required is an effective marriage of the telecommunications and Internet backbone with the physical logistics and service framework for enabling personalized co-creation experiences.

Information Technology

None of the functional needs of the modern corporation can be achieved without a *flexible* information infrastructure.

Consider Cisco. The company's innovative, networked IT system made it uniquely responsive, allowing the firm to close its books in twenty-four hours, any day of the year. But flaws in the same system contributed significantly to the company's $2 billion inventory debacle in 2001.[5]

Cisco's supply chain consisted of a few contract manufacturers (including Celestica, Flextronics, and Solectron) who ship directly to customers on demand. In turn, these manufacturers depended on large component manufacturers and chip makers (such as JDS Uniphase, Corning, Intel, and Philips Electronics) that depend on an even larger global supplier base.

Cisco had secured large supplies of scant components, based on inflated demand projections from its sales force. It did not realize that many of its customers were double ordering from Cisco's competitors, intending to purchase only from whoever delivered first. Competing for the same order, the contract manufacturers would lock up the same supplies of scarce components. Cisco's system could not tell that demand surges signaled overlapping orders.

Cisco has undertaken an ambitious, multimillion-dollar project called eHub (actually started before the debacle) designed to eliminate bidding wars for scarce components by operating in real time with another new system, Partner Interface Process (PIP), which provides unprecedented transparency to multiple orders. Cisco's manufacturing cycle will now begin when PIP sends a demand forecast to both contract manufacturers and component makers up the chain. Ultimately, Cisco hopes to automate the whole product fulfillment process, so that a customer's online transaction will simultaneously update Cisco's financial database and supply chain.

Cisco recognizes that it must accept demand volatility and the newfound customer power at the point of exchange. Companies must build

FIGURE 12 - 1

Capacity to Compete and Lead Industry Change

Line managers view information infrastructure capabilities as an impediment to building new strategic capital.

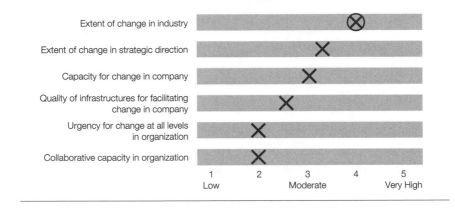

flexibility into their IT systems and into the entire manufacturing, supply chain, and logistical infrastructure. It is a necessary condition to compete in the experience space.

Working with more than five hundred senior executives in large companies over the past four years, one of us surveyed managers about their companies' abilities to respond to environmental shifts. The vast majority indicated that the quality of their firms' IT infrastructures lagged behind the need for change and thus impeded the companies' responsiveness (figure 12-1).[6]

Based on extended conversations with hundreds of industry leaders and our view of the new experience-centered co-creation space, we have identified some key requirements for a flexible IT infrastructure that companies must begin to build.

Event Orientation

An event—whether a machine breakdown, a customer query, or a change in inventory levels—is the trigger for an experience. That means our IT systems must be oriented around events that are *consumer relevant* and *managerially actionable*. They must facilitate queries and navigation based on how managers want to utilize information, not on arbitrary rules and procedures.

Contextual Navigation

A mere pile of data does not produce insight, any more than placing lettuce, tomatoes, cucumbers and salad dressing on the same table automatically produces a salad. We need contextual organization of data from multiple sources, types, and streams, all navigable via effective managerial interfaces (whether we define them as "dashboards," "cockpits," or some other metaphor). The system should facilitate event- and experience-based interaction with data so as to generate insights on which managers can act.

Multidirectional Transparency

The rapid spread of embedded intelligence demands a network that can continually gather information from points of consumer-company interaction in a form that facilitates managerial action, such that both the firm and the consumer can co-create appropriately.

Unified View

A unified view requires that IT systems must integrate data from across the experience network between applications, processes, and data sources. That means it must be event-centric and oriented toward space and time. Information must be indexed uniformly and be accessible based on the events to which it is connected. For example, a car accident sets in motion many processes involving data from many sources: police, insurance companies, onboard computers, hospitals, repair shops, and so on. The common thread is the event—the accident. The manager needs access to all the relevant information in a single unified view, including the ability to access data across many accidents to examine trends or patterns of interaction.

Support for Hypothesis Generation and Evolution of Next Practices

The new information infrastructure must not only support the best practices embedded in current business processes but also enable managers to experiment, discover, and develop the next practices. This means the ability to change the business logic embedded in applications quickly without significant resource implications. We also must create a capacity to support hypothesis generation by managers, and to help them identify weak signals and exceptions in masses of data from multiple sources. These tools will help generate contextual insights for decisions rather than merely presenting trends. For example, if Firestone had had appropriate visibility into Ford's resources (such as the nature of warranty calls and customer complaints related to tires), line managers at both companies might have been able to recognize trouble sooner.

Applications Portfolio Approach

We will always have to live with legacy systems in IT. There's no practical way to start with a clean slate every time we upgrade our IT systems—and in any case, some of our antiquated applications work just fine. Joint research with our colleague M. S. Krishnan suggests that we must develop an applications portfolio approach to evolving the information infrastructure. This requires a scorecard that evaluates each application on questions such as: What is the role of the application? Is it core or support? Are business processes stable or evolving? What is the expected degree of change in the application? What is the nature of the data? What are the information quality issues? Do we need a conformance view or an adaptation view? The answers to these kinds of questions will help determine which systems to modify, which to overhaul, and which to replace entirely.

Accommodation of Heterogeneity in Interactions

Varied company-consumer interactions require dialogue and easy reconfiguration of resources. Firms must accommodate heterogeneity in interactions while maintaining rigid controls on subprocesses. Thus, each building block (whether in products or processes) must be capable of performing at a Six Sigma level, yet allow for continuous reconfiguration.

Balance Between Innovation and Efficiency

A flexible infrastructure supports both the capacity to change (via experimentation, innovation, and flexibility) and efficiency (via support for standardization, as in subprocesses). As we have discussed, experience innovation can simultaneously embody efficiencies, if we invest judiciously in experience enablers and engage in experience (not technology) integration.

Making IT Happen: The GE Medical Example

Of all the conceptual specifications we've just listed for a modern information infrastructure, the most critical is the focus on line managers. We must shift from viewing IT as a support capability to seeing it as a critical strategic capability for becoming an experience-centric company. Building innovative contextual capabilities into the information infrastructure can help companies to innovate new experience enablers with their customers. In other words, companies can link innovation of managerial experiences with innovation of consumer experiences.

Consider, for example, GE Medical, which discovered how to use the Web to layer data services on top of its products. The resulting application, called iCenter, tracks and feeds patient data from MRI machines and other GE equipment to the radiologist (the consumer). GE also analyzes and compares the data with that from other customer sites, to see how productive a specific radiology department is compared to others using the same equipment.

GE is applying the lessons learned here to other GE divisions. For example, GE Power Systems has a similar iCenter application that lets customers analyze the performance of their turbines compared with others of similar capacity.

To help managers think further about their information infrastructure capabilities, we have summarized the challenges in the line manager-IT interface in figure 12-2.

IT infrastructure matters because it communicates the reality of consumers and their experiences to line managers. The relationship is like that between a topographical map and the actual terrain. The more accurately the map reflects the terrain, the easier for travelers to find their way. The more complex the terrain, the more detailed and accurate the map. Given the demands of the real-time enterprise, the map must correspond to the terrain as it is changing.

Most information systems force managers to use old maps, since they provide only historical analysis of data, or provide inappropriate maps that work only with a fixed set of predetermined analytical tools. Such systems complicate exploration and navigation. Managers must demand information systems that can support experimentation and innovation.

FIGURE 12 - 2

Managerial Information Infrastructure Capabilities

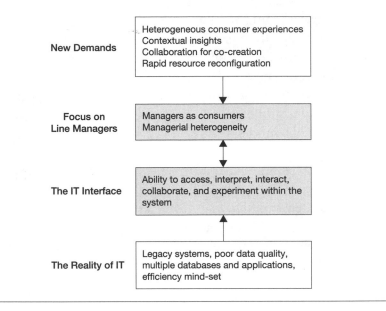

Managers also must learn fresh ways of thinking. The CIO of a large financial institution recently remarked, "We've trained line managers to think within the constraints of what our current information infrastructure can offer." The problem is endemic to many industries. For example, in a large auto company, employees simply accept that the information systems cannot readily answer the question, Which models are lagging their sales targets in specific global markets—and why? Managers must learn to think independently of the current information design and generate insight-oriented questions.

Becoming an Experience-Centric Company: The Managerial Challenges

Preparing a traditional organization for the future requires a major overhaul of its organizational structures and governance systems. In fact, no part of the company can assume that its role in the organization will be stable. As business models are revised and new challenges and opportunities emerge, the organization must repeatedly reconfigure its resources—its people, machines, infrastructure, and capital.

We urge you to jot down the most important management skills that you think will be required in the new business environment. To get you started, we have identified a few.

Managing Collaboration

Managers at every level must be trained in the art of collaboration and in dynamic negotiation for value creation. An organizational capacity to learn, nurture, share, and deploy knowledge across traditional boundaries will be a major strength. Intercultural and interpersonal competence among managers is a critical dimension of the new requirement.

Managing Migration Paths

Managers must learn to manage the migration paths of both customers and technologies. Product migration must keep pace with customer migration, if not anticipate it. For example, many users of portable computers long ago migrated to battery life, compactness, and weight as crucial product specifications, while manufacturers continued to focus on processor speed, memory, and storage. Only recently has product migration caught up with the experiences of customers.

Managing the Mind-Set

The managerial mind-set is probably the most potent tool in making the transformation to the world of co-creation. The mind-set required embraces change, is global, and accepts that the "role of the moment" is critical. Managers must understand the impact of organizational demands on individuals, the firm, and the experience network. This process is not just about an intellectual understanding of the nature and dimensions of the mind-set. It requires a deep understanding and commitment to recognize the emotional and behavioral traumas associated with changing a vast majority of individuals and teams that have worked with a different set of assumptions. This process is changing how people are socialized. The challenge is to push managers from their "zone of comfort" to the "zone of opportunity."

Managing the Skill Base

The skills for managing the new opportunity space are twofold. First, there is the substantive knowledge of the consumer and the technologies underlying the business, informed as much by personal knowledge as by "proxy analysis" via staff groups. Second is the sheer ability to get things done that require interpersonal and intercultural competence, team skills, and ongoing learning. Ambitious managers must invest in personal excellence to lead in the new competitive space.

Managing Values and Beliefs

As business relationships and models undergo dramatic and rapid change, individuals yearn for stability. The organizational pivots that provide stability are values and beliefs. While many firms have tried to articulate a system of values and beliefs, few have been successful in following them consistently. For example, a professed belief in the value of diversity is hollow if individuals within the system frequently demonstrate bias (blatant or subtle) against people on the basis of age, gender, race, ethnicity, and increasingly, intellectual heritage. For instance, suppose the dominant intellectual heritage of a bulk chemical firm is chemical engineering—how well does such a system tolerate geneticists?

Managing Teams

Needless to say, no single individual or group can accomplish all the tasks required in creating value. But team management is a complex challenge. Accountability must be clearly established even as team managers are free to change the mix of team members and tasks at short notice. Our performance evaluation and reward systems must reflect this emerging competitive reality. Managers must move toward a project management orientation for assessing performance rather than depend on more traditional quarterly and yearly reviews.

Managing Reaction Time

Increasingly, rapid reaction time and all the component skills—such as the ability to amplify weak signals, interpret their consequences, and reconfigure resources faster than competitors—will be a critical source of advantage. It's not just running faster, but thinking faster—and smarter—that makes the difference.

The Internal Governance Dilemma

Becoming an experience-centric company puts a premium on the governance process for co-creation of value. Most discussions of corporate governance focus on the relationship between the external board of directors and the top management of the company. It's an important debate. But we will focus on internal corporate governance—the relationships between the corporate center and the company's geographic, functional, and business groups. The quality of internal governance will influence the nature and the intensity of the independent scrutiny that the external board must exercise. Even more important, internal governance defines the nature of collaboration among business, geographic, and functional units, as they co-create value.

Research on internal governance in corporate America has generally focused on the relationships among the following groups:

- The corporate center and the business units. (What is the basis of relationships between the business units and the corporation? Should the corporate center act as an operating unit, as a holding company, or as something in between?)

- The corporate center and the regional units. (Should the corporation define regional strategies—for Europe, say, or for Southeast Asia or Latin America?)

- The business units and the geographic units. (Should business units have global mandates? What are the obligations of the geographic units to the business units, and vice versa?)

- The corporate-level functional groups and the business and regional functional groups. (How does the corporation maintain long-term functional excellence across various levels of functional management? What kinds of checks and balances are needed?)

The debate revolves around three generic approaches. The first focuses on organizational structure and on power and authority relationships that determine resource allocation choices. The second approach focuses on the parenting relationship between the different levels of management. The third focuses on the need for corporate values, culture, systems, and processes. All three approaches are well documented and widely known. We will not discuss them here. Instead, we will take a somewhat different approach consistent with our view of co-creation of value.

In our view, the dilemma of internal governance as we move to co-creating value involves five basic problems: the growing complexity of managing a network of relationships; managing multiple modes of collaboration; coping with rapid change in the competitive environment; the need for zero latency and decentralization; and the need to find a new balance between flexibility and accountability. Let us consider these in turn.

Growing Complexity of Networks

Corporations today must deal with a larger number of suppliers, partners, consumers, and consumer communities than ever before. Some consumers are in well-organized and powerful enterprises (such as Wal-Mart). In other cases, consumers are organized into strong thematic communities (such as the consumers of Harley-Davidson or Marlboro). Often the firm must deal with nongovernmental organizations (such as environmental and human rights groups). The needs, interests, and goals all of these groups are continually evolving and shifting.

The problem is, there are simply *too many moving parts*, governed by no set relationships around which one can organize structurally. Expecting managers to operate in such a world on the basis of a rigid corporate system is like asking the members of a jazz band to write out their improvisational riffs before they begin playing—or like asking a Carnatic musician (a performer of traditional South Indian music) how long his performance will last. The only honest answer to such a question is, "It depends." The mood of the musician, of the accompanying instrumentalists, and of the audience will all influence the content of the performance. We must recognize that while specific outcomes are unpredictable, the skill levels are not.

It's the same in the emerging world of co-creation. When the evolution of relationships can't be predicted or controlled, exclusive reliance on predetermined structural solutions is unlikely to be effective.

Need for a Collaboration Agenda

As we discussed in the previous chapter, a wide variety of collaborative modes is needed in the new co-creation sphere, including arm's-length contractual relationships, information-sharing arrangements with suppliers, and internal partnerships for deploying resources against new opportunities. This implies that managers operating at multiple levels in the organization must learn how and when to collaborate and how and when to compete. What information do we share? What information do we withhold? Who controls the products of our shared efforts? Managers must answer these and other crucial questions case by case.

We cannot restructure units for every new collaboration. Rather, we must cultivate the ability to selectively combine and disengage—Velcro provides the right metaphor. We must create a "Velcro organization" that can selectively combine and disengage resources, a prerequisite for rapid resource reconfiguration. It's not easy to balance self-interest and common interest, individual recognition and shared success, the need for a separate identity and the need for teamwork. Managers must be ready to move beyond the comforting structural clarity of an organizational chart and deal with difficult and often ambiguous relationships on a constant basis. Unless the corporation has a clear and shared agenda, continuous and opportunistic collaboration cannot work.

Coping with Rapid Change in the Competitive Landscape

Many firms are intent on standardizing their global business processes. Their leaders say, "Once we standardize our processes, we can see what everyone inside the business is doing."

That statement may be true. But it reflects an internally focused, efficiency-based point of view. Given the constant flux in the competitive environment, standardizing business processes appears counterproductive. We need the ability to continuously monitor our processes and modify them as needed. In some cases, standardization is desirable—but it's not a worthwhile goal in itself, and it's certainly not the total solution for any company.

Visibility of resources combined with flexibility in business processes should aid line managers in experience quality management by allowing redeployment of resources as a particular context warrants. The goal: a true Velcro organization wherein members can reconfigure resources easily and seamlessly.

Zero Latency and Decentralization

A decade ago, one of us was working with the leader of a large firm. In the course of the assignment, he discovered that the company was carrying more than 120 days' worth of finished goods. Asked why it was necessary to tie up so much capital in inventory, the president of the division responded, "Don't you see? We're customer-focused. We must keep inventory so that we can serve customers at short notice." This sounded impressive—but the company's service level, measured by completion of orders in the first shipment, was an appalling 60 percent. The manufacturing plants were producing stock that had little relationship to customer needs.

Today, that firm has less than five days' supply of goods in inventory, and their service level is at 98 percent. They have learned to understand customer needs and respond to them promptly—not by filling warehouses with products, but by reacting fast and flexibly. In the co-creation paradigm, inventory does not replace quick, real-time response.

Moreover, in a global organization, zero latency—the ability to continuously monitor the environment and respond rapidly—suggests a highly decentralized management approach. Managers on the front lines must have the tools to understand what is happening around them and make relevant, appropriate decisions. Operating only through a hierarchical chain of command is no longer acceptable.

Balancing Flexibility and Accountability

Business has moved a long way since the days of time-and-motion analyst Frederick Winslow Taylor. One of us remembers working as an industrial engineer with the job of fixing piece rates on a shop floor. The work was clearly defined and repetitive; the product specifications were clear; the management task was simple.

Today, things have changed. Flexibility, teamwork, continual problem solving, constant searching for process improvements, and collaboration with suppliers are the norm. Yet the greatest strength of the old fixed-process system—accountability for performance—is still necessary. Sacrificing accountability cannot be the price for flexibility, collaboration, and teamwork.

Relying on clearly defined organizational charters (focusing on accountability and simple performance measurement) is easy, but the intangible costs of overlooking the unexpected can be enormous. One manager told us, "No one gets fired for missing opportunities—just budgets." In the new paradigm, both are crucial.

Building Governance Capabilities:
Creating a System of Protocols and Disciplines

Traditionally, internal corporate governance has relied on structural solutions; clear boundaries, strict accountability, and well-planned, clearly defined processes were the primary tools. In recent years, business process reengineering and corporate culture/values have both received attention as tools for improving companies' internal functioning. As we look toward a future of co-creation, what is the right mix of governance tools for the new corporation?

Structural solutions are still important. Just as a large office building can't stand without a well-designed, load-bearing steel frame, no large firm can operate without a minimum level of bureaucracy (much as we disparage the term). And clearly defined business processes are equally important. However, as business processes get embedded within the company's information systems, they are harder to change. Formal structures and business processes are necessary but not sufficient tools for dealing with a world of change. In fact, they can become obstacles to the necessary flexibility.

A new approach to organizing activities in a large firm is emerging, one that is based on protocols and disciplines, in addition to structures and processes. To explain what this means, consider the development of Linux, the open-standard operating system that competes with Windows OS. Like Windows, Linux is continually evolving as new features and applications are developed. Unlike Windows, however, Linux is co-developed by independent programmers and users in a system controlled by no central authority. How is it that the ongoing development of Linux does not degenerate into chaos?[7]

The answer is that anyone can participate in developing bits and pieces of the system, but those who do must follow certain clear rules and protocols. The software code must be transparent, shared openly and freely with the entire community, and reviewed by an expert peer group to ensure the entire system's integrity. The Linux community incorporates any individual contribution only after this peer review and approval. These simple protocols let the entire community police its own work for excellence and reliability.

Now consider a highly decentralized network like the Web. It grows organically, allowing for great flexibility and experimentation.

It is cross-cultural. It allows for collaboration among total strangers. On the Web, thematic communities form and disappear continually. Anybody who accepts a few simple, clearly articulated social and technical protocols and standards such as TCP/IP and HTML can use the Internet.

Thus, nobody can predict what will happen on the Web. So far, we can see everything from profound collaboration on complex tasks (as in the scientific breakthroughs generated on the Los Alamos Web site) to the dissemination of pornography and the support of terrorism.[8] What if we took such a decentralized approach to corporate governance?

Governance by Protocols: The eBay Example

Pierre Omidyar wanted "to give the power of the market back to individuals, not just large corporations." So he founded eBay to alter the exchange process—buying and selling—by creating an open auction. In 2001, eBay intermediated over 170 million exchanges for $9.3 billion worth of goods in more than 18,000 categories, with revenues of over $749 million. In 2002, it generated revenues of $1.5 billion, on commissions up to 5.25 percent on transactions.[9] Clearly, eBay has succeeded in creating a platform on which to build global economic democracy. Unlike traditional exchanges, eBay does not distinguish between buyers and sellers, only between roles of the moment. I can sell my antique chair and buy a digital camera simultaneously.

In the initial stage, the eBay process focused primarily on three elements of the exchange: choice of products and services, a clear price-performance advantage because of the auction process, and ease of transactions through easy-to-use tools and clear rules. However, as people started participating, a community with its own rules gradually evolved. People acting as merchants would write thank-you notes to those acting as consumers. Buyers and sellers started grading each transaction in a "Feedback Forum." The evolving rules of engagement enabled a unique customer experience.

In its early days, eBay was simply a market for ordinary folks to sell odds and ends. But eBay's strategy has evolved through discovery and efficient innovation. Even powerhouses like IBM, Sears, and Disney use eBay to exchange their goods. eBay's business and industrial marketplace, launched in 2003, is already selling over $1 billion worth of goods. More than $3 billion worth of autos have sold on eBay, as has a $4.9 million Gulfstream jet.

Under CEO Meg Whitman, eBay has embraced the DART elements of co-creation in its governance process. Each week, eBay users exchange an estimated two hundred thousand or more messages containing tips, problems, and suggested site improvements. Such dialogue occurs freely among eBay users and employees, all but guaranteeing access to, and transparency of, information such as the track records of merchants and buyers alike. Regarding risk management, eBay has kept fraud rates low, relative to the number of transactions and people involved, by relying on its users to enforce its code of conduct. eBay has also moved fast to ensure that no one can buy or sell dangerous products such as firearms on the site.

So what are some of the basic elements of such a company-level governance system based on protocols and disciplines?

A Shared Governance Agenda

If employees do not understand where the company is going, they cannot accurately define their roles and contributions. They need a shared agenda that provides a framework for innovation and creativity so that, for important decisions, they have a single touchstone and tiebreaker: "Does this action move us closer to our goal?"

Rules for Interdependencies and Collaboration Among Managers

One business unit might decide to collaborate with a university professor on a technology problem; another might choose to negotiate its own independent supplier deal with Microsoft or Wal-Mart. Which of these engagements is acceptable? Companies must define the minimal rules of engagement for each type of relationship within the network. Like eBay, firms can start by harnessing their employees' implicit knowledge and developing simple rules that they will continually update and revise according to experiences. This approach allows for protection of intellectual property as well as clarity for managers to act independently.

Shared Values and Beliefs

Without a clearly defined and consistently practiced system of values, no large system can survive. Values provide the emotional anchor that lets individuals cope with change. A violation of these values can quickly destroy the trust of consumers, managers, investors, legislators, and regulators. Think of Enron or the Catholic Church.

A Shared View of Market Evolution

Every manager can legitimately interpret weak signals differently. A manager in California's Silicon Valley has different views of market evolution from one in Hamburg, Germany. A technical specialist's view of discontinuity will likely differ from a marketing expert's or a financial manager's. A company can leverage such diversity only when all employees share a single framework for market evolution.

Design and Development Protocols

Collaboration is impossible without clear, standardized systems for design and development. We know of one global firm that had five different e-mail systems and multiple CAD systems. Top managers talked constantly about collaborating and leveraging the firm's global reach, while operating managers laughed at the idea. With multiple e-mail and CAD systems, collaboration was impossible.

Forums for Setting Priorities

In a decentralized, global organization, priorities cannot be dictated from the top. Hence the need for forums to debate, discuss, and establish priorities. Task groups, practice communities from around the entire organization, and other ad hoc combinations of knowledge, expertise, and perspective can ensure that priorities are set on the basis of discussion. The criteria for inclusion in those groups must be merit and accomplishment, not hierarchical position.

A Shared Vocabulary

For any large firm, a vocabulary of terms with clear, shared definitions is critical. Many accounting and finance groups already practice this discipline, while human resource professionals and strategy analysts are notorious for using language loosely and vaguely. For example, the words "performance" and "accountability" are often used generically, with no specific meaning within a firm. A standardized set of terms to describe key aspects of the operation can dramatically reduce misunderstandings and missed cues.

Nonnegotiables

In establishing protocols and disciplines, senior managers must, in consultation with operating managers, establish a few "nonnegotiables."

Without clearly established rules, empowerment is impossible. For instance, collaboration invariably leads to debates about transfer prices. The problem is intractable, since no system has yet to delight both sides of any deal, to our knowledge. The approach can be very simple: "Use market prices whenever you can. When market prices are incalculable, senior management will decide." The point here is to just end the internal debates and move on to more productive activities.

This list could be expanded, but the message is clear: The importance of protocols and disciplines in managing an enhanced network cannot be underestimated.

Building a New Theory of Corporate Governance

Structural mechanisms and business processes provide the backbone and stability that companies require. But they cannot provide the flexibility that managers need to respond to emerging opportunities in a highly decentralized environment. Thus, we believe that the governance process will eventually incorporate a judicious mixture of all three elements—formal structure, business processes, and management disciplines and protocols—as shown in figure 12-3.

Co-creating value will produce significant changes in the internal governance process—changes so radical that a new theory of governance may be needed. Let's examine some of the critical building blocks of such a theory.

FIGURE 12 - 3

The Emerging Framework for Governance

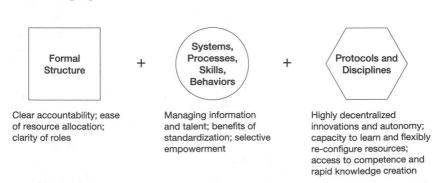

Unit of Analysis

In the traditional theory of corporate governance, the firm is the basic unit of analysis. The firm's legal boundaries determine its resources. The firm's role is to create value and extract a portion of it at the point of exchange with the consumer, where price is the basis for bargaining.

Players in the co-creation space challenge these assumptions. The nodal network of suppliers, partners, and customers may displace the firm as the unit of analysis. The firm's legal boundaries no longer determine the resources that a firm can access; the entire nodal network does. Customers help to co-create value and extract value simultaneously from the firm.

Predetermined Roles

In the traditional theory, the roles of the firm, the customer, and competing firms were clearly defined and predetermined. Now that is changing. The consumers' role in co-creating value clearly makes them part of the enterprise. Sometimes customers are passive, sometimes they actively co-create, and sometimes they compete for value. Traditional, predetermined roles are yielding to "roles of the moment."

Strategic and Operational Boundaries

Strategic and operational, rather than legal, boundaries now define the firm. The nodal firm with its extended network is an operational and strategic entity, subject to constant reevaluation and redefinition. A nodal firm may reject a supplier; a supplier may opt out of a nodal network. These relationships are flexible, and the boundaries of the network are also flexible and evolving. This may have a significant impact on the way we think about reporting results. Accounting rules, for example, are based on what the company "owns" legally. Yet the firm may effectively be using more resources than it owns. How do we account for the economic efficiency of a nodal network, rather than the efficiency of just the nodal firm? We must devise rules for accounting for access to resources that are partly owned or not owned at all by the firm that uses them.

The Definition of Self-Interest

Should firms maximize their self-interest (as traditionally defined) in every transaction, or focus instead on the benefit from multiple trans-

actions over a period of time? Is the goal of a company to win the current game—or simply to get a chance to play the next game? For example, think about the manager who purchases goods and services from
suppliers. Should he concentrate on negotiating a lowest price for the
specific purchase he makes, or on maximizing the firm's total value by
building a long-term, multiperiod, multitransaction environment that
guarantees access to competence and other resources?

Defining the Investor

The traditional theory makes a clear division between investors and
other stakeholders. The emerging theory of governance must recognize how these roles are morphing and melding. Is the employee who
owns stock options an investor? Is the consumer who helps to develop
new applications for Lego Mindstorms investing in the company and
its success? What about suppliers who share their accumulated knowledge with the firm? What about consumer communities that facilitate
the spread of the brand? We need an expanded definition of the investor. By defining the investor solely as one who provides financial
capital, we underestimate the complex mosaic of roles that is emerging
in the new paradigm.

The key dimensions of change in this evolving theory of corporate
governance are summarized in table 12-2.

The Individual: The Heart of the Matter

The new realities of value creation are challenging our thinking in
many ways. It's a promising time, reflecting the emergence of infinite
opportunities to co-create value. But if we are to compete effectively in
the new opportunity space, we must develop new ways of thinking and
acting. That, of course, has been the central thrust of this book.

Perhaps the single most important shift that companies and managers must make is to recognize the *centrality of the individual*. It does not
matter whether we are dealing with a consumer, an employee, an investor, or a supplier. The centrality of the individual must dictate our
approach. We are not merely altering our focus from an institution-
centric view of value creation to a consumer-centric view of co-
creation—though that shift would be radical enough. We are also
moving from an institution-centric view of the individual to an *individual-
centered view of the institution*. It's a change with profound implications
for the future that no one today can fully anticipate.

TABLE 12 - 2

The Transformation of Governance

	Traditional Theory of the Firm	Emerging Reality
Unit of Analysis	The firm	The nodal network
Basis for Value	Products and services	Co-creation experiences
View of Infrastructure	Physical and financial assets	Access to resources—knowledge and network
Spanning of Boundaries	Legal boundaries	Strategic and operational boundaries
Nature of Boundaries	Fixed	Evolving
Nature and Purpose of Interaction	Transaction based; maximization of self-interest in each transaction; goal is to be efficient in a known game	Series of transactions and co-creation experiences; maximization of joint interest and self-interest; goal is to keep the game evolving
Definition of the Investor	Preassigned stakeholder role	All constituents

What's more, these implications extend far beyond the world of business. Whether in government, education, health care, the arts, the sciences, or religion, today's trend toward an individual-centered view of institutions cannot be stopped. In time, it may help to create a new basis for the social legitimacy of all large institutions in our society. In the business sphere, it may finally lead us toward an economy "of the people, by the people, and for the people" (to borrow Abraham Lincoln's words). In an even broader context, it may ultimately portend the emergence of a truly democratic global society in which human rights, needs, and values are predominant—not the demands of institutions.

We see a world of co-creation emerging on the horizon, one that we hope you will co-shape actively. Welcome to the future of competition and the opportunity to co-create that future.

AIDS TO EXPLORATION

In this book, we have presented a synthesized view of what the future of business is becoming. In the Internet age of hyperlinked abundance, active readers can explore on their own terms. To aid your personal exploration, we provide a list, by no means exhaustive, of books, articles, and URLs organized by chapters.

As noted in the Preface, we have benefited from the work of the following scholars and writers, and many more.

Alderson, Wroe. *Dynamic Marketing Behavior*. Homewood, IL: Richard D. Irwin, 1965.

Becker, Brian E., Mark A. Huselid, and Dave Ulrich. *The HR Scorecard: Linking People, Strategy, and Performance*. Boston: Harvard Business School Press, 2001.

Brown, John Seely, and Paul Duguid. *The Social Life of Information*. Boston: Harvard Business School Press, 2000.

Brown, Shona L., and Kathleen M. Eisenhardt. *Competing on the Edge: Strategy as Structured Chaos*. Boston: Harvard Business School Press, 1998.

Cairncross, Frances. *The Company of the Future: How the Communications Revolution Is Changing Management*. Boston: Harvard Business School Press, 2002.

Castells, Manuel. *The Rise of the Network Society, Volume 1*. Malden, MA: Blackwell Publishing, 1996.

Christensen, Clayton M. *The Innovator's Dilemma: When New Technologies Cause Great Firms to Fail*. Boston: Harvard Business School Press, 1997.

Collins, Jim. *Good to Great: Why Some Companies Make the Leap . . . and Others Don't*. New York: HarperCollins, 2002.

Davenport, Thomas H., and John C. Beck. *The Attention Economy: Understanding the New Currency of Business*. Boston: Harvard Business School Press, 2001.

Davis, Stan, and Christopher Meyer. *Future Wealth*. Boston: Harvard Business School Press, 2000.

Dertouzos, Michael. *The Unfinished Revolution*. New York: HarperBusiness, 2001.

Doz, Yves, José Santos, and Peter Williamson. *From Global to Metanational: How Companies Win in the Knowledge Economy*. Boston: Harvard Business School Press, 2001.

Drucker, Peter F. *Managing in the Next Society*. New York: St. Martin's Press, 2002.

Evans, Philip, and Thomas S. Wurster. *Blown to Bits: How the New Economics of Information Transforms Strategy*. Boston: Harvard Business School Press, 1999.

Foster, Richard, and Sarah Kaplan. *Creative Destruction: Why Companies That Are Built to Last Underperform the Market—And How to Successfully Transform Them*. New York: Doubleday, 2001.

Ghoshal, Sumantra, and Christopher A. Bartlett. *The Individualized Corporation: A Fundamentally New Approach to Management*. New York: HarperBusiness, 1997.

Grove, Andrew S. *Only the Paranoid Survive: How to Exploit the Crisis Points That Challenge Every Company*. New York: Doubleday, 1996.

Haeckel, Stephan H. *Adaptive Enterprise: Creating and Leading Sense-and-Respond Organizations*. Boston: Harvard Business School Press, 1999.

Hagel III, John. *Out of the Box: Strategies for Achieving Profits Today and Growth Tomorrow through Web Services*. Boston: Harvard Business School Press, 2002.

Hamel, Gary, and C. K. Prahalad. *Competing for the Future*. Boston: Harvard Business School Press, 1994.

Hamel, Gary. *Leading the Revolution: How to Thrive in Turbulent Times by Making Innovation a Way of Life*. Boston: Harvard Business School Press, 2002.

Handy, Charles. *The Age of Unreason*. Boston: Harvard Business School Press, 1990.

Hayek, F. A. von. *Individualism and Economic Order*. Chicago: University of Chicago Press, 1948.

Kelley, Tom. *The Art of Innovation*. New York: Doubleday, 2001.

Kelly, Kevin. *New Rules for the New Economy*. New York: Penguin, 1999.

Kim, Chan W., and Renée Mauborgne. "Value Innovation: The Strategic Logic of High Growth." *Harvard Business Review*, January–February 1997.

Kotler, Philip. *Marketing Management*. New Jersey: Prentice Hall, 2002.

Leonard-Barton, Dorothy. *Wellsprings of Knowledge: Building and Sustaining the Sources of Innovation*. Boston: Harvard Business School Press, 1998.

McKenna, Regis. *Total Access: Giving Customers What They Want in an Anytime, Anywhere World*. Boston: Harvard Business School Press, 2002.

Mintzberg, Henry. *The Rise and Fall of Strategic Planning: Reconceiving Roles for Planning, Plans, Planners*. New York: Free Press, 1994.

Naisbitt, John, Nana Naisbitt, and Douglas Phillips. *High Tech/High Touch: Technology and Our Accelerated Search for Meaning*. London: Nicholas Brealey, 2001.

Negroponte, Nicholas. *Being Digital*. New York: Knopf, 1995.

Nonaka, Ikujiro, and Hirotaka Takeuchi. *The Knowledge-Creating Company: How Japanese Companies Create the Dynamics of Innovation*. Oxford, U.K.: Oxford University Press, 1995.

Normann, Richard, and Rafael Ramirez. *Designing Interactive Strategy: From Value Chain to Value Constellation*. Chichester: Wiley, 1994.

Peppers, Don, and Martha Rogers. *The One to One Future: Building Relationships One Customer at a Time*. New York: Doubleday, 1993.

Peters, Tom. *The Pursuit of Wow!* New York: Random House, 1994.

Pine II, B. Joseph, and James H. Gilmore. *The Experience Economy: Work Is Theater and Every Business a Stage*. Boston: Harvard Business School Press, 1999.

Porter, Michael E. *Competitive Strategy: Techniques for Analyzing Industries and Competitors*. New York: Free Press, 1980.

Rheingold, Howard. *Smart Mobs*. Cambridge, MA: Perseus Publishing, 2002.

Sawhney, Mohanbir, and Jeff Zabin. *The Seven Steps to Nirvana: Strategic Insights into eBusiness Transformation*. New York: McGraw-Hill, 2001.

Schmitt, Bernd H. *Experiential Marketing: How to Get Customers to Sense, Feel, Think, Act, and Relate to Your Company and Brands*. New York: Free Press, 1999.

Schrage, Michael. *Serious Play: How the World's Best Companies Simulate to Innovate*. Boston: Harvard Business School Press, 2000.

Schumpeter, Joseph A. *Capitalism, Socialism and Democracy*. New York: Harper & Brothers, 1942.

Senge, Peter. *The Fifth Discipline: The Art and Practice of the Learning Organization*. New York: Doubleday, 1990.

Seybold, Patricia B. (with Ronni T. Marshak and Jeffrey M. Lewis). *The Customer Revolution: How to Thrive When Customers Are in Control*. New York: Crown Publishing Group, 2001.

Shapiro, Carl, and Hal R. Varian. *Information Rules: A Strategic Guide to the Network Economy*. Boston: Harvard Business School Press, 1998.

Silverstein, Michael J., and George Stalk Jr. *Breaking Compromises: Opportunities for Action in Consumer Markets*. New York: John Wiley & Sons, 2000.

Slywotzky, Adrian J., and David J. Morrison (with Karl Weber). *How Digital Is Your Business: Creating the Company of the Future*. New York: Crown Publishing Group, 2000.

Stewart, Thomas A. *Intellectual Capital: The New Wealth of Organizations*. New York: Doubleday, 1997.

Tapscott, Don, David Ticoll, and Alex Lowy. *Digital Capital: Harnessing the Power of Business Webs*. Boston: Harvard Business School Press, 2000.

Thomke, Stefan H. *Experimentation Matters: Unlocking the Potential of New Technologies for Innovation*. Boston: Harvard Business School Press, 2003.

Tichy, Noel M. (with Nancy Cardwell). *The Cycle of Leadership: How Great Leaders Teach Their Companies to Win*. New York: HarperCollins, 2002.

Toffler, Alvin. *The Third Wave*. New York: Bantam Books, 1981.

Vandermerwe, Sandra. *Customer Capitalism: A New Business Model of Increasing Returns in New Market Spaces*. London: Nicholas Brealey, 1999.

von Hippel, Eric. *The Sources of Innovation*. New York: Oxford University Press, 1988.

Zaltman, Gerald. *How Customers Think: Essential Insights into the Mind of the Market*. Boston: Harvard Business School Press, 2003.

Zuboff, Shoshana, and James Maxmin. *The Support Economy: Why Corporations Are Failing Individuals and the Next Episode of Capitalism*. New York: Viking Press, 2002.

Chapter One

1. Prahalad, C. K., and Venkatram Ramaswamy. "The Co-Creation Connection." *Strategy and Business*, Second Quarter 2002.
   See also:
   Hagel III, John, and Arthur G. Armstrong. *Net Gain: Expanding Markets Through Virtual Communities*. Boston: Harvard Business School Press, 1997;
   Rheingold, Howard. *The Virtual Community: Homesteading on the Electronic Frontier*. Cambridge, MA: MIT Press, 2000.
2. Moore, Stephen D. "Blood Test: News about Leukemia Unexpectedly Puts Novartis on the Spot." *Wall Street Journal*, 6 June 2000;
   Landro, Laura. "Health Web Sites Usher in New Era of Patient Activism." *Asian Wall Street Journal*, 12 November 2002.
3. <http://www.medtronic.com/newsroom/media_kit_CareLink.html>;
   Carlson, Andy. "Strong Medicine." *Context*, June 2002, <http://www.contextmag.com/archives/200206/Catalyst2.asp>.
4. Kambil, Ajit, G. Bruce Friesen, and Arul Sundaram. "Co-creation: A New Source of Value." *Outlook Journal*, June 1999;
   LaSalle, Diana, and Terry A. Britton. *Priceless: Turning Ordinary Products into Extraordinary Experiences*. Boston: Harvard Business School Press, 2002;
   Peppers, Don, and Martha Rogers. *The One to One Future: Building Relationships One Customer at a Time*. New York: Doubleday, 1993;
   Pine II, B. Joseph, and James H. Gilmore. *The Experience Economy: Work Is Theater and Every Business a Stage*. Boston: Harvard Business School Press, 1999;
   Ramirez, Rafael. "Value Co-Production: Intellectual Origins and Implications for Practice and Research." *Strategic Management Journal* 20, (1999): 49–65;
   Seybold, Patricia B. (with Ronni T. Marshak). *Customers.com: How to Create a Profitable Business Strategy for the Internet and Beyond*. New York: Times Books, 1998;
   Schmitt, Bernd H. *Experiential Marketing: How to Get Customers to Sense, Feel, Think, Act, and Relate to Your Company and Brands*. New York: Free Press, 1999;
   Thomke, Stefan, and Eric von Hippel. "Customers as Innovators: A New Way to Create Value." *Harvard Business Review*, April 2002.

Chapter Two

1. Caggiano, Christopher. "Cruising for Profits." *Inc. Magazine*, Web Awards 2000, 15 November 2000, "Inc./Cisco: Growing with Technology Awards."
   See also:
   McWhirter, Douglas. "Sailing into e-Commerce." *eCRM*, December 1999;
   <http://www.sumersethouseboats.com>;
   <http://www.cisco.com/warp/public/cc/general/growing/full/sumer_cp.htm>.
2. PR Newswire Association. "Sumerset Custom Houseboats' Innovative Dry Stack Exhaust Design to Be Featured on CBS News Program '48 Hours.'" 5 September 2001.
3. Wacker, Brian. "The Great Debate: Callaway vs. the USGA." *Golf Digest*. <http://www.golfdigest.com/features/index.ssf?/equipment/the_grea_a1b45kec.html>.
4. Ibid.
5. Ibid.

6. Lohr, Steve. "Some IBM Software Tools to Be Put in Public Domain." *New York Times*, 5 November 2001.

7. <http://www.innocentive.com>.

8. Baker, Chris. "Taiwan Semiconductor." *Wired*, July 2002.
   <http://www.wired.com/wired/archive/10.07/Semiconductor_pr.html>;
   Jacob, Rahul. "Buyers and Sellers Flock to Online Asian Bazaar." *Financial Times*, 29 April 2000;
   <http://www.tsmc.com>.

9. Hyman, Gretchen. "Gateway Finds Good Use for Showroom PCs." 10 December 2002. <http://siliconvalley.internet.com/news/print.php/1554991>.

10. Lohr, Steve. "The New Leader of IBM Explains Its Strategic Course." *New York Times*, 31 October 2002;
    Ante, Spencer E. "Big Blue's Tech on Tap." *BusinessWeek*, 27 August 2001.

11. <http://www.carsharing.net/>;
    <http://www1.mobility.ch/e/index.htm>.

12. Prahalad, C. K., and Stuart L. Hart. "The Fortune at the Bottom of the Pyramid." *Strategy and Business*, First Quarter, 2002;
    See also:
    Kriplani, Manjeet, and Pete Engardio. "Small Is Profitable." *BusinessWeek*, 26 August 2002;
    <http://www.businessweek.com:/print/magazine/content/02_34/b3796>.

13. Kirn, Walter. "The 60-Second Book." *Time Magazine*, 2 August 1999;
    <http://www.lightningsource.com>.

14. Kolata, Gina. "Race to Fill Void in Menopause Drug Market." *New York Times*, 1 September 2002;
    See also:
    Brody, Jane E. "Sorting Through the Confusion over Estrogen." *New York Times*, 3 September 2002.

15. Nemecek, Sasha. "Does the World Need GM Foods?" *Scientific American*, 18 April 2001;
    "Villain or Hero, Monsanto Moving GM Food Forward," 28 March 2001, <http://www.planetark.org/dailynewsstory.cfm/newsid/10281/newsDate/28-Mar-2001/story.htm>.

16. "Poison Plants?" *Scientific American*, 5 July 1999.

17. Jonietz, Erika. "Population Inc.: Q&A with Kari Stefansson." *Technology Review*, April 2001;
    See also:
    Wade, Nicholas. "A Genomic Treasure Hunt May Be Striking Gold." *New York Times*, 18 June 2002.

18. Grady, Denise. "U.S. Lets Drug Tied to Deaths Back to Market." *New York Times*, 8 June 2002.

19. <http://www.instinet.com>;
    "No Such Thing as a Free Trade." *Economist*, 7 December 2000;
    Colarusso, Dan. "Going One-up on Electronic Traders?" *New York Times*, 23 June 2002.

20. Wade, Nicholas. *Life Script: How the Human Genome Discoveries Will Transform Medicine and Enhance Your Health*. New York: Simon and Schuster, 2001;
    Edwards, Aled M., Cheryl H. Arrowsmith, and Bertrand des Pallieres. "Proteomics: New Tools for a New Era." *Modern Drug Discovery*, September 2000;

Zacks, Rebecca. "Medicine's New Millennium: Q&A with Mark Levin." *Technology Review*, December 2001.

21. "Firestone and Ford Place Blame." 19 December 2000, <http://www.cbsnews.com/stories/2000/12/06/national/main255111.shtml>; <http://www.citizen.org/autosafety/firestone/>;
Fairclough, Gordon. "Philip Morris Tells Smokers 'Light' Cigarettes Aren't Safer." *Wall Street Journal*, 20 November 2002.

Chapter Three

1. Alderman, John. *Napster, MP3, and the New Pioneers of Music*. Cambridge, MA: Perseus Publishing, 2001;
See also:
Shirky, Clay. "Where Napster Is Taking the Publishing World." *Harvard Business Review*, February 2001.
2. Grover, Ronald, and Heather Green. "Hollywood Heist." *BusinessWeek*, 14 July 2003.
3. Leonard, Devin. "Apple: Songs in the Key of Steve." *Fortune*, 28 April 2003.
4. Strauss, Neil. "A New Industry Threat: CDs Made from Webcasts." *New York Times*, 12 December 2001.
5. Prahalad, C. K., and Richard A. Bettis. "The Dominant Logic: A New Linkage between Diversity and Performance." *Strategic Management Journal* 7, no. 6, (1986): 485–501.
6. Prahalad, C. K., and Venkatram Ramaswamy. "The Value Creation Dilemma." Working paper, University of Michigan Business School, Ann Arbor, October 2001;
Prahalad, C. K., and Venkatram Ramaswamy. "The Co-Creation Connection." *Strategy and Business*, Second Quarter 2002.
7. Fox, Loren. "Turn Your Company Outside In." *Business 2.0*, March 2001.
8. Chappel, Lindsay. "BMW Gives Z3 Buyers More Time to Change Order." *Autoweek*, 16 April 2002.
9. Wayner, Peter. "The Packaging of Video on Demand." *New York Times*, 23 September 2002;
Null, Christopher. "How Netflix Is Fixing Hollywood." *Business 2.0*, July 2003.
10. Atluru, Rajesh, Kevin Wasserstein, and Thomas J. Kosnik. "Palm Computing: The Pilot Organizer." Case 9-599-040. Boston: Harvard Business School, 1998, <http://www.hbsp.harvard.edu>.
11. "Cipla Launches New AIDS Drug." *The Hindu*, 7 August 2001.
12. McDonough, William. "How Much Can We Give for All We Get?" May 2003. <http://www.mbdc.com/features/feature_may2003.htm>;
Rubin, Harriet. "The Perfect Vision Dr. V." *Fast Company*, February 2001.

Chapter Four

1. Visit <http://www.lego.com>.
2. Pesce, Mark. *The Playful World: How Technology Is Transforming Our Imagination*. New York: Ballantine Books, 2000.
3. Keegan, Paul. "Lego: Intellectual Property Is Not a Toy." *Business 2.0*, October 2001, <https://www.business2.com/subscribers/articles/mag/0,1640,16981,00.html>.

4. Keegan, Paul. "Go Forth and Hack." *Business 2.0*, November 2001, <http://www.business2.com/articles/mag/0,1640,17435,FF.html>.

5. <http://www.technologyreview.com>; <http://www.economist.com/forums/>; Saffo, Paul. "Untangling the Future." *Business 2.0*, June 2002; "Red Herring 100: No Limits." *Red Herring*, Special Issue, June 2002; Schmidt, Charlie. "Beyond the Bar Code." *Technology Review*, March 2001; "No Hiding Place for Anyone." *Economist*, 20 September 2001; Lewis, Michael. "Boom Box." *New York Times*, 13 August 2000; Lewis, Peter. "Sony Re-dreams Its Future." *Fortune*, 25 November 2002; Shim, Richard. "Sony's Ando: PCs to Function Like a Brain." ZDNet, 5 December 2002, <http://zdnet.com.com/2100-1105-976269.html>.

6. Lohr, Steve. "A Computing Chameleon in a Little Black Box." *New York Times*, 7 February 2002.

7. See, for example: Kelley, Tom. *The Art of Innovation*. New York: Doubleday, 2001; Berry, Leonard, Lewis P. Carbone, and Stephan H. Haeckel. "Managing the Total Customer Experience." *Sloan Management Review*, Spring 2002, 85–89; Moore, Carol. "The New Heart of Your Brand: Transforming Business Through Customer Experience." *Design Management Journal*, Winter 2002; Shedroff, Nathan. *Experience Design*. Indianapolis: Pearson Education, 2001; <http://cooltown.com/cooltownhome/index.asp>.

8. Brown, Jeanette. "PRADA Gets Personal." *BusinessWeek*, 18 March 2002; <http://www.ideo.com>.

9. Buchenau, Marion and Jane Fulton Suri. "Experience Prototyping." *ACM Symposium on Designing Interactive Systems*, 2000.

10. "E-nabling the Store Next Door." *Business World*, January 2003.

11. "Digital Ink Meets Electronic Paper." *Economist*, 7 December 2000; Cameron, David. "Flexible Displays Gain Momentum." *Technology Review*, January 2002.

12. Lawrence, Stacy. "Child's Play." *Red Herring*, 17 October 2002; Pereira, Joe. "Parents Turn Teaching Tool into Must-Have Holiday Gift." *Wall Street Journal*, 27 November 2002.

13. Mucha, Thomas. "The Payoff for Trying Harder." *Business 2.0*, July 2002.

14. "The Beast of Complexity." *Economist*, 12 April 2001.

15. Rauch, Jonathan. "The New Old Economy: Oil, Computers, and the Reinvention of the Earth." *The Atlantic Monthly*, January 2001.

16. Breen, Bill. "Stock Futures." *Fast Company*, June 2002.

17. <http://energycommerce.house.gov/107/hearings/12192001Hearing458/OHara778.htm>.

18. Prahalad, C. K., and Venkatram Ramaswamy. "The New Frontier of Experience Innovation." *Sloan Management Review*, Summer 2003, 12–18.

Chapter Five

1. <http://www.intel.com/pressroom/archive/releases/CO092498.htm>; Teicholz, Nina. "Touring the Museum with a Small PC to Serve as a Guide." *New York Times*, 6 May 1999; Prahalad, C. K., and Venkatram Ramaswamy. "The Market as a Forum." Working paper, University of Michigan Business School, Ann Arbor, August 1999.

2. Billsus, Daniel, Clifford A. Brunk, Craig Evans, Brian Gladish, and Michael Pazzani. "The Adaptive Web: Adaptive Web Interfaces for Ubiquitous Web Access." *Communications of the ACM*, May 2002.
3. Pool, Robert. "If It Ain't Broke, Fix It." *Technology Review*, September 2001; <http://www.geae.com>.
4. Deford, Frank. "Faux Football." National Public Radio, "Morning Edition," 9 October 2002; <http://www.npr.org/ramfiles/me/20021009.me.14.ram>.
5. Schultz, Howard (with Dori Jone Yang). *Pour Your Heart into It: How Starbucks Built a Company One Cup at a Time*. New York: Hyperion, 1997; Bedbury, Scott (with Stephen Fenichell, contributor). *A Brand New World*. New York: Viking Press, 2002.
6. Takahashi, Dean. "Games Get Serious." *Red Herring*, December 2000; <http://www.sonyonline.com>.
7. <http://www.microsoft.com/resources/spot/default1.mspx>.
8. Fournier, Susan, Silvia Sensiper, James MacAlexander, and John Schouten. "Building Brand Community on the Harley-Davidson Posse Ride." Multimedia Case 9-501-009. Boston: Harvard Business School, 2000, <http://harvardbusinessonline.hbsp.harvard.edu/b02/en/common/item_detail.jhtml?id=501009>.
9. Ozcan, Kerimcan. *Consumer-to-Consumer Interactions: Word-of-Mouth Theory, Consumer Experiences, and Network Dynamics*. Unpublished Ph.D. diss., University of Michigan Business School, 2003.
10. Warner, Fara. "Detroit Muscle." *Fast Company*, June 2002.
11. Goldberg, Carey. "Auditing Classes at MIT, on the Web and for Free." *New York Times*, 4 April 2001.
12. Pine II, B. Joseph, and James H. Gilmore. "Welcome to the Experience Economy." *Harvard Business Review*, July–August 1998.
13. Thomke, Stefan, and Eric von Hippel. "Customers as Innovators: A New Way to Create Value." *Harvard Business Review*, April 2002.

Chapter Six

1. Peterson, Thane. "Gazing into the Future with Deere's Top Ag Man." *Business-Week*, 17 April 2000; "Technology Brings Dealers, Customers Closer Together." *Seattle Daily Journal of Commerce* Online Edition, 23 March 2000; Lane, Robert W. "Farming the Future." *Context*, August–September 2001.
2. Prahalad, C. K., Venkatram Ramaswamy, and M. S. Krishnan. "Consumer Centricity." *Information Week*, April 2000.
3. Ody, Penelope. "Survey on Supply Chain Management." *Financial Times*, 5 October 2000; Tapscott, Don, David Ticoll, and Alex Lowy. "Internet Nirvana." *Business 2.0*, December 2000; "Customer Fulfillment Networks: Beyond Supply Chains," <http://www.digital4sight.com>.
4. Griffith, Victoria. "Welcome to Tesco: Your 'Glocal' Superstore." *Strategy and Business*, Issue 26: First Quarter 2002; "Surfin' USA." *Economist*, 28 June 2001.

5. "Why Japanese Are Mad for i-mode." *BusinessWeek*, Asian Edition, 17 January 2000;
   <http://nttdocomo.com>.
6. Schwartz, Evan I. "Digital Cash Payoff." *Technology Review*, December 2001;
   Wolveton, Troy. "Citibank to Make Web Payment Service Free." CNET News.com, 15 November 2001;
   <http://news.com.com/2100-1017-275930.html>;
   Donahue, Sean. "Pay Ya Later." *Business 2.0*, May 2001.
7. Colledge, Justin A., Jason Hicks, James B. Robb, and Dilip Wagle. "Power by the Minute." *The McKinsey Quarterly* 1, 2002.
8. Herper, Matthew. "FDA Panel Backs Astra Zeneca's Cancer Drug." Forbes.com, 24 September 2002, <http://www.forbes.com/2002/09/24/0924azn.html>.
9. Kleinman, Heather. "Interview with Don Donovan, Fragrance Designer." Reflect.com, March 2001, <http://cosmeticconnection.com/reflectinterview.html>;
   Levinson, Meredith. "Getting to Know You." *CIO Magazine*, 15 February 2002;
   Cullen, Takeuchi Lisa. "Have It Your Way." *Time Magazine*, 23 December 2002.
10. <http://rei.com>;
    Fisher, Lawrence M. "REI Climbs Online: A Clicks and Mortar Chronicle." *Strategy and Business*, First Quarter, 2000.
11. <http://www.cemex.com>;
    "The Cemex Way." *Economist*, 14 June 2001.
12. "Spain's Retail Success Story." BBC News Online, 23 May 2001;
    <http://news.bbc.co.uk/2/hi/business/1346473.stm>;
    Pich, Michael, and L. Van der Heyden. "Marks and Spencer and Zara: Process Competition in the Textile Apparel Industry." INSEAD Case 602-010-1, February 2002.
13. Magretta, Joan. "Fast, Global, and Entrepreneurial: Supply Chain Management, Hong Kong Style: An Interview with Victor Fung." *Harvard Business Review*, September–October 1998;
    Tanzer, Andrew. "Stitches in Time." Forbes.com, 6 September 1999, <http://www.forbes.com/global/1999/0906/0217038a.html>;
    Lee-Young, Joan. "Furiously Fast Fashions." *Industry Standard*, 11 June 2001.
14. Schonfeld, Erick. "The Total Package." *Business 2.0*, May 2001;
    <http://www.ups.com>.
15. Jaffe, Sam. "CheckFree May Be Ready for a Healthy Bounce." *BusinessWeek*, 5 December 2000.
16. Jaffe, Sam. "Flextronics Breaks the Mold." *BusinessWeek*, 30 July 2001.
17. Prahalad, C. K., and M. S. Krishnan. "The New Meaning of Quality in the Information Age." *Harvard Business Review*, September–October 1999.

Chapter Seven

1. Prahalad, C. K., and Venkatram Ramaswamy. "The Value Creation Dilemma." Working paper, University of Michigan Business School, Ann Arbor, October 2001.
2. Prahalad, C. K., and Venkatram Ramaswamy. "The Market as a Forum." Working paper, University of Michigan Business School, Ann Arbor, August 1999.

3. Gladwell, Malcolm. *The Tipping Point: How Little Things Can Make a Big Difference*. Boston: Little, Brown, 2000;
   Locke, Christopher, David Weinberger, and Doc Searls. *The Cluetrain Manifesto: The End of Business as Usual*. Cambridge, MA: Perseus Publishing, 2001;
   Watts, Duncan J. *Six Degrees: The Science of a Connected Age*. New York: W. W. Norton, 2002.
4. Dahan, Ely. "A Bull Market in Market Research." *Strategy and Business*, Second Quarter, 2002.
5. Weingarten, Marc. "Get Your Buzz to Breed Like Hobbits." *Business 2.0*, January 2002.
6. Prahalad and Ramaswamy. "The Market as a Forum."
7. Aaker, David. *Building Strong Brands*. New York: The Free Press, 1996;
   Keller, Kevin Lane. *Strategic Brand Management*. Upper Saddle River, NJ: Prentice Hall, 2002.
8. Kapferer, Jean-Noel. *Re-inventing the Brand*. London: Kogan Page, 2001.

Chapter Eight

1. Prahalad, C. K., and Venkatram Ramaswamy. "Co-opting Customer Competence." *Harvard Business Review*, January–February 2000.
2. Sawhney, Mohan, and Emanuela Prandelli. "Communities of Creation: Managing Distributed Innovation in Turbulent Markets." *California Management Review*, Summer 2000.
3. Glanz, James. "Web Archive Opens a New Realm of Research." *New York Times*, 1 May 2001.
4. Keighley, Geoff. "Game Development a La Mod." *Business 2.0*, October 2002.
5. Croal, N'Gai. "Sims Family Values." <http://www.msnbc.com/news/835533.asp>, 25 November 2002.
6. Prahalad and Ramaswamy. "Co-opting Customer Competence."
7. Gerstner Jr., Louis V. *Who Says Elephants Can't Dance? Inside IBM's Historic Turnaround*. New York: HarperBusiness, 2002.
8. Rocks, David. "Reinventing Herman Miller." *BusinessWeek* Online, 3 April 2000, <http://www.businessweek.com/@@vkDZGocQWJbPPhIA/2000/00_14/b3675047.htm>.

Chapter Nine

1. Prahalad, C. K., Venkatram Ramaswamy, and M. S. Krishnan. "Manager as Consumer." Working paper, University of Michigan Business School, Ann Arbor, August 2002.
2. Guernsey, Lisa. "Hard Hat, Lunch Bucket, Keyboard." *New York Times*, 14 December 2000.
3. Prahalad, C. K., M. S. Krishnan, and Venkatram Ramaswamy. "The Essence of Business Agility." *Optimize*, September 2002.
4. Whiting, Rick. "Museums Exhibit Sharing Tendencies." *Information Week*, 11 May 2002.
5. Sullivan, Missy. "High Octane Hog." Forbes.com, 10 September 2002, <http://www.forbes.com/best/2001/0910/008.html>.
6. Friedman, Ted, and Jim Sinur. "Business Activity Monitoring: The Data Perspective." Gartner G2 Research Report, 20 February 2002;

Hellinger, Mark, and Scott Fingerhut. "Business Activity Monitoring: EAI Meets Data Warehousing." *EAI Journal*, July 2002;

Smith, Howard, and Peter Fingar. *Business Process Management: The Third Wave*. New York: Meghan-Kiffer Press, 2003.

Chapter Ten

1. Prahalad, C. K., and Venkatram Ramaswamy. "Managing in an Era of Discontinuities: The Challenge of Organizational Transformation." Working paper, University of Michigan Business School, presented at the International Consortium for Executive Development Research Forum, June 2001.

2. <http://www.buckman.com>;

    <http://www.knowledge-nurture.com>;

    "Balancing Act—What Do You Know? Getting Employees to Share Their Knowledge Isn't as Simple as Installing New Software: Just Ask Buckman Labs." Special Report on Technology, *Wall Street Journal*, 21 June 1999;

3. Rifkin, Glen. "Buckman Labs Is Nothing but Net." *Fast Company*, June 1996.

4. Stepanek, Marcia. "Spread the Knowhow." *BusinessWeek*, 23 October, 2000.

5. Davenport, Thomas, and Laurence Prusak. *Working Knowledge*. Boston: Harvard Business School Press, 2000;

    Ikujiro, Nonaka, and Toshihiro Hishiguchi. *Knowledge Emergence: Social, Technical, and Evolutionary Dimensions of Knowledge Creation*. New York: Oxford University Press, 2000;

    Krogh, Georg Von, Ikujiro Nonaka, and Kazuo Ichijo. *Enabling Knowledge Creation: How to Unlock the Mystery of Tacit Knowledge and Release the Power of Innovation*. New York: Oxford University Press, 2000;

    Polanyi, M. *Personal Knowledge: Towards a Post-Critical Philosophy*. Chicago: Routledge, 1962;

    Polanyi, M. *The Tacit Dimension*. New York: Doubleday, 1966;

    Brown, John Seely, and Paul Duguid. "Organizational Learning and Communities of Practice: Toward a Unified View of Working, Learning, and Innovation." *Organization Science* 2, (1991): 40–57;

    Wenger, Etienne. *Communities of Practice: Learning, Meaning and Identity*. Cambridge, U.K.: Cambridge University Press, 1999;

    Zack, Michael. "Managing Codified Knowledge." *Sloan Management Review*, Summer 1999.

6. <http://www.archimuse.com>.

7. "Of High Priests and Pragmatists." *Economist*, 21 June 2001.

8. Rumizen, Melissa. "How Buckman Laboratories' Shared Knowledge Sparked a Chain Reaction." *The Journal for Quality and Participation*, July–August 1998.

9. Collison, Chris, and Geoff Parcell. *Learning to Fly: Practical Lessons from One of the World's Leading Knowledge Companies*. New York: John Wiley and Sons, 2001;

    Collison, Chris. "Making Connections: BP's System for Connecting People and Generating Tacit Knowledge." *IHRIM Journal* (International Association for Human Resource Information Management), March 2000.

10. Barrow, David C. "Sharing Know-How at BP Amoco." *Research Technology Management*, May–June 2001.

11. Prokesch, Steven E. "Unleashing the Power of Learning: An Interview with British Petroleum's John Browne." *Harvard Business Review*, September–October 1997.

12. Echikson, William. "When Oil Gets Connected." *BusinessWeek*, 3 December 2001.
13. Collison, Chris. "Connecting the New Organization." *Knowledge Management Review* 7, March–April 1999.
14. Buderi, Robert. "Intel Re-vamps R&D." *Technology Review*. October, 2001.

Chapter Eleven

1. Prahalad, C. K., and Venkatram Ramaswamy. "The Collaboration Continuum." *Optimize*, November 2001.
2. Brown, Shona L., and Kathleen M. Eisenhardt. *Competing on the Edge: Strategy as Structured Chaos*. Boston: Harvard Business School Press, 1998.
3. von Hayek, Friedrick A. "Competition as a Discovery Procedure." In *New Studies in Philosophy, Politics, Economics, and the History of Ideas*. Chicago: University of Chicago Press, 1968.
4. Weick, Karl E. "Improvisation as a Mindset for Organizational Analysis." *Organizational Science* 9, no. 5 (1998): 543–555.

Chapter Twelve

1. Shedroff, Nathan. *Experience Design*. Indianapolis: Pearson Education, 2001.
2. Moore, Carol. "The New Heart of Your Brand: Transforming Business Through Customer Experience." *Design Management Journal*, Winter 2002.
3. Prahalad, C. K., and Venkatram Ramaswamy. "Co-opting Customer Competence." *Harvard Business Review*, January–February 2000.
4. Prahalad, C. K., Venkatram Ramaswamy, and M. S. Krishnan. "Consumer Centricity." *Information Week*, April 2000.
5. Kaihla, Paul. "Inside Cisco's $2 Billion Blunder." *Business 2.0*, March 2002.
6. Prahalad, C. K., and M. S. Krishnan. "The Dynamic Synchronization of Strategy and Information Technology." *Sloan Management Review*, Summer 2002.
7. <http://www.linux.org>.
8. Garfinkel, Simpson L. "The Web's Unelected Government." *Technology Review*, November–December 1998;
   Lee, Tim-Berners, with Mark Fischetti. *Weaving the Web: The Original Design and Ultimate Destiny of the World Wide Web*. San Francisco: Harper, 2000;
   Lessig, Lawrence. *The Future of Ideas: The Fate of Commons in a Connected World*. New York: Random House, 2001.
9. Hoff, Robert. "eBay: The People's Company." *BusinessWeek*, December 2001, <http://www.businessweek.com/@@Ep*L84cQW5bPPhIA/magazine/content/01_49/b3760601.htm>;
   Patsuris, Penelope. "The eBay Economy." Forbes.com, April 2003, <http://www.forbes.com/2003/04/16/cx_pp_0416ebaylander.html>.

Index

About the Authors

C. K. Prahalad is the Harvey C. Fruehauf Professor of Business Administration at the Michigan Business School. He is coauthor of the landmark bestseller *Competing for the Future* and widely regarded as one of the foremost strategy thinkers in the world. His research has consistently focused on "next" practices.

Venkat Ramaswamy is the Michael R. and Mary Kay Hallman Fellow of Electronic Business and Professor of Marketing at the Michigan Business School. His eclectic interests span innovation, customer experiences, communities, new market creation, networks, information and communications technology, human resources, and strategy. His research focuses on new frontiers in experience innovation, consumer-company interactions, experience quality management, infrastructure for experience networks, and co-creating value.

Prahalad and Ramaswamy have coauthored several articles in the *Harvard Business Review, Sloan Management Review, Strategy and Business, Information Week, Optimize,* and other publications.